Communities

in Economic

Crisis

Appalachia and the South

Edited by

JOHN GAVENTA

BARBARA ELLEN SMITH

ALEX WILLINGHAM

Temple University Press

Chapter 8, "Betrayal of Trust: The Impact of Economic Development Upon Working Citizens," by John Bookser-Feister and Leah Wise, © 1989 Southerners for Economic Justice, Inc.

Temple University Press, Philadelphia 19122
Copyright © 1990 by Temple University. All rights reserved
Published 1990
Printed in the United States of America

The paper used in this publication meets the minimum requirements of American National Standard for Information Sciences—Permanence of Paper for Printed Library Materials, ANSI Z39.48-1984.

Library of Congress Cataloging-in-Publication Data

Communities in economic crisis : Appalachia and the South / edited by
    John Gaventa, Barbara Ellen Smith, Alex Willingham.
        p.   cm. — (Labor and social change)
    ISBN 0-87722-650-4 : (alk. paper)
    1. Appalachian Region—Economic conditions—Case studies.
    2. Economic development projects—Appalachian Region—Case studies.
    3. Southern States—Economic conditions—1945–   —Case studies.
    4. Economic development projects—Southern States—Case studies.
    I. Gaventa, John, 1949–   . II. Smith, Barbara E., 1951
    III. Willingham,   Alex W., 1940–   . IV. Series.
    HC107.A127C65   1989   89-4575
    330.974'043—dc20   CIP

This book must be returned immed-
iately it is asked for by the Librarian,
and in any case by the last date
stamped below.

Labor and Social Change,

a series edited by Paula Rayman and Carmen Sirianni

CONTENTS

Case Studies from the Deep South

PART II
Visions for the Future

Development by Corporate Design

Visions for Change

PREFACE

Involvement in the struggle for economic justice is the thread that binds together the many contributors to this book. While the book is mainly by Southerners and is about our region, the realities we describe are not unique. The present economic problems of Appalachia and the South are rooted in the broader restructuring of the economy that affects communities throughout the nation.

"Economic restructuring"—particularly the shift from a manufacturing to a predominantly service-based economy—has been the subject of extensive academic research, policy analysis, and political debate. All too often absent from this outpouring of information, however, are the voices of people at the grassroots: those who are the first to experience the economic transformation personally and who are struggling to deal with its consequences. There seems to be an enormous gap between the "official" diagnoses of and prescriptions for the economic crisis, emerging within academic and policy circles, and the everyday struggle to survive and maintain one's community within a dramatically changing world. It was concern for this "knowledge gap" about the economic crisis that motivated us, the editors, to begin the process that led to this book.

Each of us experienced the issue in different ways. In 1986, John Gaventa, working as research director at the Highlander Research and Education Center in New Market, Tenn., was asked by the Commission on Religion in Appalachia (Knoxville) to help organize a series of hearings on the economic crisis for church groups concerned with poverty and justice issues in the region. As the hearings group went from the coalfields of West Virginia to declining manufacturing towns like Chattanooga and Pittsburgh, he was struck with the rich oral testimonies and community-based analyses of the workers, community organizers, and activists who spoke.

Barbara Ellen Smith, meanwhile, working as research director for the Southeast Women's Employment Coalition in Lexington, Ky., had just completed a participatory research project that involved grassroots women in the South in analyzing their own economic futures—a process that revealed a knowledge and reality also quite different from the dominant images of Southern women. Alex Willingham, research director at the Southern Regional Council in Atlanta, who had been studying and working for voting rights in the South, became increasingly concerned with how the political power that blacks had gained in the region might be converted to economic equality and how those political gains were now being lost through economic decline.

On the initiative of the Highlander Center, the three of us decided to ask others who represented the diversity of the region to discuss and analyze their experiences with the changing economy. We invited a broad group of community-based researchers and activists to Highlander for two workshops, one in the fall of 1986 and one in the spring of 1987. The participants were concerned with different sectors of the economy—coal, textiles, banking and other services, farming, paper; from different racial and ethnic backgrounds—black, white, Native American, Creole; from different forms of organization—trade unions, community advocacy organizations, community business enterprises, public interest groups, colleges and universities; from different educational backgrounds; and with different forms of knowing—through personal experience, activism, or scholarship.

From the start, we viewed this diversity as our greatest strength. It would enable us, we hoped, to probe deeply into the interaction of class, race, and gender in a period of economic transformation, and to relate our various perspectives to the broader debate about the growing economic crisis. Our diversity would also enable us to explore, in a microcosm, the analytical and strategic differences that frequently divide efforts at change. Could we identify a common analysis of the economic crisis that underpinned our separate work? Was there a way of linking our specific issue- and constituency-oriented work to a broader strategy and a broader movement? Could our various perspectives, our various ways of knowing, strengthen and inform one another?

In many ways, the workshops were difficult; they served as much to clarify differences as to develop commonalities. Some dealt with the loss of traditional jobs in coal, textiles, and agriculture; others were concerned with organizing the new service jobs. Some were driven to analyze and influence the dominant formal economy; others sought to preserve and develop the informal sectors of the economy, especially among women and in black and indigenous communities whose forms of production and exchange had in large part been excluded from the dominant economy to begin with. There were debates over strategy: should we even attempt to transform policy, or did we need to concentrate on building grassroots power? Was it better to develop alternative community-based enterprises or to organize workers against the objectionable practices of large corporations? How did the politics of class, race, and gender affect not only our strategies for change but our personal and organizational ways of knowing and working?

There were parallel debates over knowledge. We hoped that the workshop discussions would eventually lead to a book. But was this book a worthwhile enterprise? Who was its audience and whose interest did it serve? Was it intended to inform policymakers and university students or to broaden the consciousness and action of those engaged in social change? How could it incorporate the experiential and the analytical, the active and reflective, the cultural and the political, the local and the global?

As editors, we became increasingly aware of the difficulties of the project. We retreated from the attempt to develop a common analysis from the diversity of experience and approaches. Rather, we began to feel that it was precisely the *differences* in the authors' experiences, analyses, and efforts at economic change that could make an important contribution to a broad audience of people who were struggling with similar questions elsewhere.

Participants in the workshops were invited to contribute to this volume. Some chose not to, feeling that writing was not a personal or political priority. Some people who were not normally writers jumped at the chance to reflect on their experiences. Others, mainly in the more scholarly occupations, were excited about continuing to link their analysis to action.

We made the process as participatory as possible. After drafts of the articles were developed, most of the contributors came back to Highlander to critique one another's efforts and to discuss as a group how to frame the themes for the overall volume. We struggled with ways of blending the wide range of voices; with learning from both the commonalities *and* the differences in our work. We sought to recognize the expertise that each contributor brought by virtue of scholarship or practical experience. We tried to create a book important not only for what it says, but also for who says it.

In the end, we hope that the essays in this volume reflect the richness, strength, and diversity of Southern communities, which the process of creating the book taught us again to respect. We hope that they help the reader learn how grassroots communities survive and create change in times of economic crisis. We especially hope that the case studies of struggles for economic dignity and development at the grassroots inspire creative responses to economic crisis and new visions of economic justice.

ACKNOWLEDGMENTS

T his anthology has been just over two years in the making. During that time we have received the help of many. Our thanks go first and foremost to each of the contributors, who worked with us patiently. Many did far more than draft their own essays. They participated in workshops, read and critiqued other essays, and made suggestions for the overall project.

We are grateful, of course, to each of our organizations for support of this endeavor—Barbara Ellen Smith, to the Southeast Women's Employment Coalition; Alex Willingham, to the Southern Regional Council; and John Gaventa to the Department of Sociology at the University of Tennessee in Knoxville and to the Highlander Research and Education Center. The project would not have been possible without the additional support of the Office of Rural Poverty of the Ford Foundation, to which we are also grateful. Thanks also to Loretta McHan and Karen Jones for word processing assistance in the final editing stages, and to Michael Ames and Mary Capouya of Temple University Press for their constant enthusiasm about the project.

We especially appreciate the support we received from our families: Dan, Juliet, Jennett, Kwame, Lumumba, Kyle, Richard, Jacob, Jonathan, and Megan. This project was one of many competing demands for all of us. During its course, Barbara bore two children, Alex survived serious illness, and John began teaching at the university—each of which experiences carried its own trauma.

Most of all we thank the grassroots communities whose stories and struggles are shared in this volume. Their efforts to achieve economic justice in the face of deepening adversity continue to strengthen us all.

JPG
BES
AWW

Communities in Economic Crisis

Appalachia and the South

INTRODUCTION

I don't know the answer to the economic crisis, but I know that it has to come from the people. It has got to come out of the hands of the so-called system and the so-called powerful people and come back to the people—the dinner buckets of America and the dinner buckets of Korea and the dinner buckets of the Philippines.

—*Maxine Waller,*
Ivanhoe Civic League,
Ivanhoe, Virginia

Change is afoot in communities across Appalachia and the South. For nearly a decade, poor and working-class Southerners have endured the most severe economic dislocation since the Great Depression. Despair and resignation have been common responses among some to unemployment, eviction, and a reduced standard of living, but now defiance and solidarity have begun to spread. Maxine Waller, a thirty-eight-year-old woman from southwestern Virginia, gives voice to this shift in the political mood, now emerging in communities across the region.

According to current statistics and economic trends, there is little cause for hope. The present hardship is not the temporary result of a downturn in the business cycle; it is part of a fundamental, international restructuring of the economy. Coalminers in West Virginia can no longer expect an upturn in the market to restore their dangerous jobs; their layoffs are permanent. Factory workers in the Carolinas can no longer count on $5 an hour in the local electronics or textile plant; production has moved overseas. And rural black communities in the Deep South can no longer hope a branch plant will come in search of their cheap, nonunion labor; hazardous-waste disposal is one of the few industries even considering their location.[1]

The impact of this economic crisis has been magnified by a simultaneous political assault on poor and working-class people. Federal reductions in social welfare programs—from Aid to Families with Dependent Children (AFDC) to housing, from job training to student aid—have further whittled away the narrow base of resources by which poor people survive. These reductions have been particularly acute for poor people in the South, where poverty rates are

3

the highest in the nation and state governments have never been generous in their allocations for social welfare.[2] And all this has occurred at a time when the movements that once gave power and hope to their participants—civil rights, welfare rights, coalminers' union insurgency—are no longer as strong as they once were. Finding themselves held hostage to economic crisis, communities are tempted by political despair.

Yet it is precisely the depth of this crisis that has begun to generate a new vision and activism. The manifest failure of the economic and political systems to provide decent jobs, adequate housing, affordable medical care, and other necessities has begun to open those systems up to fundamental questions. Who is benefiting from current economic trends? What are the obligations of corporations to the communities where they locate and to the workers they employ? Perhaps most fundamentally, who should control the economy, and to what end?

This book gives voice to those seeking to answer these and other questions through community and workplace organizing across the South. Their efforts are richly diverse: Lumbee Indians organizing against toxic wastes in eastern North Carolina, women coalminers seeking new avenues to equity in the workplace, and rural blacks advocating for community economic development through local political mechanisms, to name a few. They are bound together by their common economic crisis, their common effort to transcend conventional definitions of *development,* and their common challenge to traditional structures of economic power and control. They offer some strategic responses and visionary alternatives to the economic crisis that is bleeding our region, our nation, our world. They offer some answers from the people of Appalachia and the South, from "the dinner buckets of America," for all who seek a more just and democratic economy.

Dimensions of the Crisis

Each decade since 1960 has brought a different popular image of the Southern economy. During the 1960s, there was a tendency to view the South and Appalachia as regions outside the social and economic mainstream. Indeed, maps of socioeconomic conditions in the United States at that time revealed "pockets of poverty" in which Appalachia and the Black Belt South stood out, along with the Indian reservations of the Southwest, as the nation's poorest regions. The assumption was that the mainstream economy was healthy; the depressed regions were simply those "left behind." "For all practical purposes," wrote the President's Advisory Committee on Rural Poverty, "most of the 14 million poor in our poverty areas are on the outside of our market economy. . . . They are on the outside looking in, and they need our help."[3]

Integrating these areas into the mainstream economy, not transforming that economy, was the problem.

Then, during the 1970s, the image of the region began to glitter and shine: the South had become the Sun Belt. With growing employment, income, and population, especially in metropolitan areas, the region beckoned like an oasis, especially when contrasted with the declining "Frost Belt" or "Rust Belt" of the industrial North. The relative prosperity seemed to vindicate the development strategy of "smokestack chasing," or industrial recruitment, which Southern state governments pursued with a vengeance.

Within a decade, however, the image had changed again. In the early 1980s, a series of policy reports began to warn of a pattern of uneven development in the South, especially in rural areas. MDC, a research and consulting firm in North Carolina, wrote of "shadows in the Sunbelt" in an influential report on the Southern economy. Picking up the theme, the 1986 Commission on the Future of the South referred to the region as "Halfway Home and a Long Way to Go":

> The sunshine on the Sunbelt has proved to be a narrow beam of light, brightening futures along the Atlantic Seaboard, and in large cities but skipping over many small towns and rural areas. The decade's widely publicized new jobs at higher pay have been largely claimed by educated, urban, middle-class Southerners. Although their economic progress has lifted southern per capita income to 88 percent of the national average, millions of us—approximately the same as in 1965—still struggle in poverty.[4]

This time, the South's economic troubles could not plausibly be attributed to its failure to integrate with the mainstream economy. By the mid-1980s, socioeconomic maps of the United States revealed a picture very different from that of the 1960s. A series of reports began to warn of a bicoastal economy, divided between "healthy economies" along the coasts, where service industries were locating, and a problem-plagued heartland, where the country's traditional agricultural, industrial, and mineral base was in decline.[5] Eighty percent of the poorest counties in the country could be found in seventeen states that formed a giant V or wedge in heartland America, stretching from the steel towns of northern Appalachia, down through the coalfields of central Appalachia and the mill towns of the Piedmont, on through the deeper South and then back up north to encompass the Rust Belt areas of the Midwest and the Farm Belt of the Great Plains. Rather than growing smaller through integration into the national mainstream, the traditional pockets of poverty had expanded. Now the crisis is not of a regional economy "on the outside looking in"; it is of the mainstream economy itself.

It is by now commonplace to say that the agricultural and industrial America of the past is being transformed to a service-based and finance economy. In the five years between 1979 and 1984, 11.5 million workers nationwide lost their jobs as company officials shut down or relocated plants. In such economic restructuring, the jobs in traditional sectors such as mining, manufacturing, and agriculture have declined the most.[6]

Some analysts view this process of economic transformation as a positive phenomenon.[7] The loss of industrial jobs, they argue, is outstripped by the growth of the new service-sector jobs. Though workers may experience some short-term dislocation, over the long run the economy will be better off as more and more jobs are created. But other analysts question this view of economic growth. According to a study by the U.S. Office of Technology Assessment, only 60 percent of the workers affected by plant closings and layoffs nationwide have been able to find other jobs, and many have taken a wage cut in doing so. Moreover, a recent study for the Joint Economic Committee of Congress found that, between 1979 and 1985, 44 percent of new jobs created in the United States paid poverty-level wages.[8]

Although obscured by the persistent image of a Sun Belt boom, these trends have a special scope and meaning in the South. Once a haven for northern industries seeking low-wage, nonunion labor, the South is now being deserted for cheaper production sites in Mexico, South Korea, and Taiwan. Responding to the squeeze of intensified global competition, corporations are automating production, closing less profitable plants, and moving some facilities out of the country altogether. Moreover, the rural areas of the region have long been dependent on natural resource–based industries such as textiles, coal, timber, paper, poultry, and tobacco; entire communities, indeed, entire states, have depended on a single one of these industries for their economic survival. These are precisely the sectors hardest hit by the ongoing restructuring of the economy.

In the Appalachian coalfields of the upper South, for example, expansion in the wake of the Arab oil embargo created a short-lived employment boom during the mid-1970s. These prosperous times, which lured many Appalachian migrants back to the region, now seem like a dream. Coal-dependent communities have become ghost towns as employment in the industry has plummeted by 40 percent since 1978.[9] Technological innovation and a dramatic rise in productivity suggest that the reduced employment is structural and permanent.

The rolling Piedmont region, which skirts the Appalachian mountains to the south and east, is the industrial heart of the South. North Carolina, for example, has the highest proportion of its labor force employed in manufacturing of any state in the nation. Premier among the Piedmont's industries are textiles and apparel. New technology, combined with plant closings and re location overseas, has also taken a heavy toll on jobs here: between 1980 and 1985, 250 textile plants closed and 248,000 jobs were eliminated.[10]

South of the Piedmont lies the area that most people think of as "the South": the rural agricultural region that was once the scene of sprawling plantations and an economy based on slave labor. This past lives on in the form of a highly unequal distribution of wealth, an impoverished black population, and a scarcity of economic opportunity. Dependent on agriculture and low-wage, labor-intensive manufacturing, the Deep South has experienced double jeopardy during the present crisis: a higher percentage of farmers declared bankruptcy or went out of business here than in any other region of the United States, and the industries that once sought the area's cheap labor now find it overseas.[11]

To be sure, jobs in other industries are emerging even as opportunities in the South's traditional sectors—manufacturing, mining, and agriculture—are on the decline. The restructuring of the economy is bringing about a new international division of labor, in which the United States is becoming more exclusively a center of finance, business and personal services, and retail trade. For laid-off workers and their communities, however, this trend holds scant hope. Most of the growth in service employment is concentrated in urban areas, not in rural communities where the job loss has been so devastating. Those who do find employment in these "new" sectors rarely earn what they made even in low-wage manufacturing. Production workers in the textile industry, for example, average more than $2 an hour more than waitresses.[12] Moreover, in many rural areas of the South, service-sector growth has taken the form of increased tourism. This industry not only perpetuates historic problems of seasonal jobs and low wages; it also tends, because of rising property taxes, real estate speculation, and the breakup of rural communities, to dispossess people from their land and culture.

Under the Reagan administration, internationalization of the economy was accompanied by militarization of the economy. The $150 billion increase in defense appropriations since 1980 has of course generated jobs; however, it is difficult to assess the direct employment impact in the Southern economy. Many Southern military contracts are not for weapons or military hardware, but for T-shirts, socks, cigarettes, and other nonweaponry items.[13] Despite the overall increase in defense spending, job opportunities in these industries have shrunk dramatically. Perhaps the greatest employment impact of the enormous defense budget has been on military enlistment: lacking job opportunities in their hometowns, young women and men all over the South have joined the armed forces. Perversely enough, military enlistment may be considered the largest employment and training program of the Reagan era.

These are the economic trends that the workers and communities depicted in this volume are combatting. In broad outline, they are the same trends that confront people all over the country. Southerners, however, are struggling to counter these trends within the context of their own regional history—a history characterized by a race-based political economy, virulent anti-unionism, and entrenched political conservatism. This makes their struggles distinctive, but it also makes them specially relevant. The relatively low wages, difficult working conditions, and nonunion status of Southern workers are becoming the standard for workers across the country. The organizing strategies and lessons of Southern workers and their communities thus have a special national meaning today. Their toughness and dignity in the face of tremendous odds offer hope and inspiration for us all.

We're Here to Stay: The Response of Workers and Communities

Although the common problems of unemployment, lowered wages, and a reduced living standard may be found throughout the South, the character and impact of the crisis differ among various areas within the region. For example, in the central Appalachian coalfields, a single dominant industry with a predominantly male work force and a long history of militant trade unionism set the context in which people are seeking a more just economic future. Issues of gender equity and strategies involving labor solidarity are apparent in this subregion. By contrast, the Black Belt counties of the Deep South present a context of stark racial oppression and economic dependence on agriculture, with the inspiration for political activism coming largely from the recent civil rights movement. Issues of racial equality and strategies involving the mobilization of black political power predominate here.

Because of this diversity, the chapters in Part I of this volume are organized by subregion: Central Appalachia, the Piedmont, and the Deep South. Each chapter analyzes a specific organization or group as it wrestles with the consequences of economic crisis. The chapters in Part II evaluate two divergent paths of development for the region. The first section focuses on "Development by Corporate Design"; it contains chapters that analyze broad issues, such as industrial recruitment and service-sector growth, through the experiences of specific groups of people. The second section, "Visions for Change," amplifies the alternative visions of the economy and the new definitions of development that are implicit in current grassroots organizing. The book concludes with a Resources section that lists the key organizations discussed in the text; brief organizational descriptions, plus phone numbers and addresses, are included.

Mike Yarrow's piece, "Voices from the Coalfields" (Chapter 3), explores how miners and their families experience and interpret the massive layoffs and deterioration in working conditions that occurred from 1978 to 1988. Through extensive personal interviews, Yarrow allows those who live the crisis to describe the struggle to survive and maintain dignity, make sense of a drastically changed world, and challenge the corporate offensive against past gains.

John Bookser-Feister and Leah Wise also use the statements of workers themselves to document the climate of fear that pervades the furniture, textile, pharmaceutical, and other plants of the North Carolina Piedmont. "Betrayal of Trust" (Chapter 8) shows how random, at-will terminations, grossly unhealthy working conditions, and other abuses flourish in a state where economic and political elites have viciously and successfully fought unionization and progressive labor legislation for decades.

John Gaventa's essay, "From the Mountains to the *Maquiladoras*" (Chapter 7), takes an in-depth look at one textile company and its relentless search for cheaper production sites. This detailed study of capital flight and its impact on the workers and community left behind provides insight into the economic blackmail that threatens the organizing efforts of people all over the South, and reinforces the "climate of fear" documented by Bookser-Feister and Wise.

Articles from the section on the Deep South add an additional layer of complexity to the analysis. Rickey Hill's exploration of race, economic development, and black political life in Bogalusa, Louisiana (Chapter 11), reveals patterns quite similar to those in many textile and coal towns farther north: an economy dependent on a single industry (paper), a dominant corporation with a paternalistic and racist approach to civic life, and a recent history of automation, layoffs, and increased hardship, especially for working-class residents. By contrast, Alex Willingham's analysis of Burke County, Georgia (Chapter 10), shows the ambiguously progressive role of major corporations that located plants in this extremely poor, agriculturally dependent Black Belt county. By ignoring the county's rigidly racist social code and, most important, by providing an independent economic base for black employees, corporations like Continental Can and Union Bag inadvertently facilitated the growth of black protest and political power.

The essay by Hal Hamilton (Chapter 6) rounds out the analysis of the economic crisis by adding the voice of small farmers. Hamilton analyzes the complex forces, including federal farm policy and the internationalization of the tobacco industry, that are undermining the livelihood of small tobacco farmers in the "Burley Belt" of central Kentucky.

Even as traditional ways of making a living decline, Southern policymakers and corporate officials promise a bright new future based on recruitment of

new industry and the growth of service employment. Carter Garber takes the
bloom off the mythical rose of industrial recruitment by analyzing in detail the
heavy costs and questionable benefits of the much-heralded Saturn plant in
Tennessee (Chapter 14). Robert D. Bullard, in Chapter 15, demonstrates how
frequently racism has guided decisions on siting of hazardous-waste facilities—one of the only industries seeking to locate in many communities of
color across the South. Cindia Cameron focuses on one large segment of the
"new" service work force—women office workers—and the organizing
efforts of the group called 9to5. She describes (in Chapter 16) the restructuring of the office and the marginalization of office workers (through increased
part-time employment, reductions in fringe benefits, and other changes), and
analyzes how these trends create obstacles to organizing as well as new political opportunities.

    In response to these problems of capital flight, economic marginalization,
and environmental danger, working-class people across the South have initiated a kaleidoscope of organizing efforts. Most of these efforts have taken the
form of community-based organizations. Some focus on organizing and ad-
dressing the needs of a specific constituency: the Community Farm Alliance,
for example, works with farmers in Kentucky (see Chapter 6); the Workers'
Rights Project organizes primarily among workers in South Carolina (see
Chapter 9); and the Coal Employment Project works with women coalminers
(see Chapter 4). Other groups have defined their constituency more broadly:
all citizens interested in progressive economic change. Groups like Kentuckians For The Commonwealth (described in Chapter 2) and the Ivanhoe
Civic League (see Chapter 1) are examples.

    Regardless of organizational form, all these groups seek to expand the
economic opportunities and benefits available to their constituents. Two distinct strategies for achieving this goal are apparent in their work. Certain
groups have built local economic institutions—small businesses, co-ops, and
so forth—in a self-help approach to development. Others have challenged
economic priorities and practices in the mainstream economy. Some have
done both.

    The appeal of these grassroots struggles is not limited to the most op-
pressed, most impoverished segment of the population. Indeed, there is wide
diversity in the race, gender, class, and other characteristics of those who have
initiated economic change. Three groups that sought to build up their local
economy through business development illustrate this diversity and its potential implications. The relatively well-to-do white women who founded the
Mayhaw Tree, in southwestern Georgia (see Chapter 13) turned a distinctive
local product that women had made for generations—mayhaw jelly—into a
profitable community development venture quite rapidly, though not without

opposition. The Ivanhoe Civic League, a group of predominantly working-class women and men in southwestern Virginia, sought—so far unsuccessfully—to develop vacant county property into a recreation center. The struggle in Ivanhoe continues, with those who originally pursued their grassroots vision of development becoming increasingly politicized by their experiences (see Chapter 1).

Burke County, located in the Georgia Black Belt, offers a third scenario in community-based development (see Chapter 10). Here, during the 1960s, self-help proponents in the black community formed the East Georgia Farmers' Cooperative to expand the marketing capacity of black farmers. Within the context of extreme racial oppression and white minority political rule, however, such a community development strategy gradually began to seem accommodationist, at least in the eyes of more radical black activists. In recent years, Burke County became a center of successful voting-rights activism and litigation. Black leaders now pursue economic development in the context of black political power.

In contrast to these self-help development strategies, many organizations have chosen direct challenges to corporate practices and government policies in the dominant, mainstream economy. Political pressure and the legislative process have been their primary strategies; corporate campaigns and workplace organizing have receded in importance in recent years as their effectiveness has diminished and the threat of retaliation has increased.

Worker-based groups such as the Coal Employment Project (CEP), Workers' Rights Project, and 9to5 have sought to influence employment conditions through legislation. CEP has been a spearhead of the national drive for a parental-leave law, and the Workers' Rights Project has sought to prohibit retaliatory firings of injured workers. The group called Kentuckians For The Commonwealth has organized a wide spectrum of citizens who are pressuring lawmakers and public officials about tax reform, environmental protection, and democracy in the legislative process. On a more local level, Clergy and Laity Concerned in Robeson County, North Carolina, helped to galvanize opposition to locating a commercial hazardous-waste treatment facility in this poor, triracial county. The history of this struggle is recounted in Chapter 12.

In pursuing its organizational vision, each group confronts economic forces and institutions that are international in scope and often seemingly invincible. To challenge the closing of a local textile plant is, ultimately, to challenge the global mobility of capital. To take on the pricing structure of burley tobacco is to take on a highly concentrated, multinational industry. To fight the layoffs associated with automation is to fight an international trend toward reduced labor costs.

Some groups have, therefore, deliberately sought information, relationships, and influence across national borders. Members of the Ivanhoe Civic League have participated in classes that explored the international aspects of their local economic situation. The Community Farm Alliance has sought to influence federal policy on international issues related to agriculture, such as foreign trade. The Coal Employment Project has sponsored exchange visits between British and American coalminers. Ann Seidman picks up this theme of internationalization in her essay on the economic connections between the southeastern United States and southern Africa (Chapter 17); she also suggests ways to build international understanding, solidarity, and, ultimately, a world at peace.

Each group must also fight against a powerful undertow of apathy and resignation among its own constituents. The fear and desperation of hard times have generated a tendency to "accept whatever we can get" that will produce income and jobs—be it a hazardous-waste facility, a minimum-wage restaurant, or an unhealthy work environment. Several organizations have been able to overcome attitudes of powerlessness and political inertia by appealing to deeply held cultural values and relationships, which in many cases have been violated by the actions of corporate and public officials. For example, the Lumbee Indians who joined in opposition to the hazardous-waste facility in Robeson County did so out of their fierce love for and longstanding economic and spiritual relationship with the threatened Lumbee River. Native American dance, music, and regalia were used to maximum effect in their organizing activities. The importance of the cultural roots of resistance is amplified in Chapter 19, where Deborah Clifton Hils contrasts the values of her Louisiana Creole culture with those inherent in industrial development.

Even as organizations have flourished because of their cultural roots, many have also sought to overcome the oppressive aspects of their heritage, particularly the deep-seated prejudice associated with race, class, and gender. Women, for example, have been central, visible leaders in community organizations such as the Ivanhoe Civic League, the Mayhaw Tree, and Kentuckians For The Commonwealth. Women's economic needs have risen to the top of the agenda of some organizations. In Chapter 5 Chris Weiss pursues this theme by analyzing the damaging consequences of development schemes that ignore women's activities and needs and by arguing for placing women's leadership and concerns at the center of economic decision making.

Despite the diversity of issues, strategies, and constituencies here, common visions inspire the work of many of the organizations represented in this book. Every group is making it possible for poor and working-class people to appropriate some control over their economic lives. Every group is reaching for a new definition of *development* by advocating the economic interests and future of its constituents—ordinary people who are typically ignored when policymakers craft development plans or when corporations decide on plant locations. These groups do more than seek a humane and equitable economic future; to varying degrees, they also seek to appropriate *power* over that future. They seek economic democracy.

All the contributions in the second section of Part II take up the challenge of articulating this vision of a more just and democratic economy. Wendy Luttrell's piece (Chapter 18) analyzes the historical process by which the economy came to be seen as an external, mysterious force that could be neither understood nor controlled by ordinary people. She explores the ways economic education can be used as a vehicle for reappropriating that control and understanding.

The final three chapters analyze the relevance of national economic renewal programs to the South (Chapter 21), put forth a visionary proposal for an economy centered on human services (Chapter 20), and offer suggestions for strategic initiatives that can move us in the direction of economic democracy (Chapter 22). None of these articles purports to be a unifying manifesto or a blueprint for collective action. Our efforts have not yet reached the point when such a document can be written. Each of the last five chapters, like those in the rest of the book, provides a piece of a vision that can be made real only through a much wider and stronger movement. They are offered in the hope of moving us all closer to the day when such a movement becomes possible.

NOTES

1. Recent analyses of the region's economy include *Economic Transformation: The Appalachian Challenge* (Knoxville, Tenn.: Commission on Religion in Appalachia, 1986); *Shadows in the Sunbelt* (Chapel Hill, N.C.: MDC, 1986); Stuart A. Rosenfeld, Edward M. Bergman, and Sarah Rubin, *After the Factories: Changing Employment Patterns in the Rural South* (Durham, N.C.: Southern Growth Policies Board, 1985); *Women of the Rural South: Economic Status and Prospects* (Lexington, Ky.: Southeast Women's Employment Coalition, 1986).

2. See two publications by the Southern Regional Council: *Patterns of Poverty* (Atlanta, 1984) and *Public Assistance and Poverty* (Atlanta, 1985); both were prepared by Steve Suitts.

3. "Comparing Appalachia's Counties with the Nation's," *Appalachia* 19, nos. 2–4 (Spring 1986): 8–10. National Advisory Committee on Rural Poverty, *The People Left Behind* (Washington, D.C.: U.S. Government Printing Office, 1967). See also the review by Peter Dorner, "Fourteen Million Rural Poor," *The Yale Review* 68 (1969): 282–92.

4. MDC, *Shadows in the Sunbelt;* Report of the 1986 Commission on the Future of the South, *Halfway Home and a Long Way to Go* (Durham, N.C.: Southern Growth Policies Board, 1986), 5.

5. "Comparing Appalachia's Counties . . ."; U.S. Congress, Joint Economic Committee, *The Bi-Coastal Economy: Regional Patterns of Economic Growth During the Reagan Administration,* study prepared by the Democratic staff, July 1986.

6. U.S. Congress, Office of Technology Assessment, *Technology and Structural Unemployment: Reemploying Displaced Adults,* OTA-1TE-250 (Washington, D.C.: U.S. Government Printing Office, 1986), 5.

7. For a review of the various perspectives on the quality of new jobs, see Gary W. Loveman and Chris Tilly, "Good Jobs or Bad Jobs: What Does the Evidence Say?" *New England Economic Review* (January/February 1988): 46–65.

8. U.S. Congress, Joint Economic Committee, *The Great American Job Machine: The Proliferation of Low-Wage Employment in the U.S. Economy,* study prepared by Barry Bluestone and Bennett Harrison, December 1986. Also see their book, *The Great U-Turn: Corporate Restructuring and the Polarizing of America* (New York: Basic Books, 1988), and U.S. Office of Technology Assessment, *Technology and Structural Unemployment.*

9. *Coal Data,* selected years (Washington, D.C.: National Coal Association).

10. Stuart Rosenfeld, "A Divided South," in *Everybody's Business: A People's Guide to Economic Development,* a special edition of *Southern Exposure* 14, nos. 5–6 (September/October and November/December 1986): 12.

11. See Lionel J. Beaulieu, *The Rural South in Crisis: Challenges for the Future* (Boulder, Colo.: Westview Press, 1988).

12. See Rosenfeld, Bergman, and Rubin, *After the Factories*; U.S. Department of Labor, Bureau of Labor Statistics, *Employment, Hours, and Earnings, United States, 1909–84* (Washington, D.C.: U.S. Government Printing Office, 1985).

13. Tom Schlesinger, with John Gaventa and Juliet Merrifield, *Our Own Worst Enemy: The Impact of Military Production on the Upper South* (New Market, Tenn.: Highlander Research and Education Center, 1983).

Part I

CASE STUDIES OF
CRISIS AND STRUGGLE

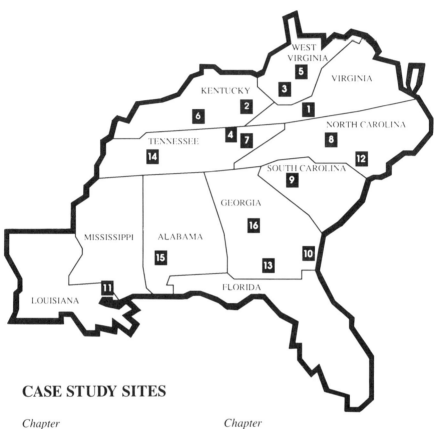

CASE STUDY SITES

Case Studies
from Central Appalachia

BENEATH the rugged mountains of central Appalachia lies some of the highest-quality bituminous coal in the world. Geology has also endowed the area with oil, natural gas, carbide, and other natural resources. Extractive industries based on these resources—above all, bituminous coalmining—have been the dominant force in the area's economic and political life for a century.

Unlike much of the rest of the South, the central Appalachian coalfields, particularly in West Virginia, have a long tradition of strong trade unionism. Bloody confrontations over union recognition erupted at Matewan, Paint Creek, Harlan, and elsewhere during the first decades of this century. Unionization represented a vehicle not only for protecting miners around workplace issues, but also for challenging the coal industry's monolithic domination of health care delivery, school systems, county governments, and other community institutions.

Today, massive layoffs and an anti-union offensive by certain companies are testing the strength of the United Mine Workers of America (UMWA). Introduction of longwall technology (which shears the coal away from the seam along a "long wall"), coupled with a determined productivity drive that theatens hard-won health and safety practices, has made possible higher production with a greatly reduced work force. As Mike Yarrow describes in Chapter 3, some coal companies, most notably A. T. Massey, have taken advantage of miners' diminished bargaining leverage and attempted to operate nonunion even in the UMWA's stronghold in southern West Virginia.

For women, the singular domination of extractive industries with male work forces traditionally meant virtual exclusion from the formal economy. In Chapter 4 Betty Jean Hall describes the activities of the Coal Employment Project, which reversed this historic pattern by gaining access for women to jobs in the coalmines. Other organizations have celebrated and built on women's traditional activities in the informal economy (home-based production of food and clothing, for example), and their successes have often been critical to economic survival in the fickle, boom-and-bust economy of the coalfields. Women and Employment, described in Chapter 5 by Chris Weiss, has encouraged small-business development by women and has been an advocate for women's role in economic development decision making.

Hardship has also spurred the formation of other community-based organizations, often led by women, which seek to democratize economic control. The Ivanhoe Civic League of southwestern Virginia, led by Maxine Waller and described in Chapter 1, has sought to diversify the local economy and to redefine *development* to include local leadership and control. Kentuckians For The Commonwealth, a broad-based group discussed in Chapter 2, seeks to open up state policymaking processes to ordinary citizens and relieve underfunded public services through more equitable taxation of company-controlled land. In a region where labor struggles, usually led by men, predominated in the past, community organizations, often led by women, have emerged.

CHAPTER

1

"It Has to Come from the People": Responding to Plant Closings in Ivanhoe, Virginia

Maxine Waller, Helen M. Lewis, Clare McBrien, and Carroll L. Wessinger

In September 1986 the people of Ivanhoe, Virginia, formed the Ivanhoe Civic League for one purpose: to stop Wythe and Carroll counties from selling an abandoned, overgrown industrial park. The park had been left to the local industrial development authorities twenty years earlier, when National Carbide, long the town's major employer, closed down its operation. The announcement that the property was for sale was the signal that local economic development officials were giving up all hope of locating another industry for the community.

In response, the residents of Ivanhoe began a citizens' campaign to revitalize the dying town. Their efforts made the national news, including an emotional fundraising event called "Hands Across Ivanhoe," in which 3,000 people paid $3 each to stand in the cold rain and hold hands in support of their community.[1] People who had grown up in Ivanhoe and moved away came home or sent money. The editor of *Appalachia*, the Appalachian Regional Commission's publication, wrote, "It gives us hope that something can be done to breathe life back into our home towns—rural America."[2]

Initially, the main strategy was to recruit a major new industry, to do what the industrial development authorities had been unable to do. As this is written, the people of Ivanhoe still do not have a new industry. Nevertheless, they have accomplished a great deal: they have waged a campaign to educate themselves about the economy, to develop their own community-centered development, to start a literacy and training center, to make officials accountable to them for the development of their community.

Ivanhoe is a small rural mountain community in southwestern Virginia. It straddles Wythe and Carroll counties, and is the poorest area in both. For a hundred years Ivanhoe was a booming center for mining iron, lead, zinc, and manganese. Two of the largest industries in southwestern Virginia were located here: National Carbide and New Jersey Zinc Company. In 1966, National Carbide closed, taking 450 jobs with it. In 1981, 350 more jobs were lost when New Jersey Zinc closed. Closings of furniture plants and sewing factories in surrounding counties have left the area economically devastated.

At its height, in the 1940s, Ivanhoe had around 4,500 residents, racially and ethnically mixed. It had a school, railroad, hotel, stores, theater, doctor, and restaurant. Now Ivanhoe has about 1,300 residents. The school, stores, theater, and railroad are all gone. Employment opportunities are very limited. Those who found work after the factories and mines closed commute an average of 63 miles—to jobs with lower pay and fewer benefits.

The first accomplishment of the Ivanhoe Civic League was blocking the sale of the industrial park. In 1986 the local industrial development authorities agreed to delay the sale for two years, to give the league itself time to recruit an industry to the park. This was the beginning of a vigorous campaign that included trips to Richmond to talk to the governor and legislators. The community recruited a small manufacturing industry to the old Carbide building, but the company was unable to raise sufficient capital to employ more than three people. County developers steered other potentially interested industries away from Ivanhoe to the newer growth areas located along the interstates.

Ivanhoe is located on the New River, one of the cleanest fresh-water rivers in the East. When the factories in Ivanhoe were operating, a railroad ran along the river valley, through the national forest. Now the state is developing the area along the old railroad bed into the New River Trail, a state park for hiking and biking. The industrial park is located at the head of the new trail.

During the first summer, League members and community volunteers cleaned up the land along the river by the industrial park. They named it Jubilee park, from the biblical theme of the Jubilee year. Like the people in Leviticus, they claimed it as sacred land to commemorate their repossession of it, and had a week-long Fourth of July festival in 1987 to celebrate their revived determination, to raise funds, and to mobilize the community.

After the Jubilee celebration, the Civic League began a campaign to secure the land for a permanent recreation park. As it became more and more obvious that recruiting an industry to their small rural community was unlikely, they began to plan Jubilee Park as an alternative, a community-owned enterprise. The park would have camping, bike and raft rental, and a convenience store, providing both jobs and recreation for the community, and recreation for tourists. League members hoped to use the income to finance further economic development. But they soon met resistance from the local authorities. The officials had given the community two years to find an industry for the industrial park land, but they refused to count Jubilee Park as "industry," holding to the traditional view that economic development is what happens when a factory comes into a community from the outside. Furthermore, they would not allow the Civic League to lease or buy the land.

After several frustrating encounters with the local governments and industrial development boards, the Civic League experienced a sense of powerlessness. But their discouragement led to a new determination: if anything was going to happen in Ivanhoe, it would be because the people made it happen.

In the league's small office in an abandoned building they had renovated, the group organized a six-week series of economic workshops for the community, where they read and discussed studies of rural economic development.[3] They carried out a community survey, which led them to change their major focus from "chasing smokestacks"—trying to bring a factory into town—to looking at smaller local development based on their own needs and resources. They also changed their goals from industrial recruitment to broader community development. They had already organized a senior citizens' program and a youth recreation program, but during the six weeks of the workshop they began literacy classes and GED training. Later, they renovated the old company store and named it "Ivanhoe Tech," a community-controlled education center. They now see themselves working to develop a new model of community development, one that is more self-sufficient and locally based. From an initial goal of getting *any* development, they are now creating their own.

Maxine Waller is the energetic and creative leader of the Civic League. Here she tells us what happened in Ivanhoe.

"I Wanted GM and I Wanted GE and I Wanted IBM"

I started out as an idealist. I believed in everything the American system said I should believe in. I was trying to be a true American—live my life, go to work and come home, go to the grocery store and pay the bills. When we lost the mines, we lost our jobs, I thought it was because we had done something wrong. Somehow we had made this gigantic mistake and made the company look bad or do bad or be bad because we had a union.

I have learned a lot, and one of the things I learned was that the company was in the black. They were making money but they could get more money by leaving us stranded without jobs, because our government gave them all these wonderful tax breaks and all these credits. So I found out that the American system is not made for the American people, in a sense. There's more poor people than rich people but rich people are in control. And one day you wake up like me, a thirty-eight-year-old woman, and you realize that you have done all those things you are supposed to: you paid your taxes; you sent your children to school. You just accept. Then one morning you realize it was the right way for the multi-rich people, for these rich people who live in these wonderful houses, that aren't hungry and aren't cold, but it's not the right way for you. Some people just go back and accept it again—but I am not going to accept it.

I am going to bring about some changes. I know I am still going to have to pay taxes and I am still going to have to deal with the government, but I am going to bring about changes in my own life, and I am going to be in control. I am going to teach my children there is a difference between being an American and being part of the so-called system, and that the Constitution does grant us rights. But we have got to bring about some changes. I am going to bring about changes with my children and my neighbors' children and anybody else that will listen to me.

First thing that I had to do was accept the fact that I couldn't change everything overnight. We didn't get in this situation overnight. Then I realized along the line that it was a world problem. The depression is a world problem, and there are people all over the country and all over the world bringing about these little changes just like we are. We are going to work here in our community, but as time goes on, it will spread out to other communities and other people will learn from it.

I was really blind. We wanted this wonderful factory and it had to have smoke coming out of it and it would employ the people. I just knew that was the answer for us, so I went out to get this factory. I kept trying to find a factory and there wasn't none to find. I kept knocking on doors and I called people and I worried the hell out of some people trying to figure some way to get a factory to come. I wanted this white knight waving an American flag to come down the street and have all these wonderful jobs. I wanted GM and I wanted GE and I wanted IBM to come in here and save us, but that didn't happen.

"With My Bible Under One Arm and My Dictionary Under the Other"

The first thing that happened was that we were treated as radicals, as bad children. Our governments in Wythe and Carroll counties kept throwing out all these big educated words that mean nothing and all these theories that mean nothing to nobody. That's not living and eating and sleeping and walking and thinking. That's not reality. They do that to throw the poor people off. They have this other language and they think you don't understand it. But hell,

I've got a dictionary and that was my main thing. I carried it under my arm. My Bible is under one arm and my dictionary under the other. I figured what the Lord didn't straighten out for me, the dictionary would.

I was always looking up these words. I would go to all these damn meetings, and they would throw out all these big words and I would get my dictionary to look them up and that would throw them off completely. I would say, "I didn't understand what you said and I'm going to look it up and see what it means." And I'd read the damned definition to them. When I got *Robert's Rules of Order* on how to run a meeting, that really just floored them all. I was standing up before 140 people, and the Senator was beside me and the delegate beside me and the head of economic development in southwest Virginia, and they are all sitting there in their little three-piece suits. I was reading this *Robert's Rules of Order* and then I just shut it and said, "According to *Robert's Rules of Order* I can do any damn thing I want to."

So that's the way it is, because this is a people movement and we are doing what suits us and not what suits Robert or anybody else. And that's when I really got a grasp on it. It didn't make a damn if we didn't do things just exactly right as long as we did things right for us, if it was right for the people. And that's what we have been doing all this time.

I went to Tennessee to the Highlander Center in January or February of 1987. I had applied for a SALT fellowship, which is Southern Appalachian Leadership Training Program. I was really upset because I wasn't trained with anything, I didn't know what I was doing, just haphazardly doing stuff. I felt like I needed some extra school but I didn't want to go over to the college because that is the kind the political system has and they used *Robert's Rules of Order* and they were going against everything we were trying to do. Nothing had to do with the people.

I went to the Highlander Center and they asked me why I was there. I said I wanted a factory to employ the people because the people were tired and cold and hungry and they wanted a job. And I wanted a factory and that was it. If someone could find me a factory, then I would be happy. I spent the weekend out there, talking and listening to other people. They were in the same boat as me. Part of them had a factory and didn't want it because it was the wrong kind of factory. I thought, "Oh, I just want any kind of factory," and they kept saying, "No, you don't, you don't want one that kills the people," and I thought, "Are there factories that kill people?"

I got to reading wonderful articles, and resource books, and then I read the Bible. All the time I read the Bible. I read *Unexpected News: Reading the Bible with Third World Eyes.* I didn't even know there *was* a Third World. I still haven't figured out who said there was a Third World and who decided that the United States was the first world. I read *Colonialism in Modern America: the Appalachian Case.*[4] I got to reading about all these things in Appalachia and I also got to traveling around in the Appalachian mountains, so I had some eye-opening experiences. I went to Kentucky and I saw strip mining. I went to Kentucky, and I saw these beautiful, beautiful mountains that God made being destroyed by man. Only God can make a mountain and man should leave it alone. There is no reclaiming a mountain after man has destroyed it.

I saw the video of *Global Assembly Line*. I was crying because I was so mad—they were shooting people in the Philippines, and all they wanted to do was work. You know, here in Ivanhoe all we wanted to do was work but everybody says we want to be on welfare. You can go over to Wytheville and over to the government offices and they say, "All those people over there want to do is be on welfare." But you know when we did the survey here, didn't nobody say they wanted to be on welfare and didn't nobody ask to be a millionaire. But the American system is set up so that people are on welfare.

I began to see it was a world problem more than just an Ivanhoe problem and more than an Appalachian problem. I went to Dungannon, Virginia, and I went to Trammell, Virginia, and I learned a really wonderful lesson about getting independent and dependent at the same time. I learned it is easy to get dependent on someone else. I decided that we would be diversified, and that we would keep control. When outsiders came in, we would keep control. We wouldn't just let anybody come in and take charge. I had seen that happen to a lot of little places in Appalachia. They were defeated—the same people who had helped them be independent made them dependent again. So we had to be independent and we had to be in control. The people of Ivanhoe—if it is good or if it is bad, if it is a failure or if it is a huge success—the people of Ivanhoe have to be in charge. We will do it together.

I had to realize that all people are not going to see the same way, and it is going to take a while for some people to see. There is not anybody that I haven't in some way tried to work with; they are part of the community even though they go around saying we are doing wrong. "We didn't get no factory." I don't know how many times I have heard "We didn't get no factory."

"It Has to Come from the People"

We made some comparisons between the kind of development we used to have under Carbide and New Jersey Zinc and the kind of development we wanted to have. And people started talking about all the awful parts of working for these industries and how they wanted a different kind of industry. That was a change for some people in that room. M. H., in particular, came forth and said, "If we have to have that same kind of industry I don't want it. I worked for it."

That was the turning point for education. That was when everyone said that we want to get the kind of industry *we* want, one that is good for us, and one that we can live with. We don't want the kind we have had. We were uneducated then, so we better get a better education. But we don't want the education they are teaching over at the college, because that teaches us to go along with what has been done. We want something different.

People started reading those articles on the "buffalo hunt" and others.[5] See, many years ago there really were buffalos and they skinned this buffalo and they used the skin, the horns, the eyes, the head, everything, and they ate it but they didn't kill more than they needed. Then men came along with get-rich schemes—power. They could make money by selling the skins so they went out and killed the buffalo and just got the skin and left all the meat, the carcasses out on the prairie, and then there weren't any more buffalo. In the 1940s and 1950s and 1960s they went up north and they went buffalo hunting there for industries and said, "If you will come down south, we will work for you for a little bit of nothing and we will make you rich people. You just come on down south. You will have a wonderful home with us."

So the industries moved down and they left all these vacant buildings up north and that was like the carcasses and meat of the buffalo. They brought the buffalo skins down here and put them up like little teepees, little factories everywhere, and everyone went to work but we didn't have a union so they didn't treat us right and we had to do this slave labor for a little bit of pay. We became dependent. And the people up north were in the same boat so some of them came down south to try and keep working. Only thing was, when they came down south they worked for about half what they worked for up north. Then because we lured them down here they knew somebody else would lure them someplace else.

So you see we went buffalo hunting and the Northern people were crippled by what we did to them. We deindustrialized them, then we industrialized the South, and now the South is almost crippled by what has happened, so this is called an economic crisis.

I don't know the answer to the economic crisis but I know that it has to come from the people. It has got to come out of the hands of the so-called system and the so-called powerful people and come back to the people—the dinner buckets of America and the dinner buckets of Korea and the dinner buckets of the Philippines.

"Who Made the Decisions?"

Another eye-awakening time in my life was in May 1987 at Highlander. I had brought two people with me, and the people at Highlander asked us, "Who was in charge of Ivanhoe, the political system in charge of the bank? Who made the decisions about Ivanhoe?" And we got to writing out and talking and asking ourselves who owned the land, what politicians voted for us or voted against us, who had control, and the rest. And we found out that the powers of the two counties were the powers in the banks, all business people, insurance, the lawyers, doctors, all those people. The people in charge are also the people we depended most on, the people that hold the life line to us. We found out that there was no separation between them; there weren't two groups of people, they were the same people. That was an eye-opener for all of us—to find out that someone who had played a big political part in our lives was the landlord here.

That was one of the reasons I wanted the classes in economics because I couldn't understand the economy of Ivanhoe. I didn't understand that none of our money stays here, so why shouldn't we be poor? I found out if you have money and put it in a place and it stays in the community and turns over two or three times, that's what makes the community economically stable. We live here but we pay rent to people outside and it goes out of Ivanhoe—we never bring it into our town. That's the reason we are economically depressed.

I don't think it is going to be a fast process to bring things around, but I am really convinced that we will do it. It is going to be a lifetime and more than my life. I think this is something that will pass on to my children and their children because this is happening all over the country. You wake up one day and these industries have gone and left these communities and there is nothing there to support them.

I've had a lot of problems being a woman, first by not being taken seriously. "Pat her on the back and she will go home." And "Hush." But I didn't—I didn't go home and I didn't hush. They patted me on the back and called me "honey" and "darling," and I resent those words, because I'm not anybody's honey and I'm not anybody's darling. I'm a person and the way they were treating me was, "Go home and make little brownies for the PTA meeting. We'll take care of this, honey, we know what we are doing." Being a woman has opened a lot of doors, but in the community it has created some resentment from mountain men, especially the older men who believe that a woman should be seen and not heard. She should go to church and she should be at home and cook the meals. My husband doesn't feel that way—I am really blessed with that. So far I have been able to turn everything around and present things in a way that people could see that it was right. They couldn't say it is because she is a woman that this happened or that happened, because it wasn't that.

"So Who Is Educated?"

Ivanhoe is what I am working for. It is hard for me to even begin to think that I could ever sit here and think like I think now, but it's because of this education process I have been through. I have some strikes against me because I am a woman and because of not being educated, not educated in the system. I don't have little papers to go with my education, but I've got an education all right. I've got a wonderful education because I read and I research and I do all these things but they are not things I can write on a piece of paper and add "XYZ" behind my name.

When I started out I thought like them: economic development was a factory. And what has happened? I have left them behind. I didn't realize that until right now, but I am superior in my thinking, and these people are in charge of economic development. I realize that you can't go out and get these little factories no more. And these are educated people in charge of economic development and they are still looking for factories, and I realize you can't get them. So who is educated?

I used to feel so inferior to these people; they had their little suits and they go to the club for lunch, but now I don't feel inferior to them. I feel superior to them. Theirs is an educated ignorance. They are educated to the point that they are ignorant. I can't feel equal to them. I can't be equal to them because I have an open mind. People in Ivanhoe are receptive to new ideas, new thoughts. But these people are not. Is it because they are not cold and hungry? Is it because they have plenty to eat and plenty of money? Is it because we don't have those things, is that why we are grasping and doing so much and being so receptive to everything and they are not? Because they are comfortable and we are uncomfortable?

They don't have to listen to us because they are not dependent on us and we are dependent on them—or they *thought* we were. But somewhere along the line, someday they are going to wake up and they are going to find out that this bunch of people here, this core bunch of people in Ivanhoe, are going to be *independent*. They keep thinking we are going to die and we are going to quit and they are going to break us apart. They have done everything to throw us off.

We questioned who the kings of the world were. How did you get so much power? Who decides? Who made these decisions and why? Did you make these decisions because it was good for us, the taxpayers, or did you make these decisions because it was good for you? And how much taxes do you pay? And who buys lunch at the club? We asked them a lot of stuff. So we have kind of shook their castle—cracked the base of it.

The political powers would like to see our group separated, because we banded together and we have stayed together for so long and have been such a strong force. If part of us stand on one side and part on the other, that's exactly what they want. And that has happened all over the world.

In August 1987 I talked with the assistant county administrator, and he said—as long as I live I will remember these words—"Maxine, what's wrong with you is you have never learned to work within the system." And I said right back to him, "If the system, the so-called system, is set up to make people cold and make people hungry and uneducated and to die in poverty, then God help the damn system. Because the system is wrong. There needs to be a new system because this one is not working."

We don't have many successful models to follow. We are brand-new at it. We are giving birth to a new way of life for the Appalachian people. I feel like we are nurturing a baby and we are going to have to be stronger than most people. I think we are progressive. We are dealing with something entirely different from what has been done before. We have been so creative. I think this is the right place to be and the right time, and I think we will be a role model in economic development. We have gone out of the system and started thinking in terms of reality. We have a stronger momentum, a stronger movement right now. The time is right.

NOTES

1. For an example of national news coverage, see "Virginia Town Staves Off Disaster," *Washington Post,* February 11, 1987.

2. Jack Russell, *Appalachia* 20, no. 2 (Fall 1987).

3. The discussions began when the members of the Ivanhoe Civic League contacted Carroll L. Wessinger, a Lutheran minister, and Clare McBrien, a local Catholic church worker, for assistance. In turn, they contacted Helen M. Lewis of the Highlander Research and Education Center because of her work in economic education in other communities. Highlander's approach to economic education is described in Chapter 18 and in several publications available from the center (see Resources).

4. Robert McAfee Brown, *Unexpected News: Reading the Bible with Third World Eyes* (Philadelphia: Westminster Press, 1984). Helen Matthews Lewis, Linda Johnson, and Donald Askins, *Colonialism in Modern America: The Appalachian Case* (Boone, N.C.: Appalachian Consortium Press, 1978).

5. This is a reference to a report discussed during the six-week economics class, *Shadows in the Sunbelt,* prepared by MDC, Inc., an economic development research group in North Carolina (Chapel Hill, 1986). In the report, MDC compares the strategy of industrial recruitment or "smokestack chasing" to "the great buffalo hunts of the last century. . . . The stampede of plants to the South is definitely over—especially in rural areas that lack a skilled workforce, transportation, infrastructure, and cultural amenities. Yet the hunters continue in their pursuit, hoping to bag one of the remaining hides" (p. 10). The report urges the South to go "beyond the buffalo hunt" to seek new strategies for community-based economic development.

CHAPTER

2

People Power: Working for the Future In the East Kentucky Coalfields

Kristin Layng Szakos

Mountains laid bare and barren by strip mining; absentee mineral owners in far-away boardrooms making decisions that take no account of the
needs of the people living on the land; poor schools turning out poor people
dependent on coalmining for their livelihood; mechanization in the mines
driving unemployment rates over 30 percent—these problems of central Appalachia have been well documented in the books and articles that have been
pouring out since the region was "rediscovered" twenty-five years ago during
the War on Poverty.[1]

Less noted are the stories of the people working to solve the problems and
change the structures of Appalachian power. This chapter tells some of those
stories, rays of hope for the future.

The people in eastern Kentucky are much the same as those anywhere.
They want to be safe and secure, they want to make their world a decent place,
and they want to provide a good life for their children. But in this area, which
is dependent on a single industry—coal—for its economic health, they face a
special set of obstacles to their search for the good life.

The state government has long supported the welfare of the coal industry
at the expense of its residents, leaving poor roads and bridges, poor schools
and poor services as millions of dollars' worth of coal leave these rolling
mountains every year, loaded onto trucks, barges, and railroad cars.

Until 1988, Kentucky was the only major Appalachian coal-producing state that did not allow local governments and school districts to tax the vast mineral wealth as property, and the state property tax on coal was so small that local and appeals courts recently ruled that it was really an unconstitutional tax exemption. Because the owners of minerals in Kentucky are often different from the surface-land owners (vast mineral reserves were sold at the turn of the century while much of the surface stayed in the hands of local residents), the surface owners—whose land *is* taxable—have had to bear the burden of supporting state and local government and schools. The mineral owners (mostly absentee corporations, as a 1980 study[2] showed) paid little or no property tax. In the eastern Kentucky mountains, where the state's mineral resources are concentrated, this loss of taxable property results in county and school budgets that are hopelessly tight.

- Eastern Kentucky ranks near the bottom of the nation in the quality of public education, according to the Kentucky Education Association. Teachers are underpaid, buildings overcrowded, and students sell candy and light bulbs to pay for school cleaning supplies and textbooks. Half the students who begin high school in eastern Kentucky drop out before they graduate, and many who do finish perform poorly on standardized tests. In the 1980 census, Kentucky showed the nation's highest rate of adult illiteracy.

- According to studies by the Citizens Education and Water Monitoring Project, sponsored by Kentuckians For The Commonwealth, more than one of every five water wells in eastern Kentucky has been contaminated or lost through mineral extraction. Tax money is not available to provide public water systems. Plastic jugs are still the primary water source for many families whose wells have been damaged.

- Overloaded, uncovered coal trucks, often weighing forty to fifty tons, spill coal on the roads and tear at the surface of paved roads, creating a washboard surface dotted with potholes. Tax money is not available for road repair.

- Public funds are not available for fire departments in most eastern Kentucky communities. While volunteer firefighters collect donations and sell baked goods at local fairs to purchase trucks and hoses, insurance rates on unprotected homes skyrocket.

- Public libraries are small, understocked, and understaffed, and most smaller communities do not have a library at all.

For years, the coal industry has kept dissent to a whisper by arguing that it will take care of the people of eastern Kentucky—providing jobs, paying taxes for roads and services, and donating land for schools. Economic fear has long kept many Kentuckians—and their government—quiet about the tax inequities and environmental damage associated with the mining industry.

Largely as a result of this community cooperation and low taxation, the mid-1980s were banner years for the coal industry. The year 1987 saw record production levels by the larger companies, with corresponding record profits. Yet unemployment in coal counties is among the highest in the nation, roads are pitted and dangerous, local governments must choose between operating water systems or jails, and Kentucky's schools are the poorest of all the states.

If anything, the region is worse off now than it was in 1964, when President Lyndon B. Johnson came to Martin County to declare his War on Poverty. Then, many people farmed, granting themselves some measure of independence. And those who did not could travel to Detroit, Cincinnati, or Chicago to find other work. Today, as those areas struggle with their own economic crises, there is nowhere else to go.

Although the region continues to be dependent on the coal industry, growing numbers of Kentuckians are beginning to see through the promises and threats of the industry, and are realizing that if they want good things for their state, they must get them themselves—even if it means fighting the industry and the state itself to do it.

Kentuckians For The Commonwealth

Citizens' groups in Martin and Harlan counties, who had been working independently for many years on taxation and environmental issues, came together in late 1981 to combat the inequities the coal industry had brought to their state. The Kentucky Fair Tax Coalition, as the new group was called, helped to form citizens' groups in other counties to address local issues and encouraged the groups to work together on statewide problems. While members of a local group worked to keep a coal company from polluting local streams, for example, the coalition would work with them to change state regulations concerning water pollution by coal mines.

In 1988, the coalition was renamed Kentuckians For The Commonwealth (KFTC). It now has more than 2,400 members throughout the state who are beginning to break the stranglehold of the coal industry and to broaden citizen participation in the decisions that affect their lives.

Although people have fought injustices in Kentucky for generations, never before has there been such a large and concerted effort to change the structures that have kept the coal industry's hold strong. KFTC members worked hard to remove the exemption from property tax enjoyed by mineral owners, to establish rules to make the state legislature more responsive to voters and less responsive to cash, to improve public access to schools and school boards, and to protect the environment from coalmining, oil and gas extraction, and toxic wastes.

Through all its work, KFTC has emphasized leadership development, teaching people to participate effectively in community and public affairs. In this way, citizens will continue to have an impact on the policies that affect them, long after the coal is gone.

The heart of KFTC's leadership development philosophy can be found in the preface of the organization's leadership training manual. Devised by staff members from their experience in working with groups and adopted by the KFTC steering committee, the preface outlines the ideal of citizen leadership within the organization.

Everyone has the potential to lead, but most people are discouraged from taking leadership roles. Our social and economic systems prevent ordinary people from recognizing and developing their talents and skills for leadership by celebrating the rich, powerful and well-educated as leaders. Too often society ignores the contributions of homemakers, retirees, laborers, and others in making their communities better places to live. To break these barriers, KFTC's leadership training program is intended to draw out an individual's potential and encourage ongoing skills development by practice and direct application in real situations.

Training sessions consist of practice, role playing, discussion, and evaluations. Sometimes they are led by staff, sometimes by more experienced members. Through this practical and methodical training, KFTC members learn to lobby legislators, write letters to the editor, raise money, run meetings, talk to the press, and hold public forums. So effective has the leadership training been, in fact, that staff control, so common in some citizens' groups, would be difficult to wield in KFTC. At the annual membership meeting, staff members are banned from the room during the business meeting and elections!

Steering committee members elected by each county chapter help set the yearly goals for the organization, using recommendations from chapter meetings, and the annual platform is adopted at the annual membership meeting. The steering committee sets priorities for staff time, and must approve any major organizational move.

The People of KFTC

Willa Hood

KFTC members have come to the struggle for different reasons. For Willa Hood, librarian at the Leslie County Public Library, conditions at work led her to question, and ultimately work to change, the current taxation system in Kentucky.

"We do not have enough space or volumes to serve our county population, according to the state's minimum standards for libraries," she told participants at a public hearing in Hazard in 1986. "We're short by 9,412 volumes and by 9,000 square feet. The salaries of the library staff are far below that of the business sector. We also have no retirement program and no medical coverage."

The problems at the library stem from lack of money, she said. With federal cutbacks during the Reagan administration, federal funding has been cut from 41 percent to 16 percent of the Leslie County library's budget. Because the library district could not tax the valuable coal property in the county before 1988, it has so far been unable to compensate for the loss.

"We need to be increasing services and adding staff," she said. "We have a lot of equipment that is getting old and needs to be replaced. Instead of adding services and space and materials and staff, we will be cutting back unless we receive more funding."

Hood became one of KFTC's earliest members because she believed that the efforts of the group to enact an unmined minerals tax were crucial to saving the region's economy.

> Libraries are not only affected by the economy, but we also have an effect on the economy. The strong educational role that the library plays in the county can only have a positive effect on the economy.
>
> Information is power, and we must be constantly alert to and strongly opposed to anything that poses limitations on free access to information and opportunities that public libraries offer. Otherwise, information will become available only to those who can afford it. And if this happens, the powerful will then be more powerful and the powerless will become less powerful. Let us do what we can to ensure that this does not happen.

The work of Willa Hood and other KFTC members has had an impact. The state supreme court recently ruled that coal's exemption from property taxation was unconstitutional, opening the way to increased revenues for counties, schools, and public libraries.

Everett Akers

A big man in a powder-blue suit, his thick white hair combed to the side, Everett Akers at seventy-two was an impressive man. A businessman, a venture in coin-operated machines had led him in the late 1960s to a term in the state legislature, where, he later admitted, his only goal was to pass legislation related to coin-operated machines.

In the legislature, Akers discovered that his constituents didn't know what went on in the state capital. Television stations serving Kentucky's eastern mountains all originated in West Virginia. People back home were familiar with West Virginia politics, but many knew nothing about their own government. He returned to Floyd County after one term, determined to bring Kentucky news to eastern Kentucky. He built a giant television tower to receive broadcasts from Lexington and began business as a cable television operator.

The new business did not last long. Soon after the tower went up, Triple Elkhorn Coal Company, which had obtained a deed to the coal under Akers's land, brought in strip-mining machinery and began to tear into the mountain behind his house, damaging the tower beyond use. "They put me out of business and made their millions off my land," Akers says.

The document that allowed Triple Elkhorn to destroy Akers's land and business was a broad-form deed. Like thousands of such deeds signed at the turn of the century in Kentucky and other Appalachian states, it conveyed the coal under the land to a mineral company. Under Kentucky law, a company with a broad-form deed could strip mine without permission to within 300 feet of the surface-property owner's house, and the surface owner's rights were subservient to the mineral owner's.

When the deeds were signed, strip mining was unheard of in eastern Kentucky. Little did the farmers who sold the coal—or had it swindled from them—imagine that their farms could be torn apart by huge machines in the 1980s. But with the advent of strip mining, companies had the right to tear apart forests and farms to get to their coal, destroying the property of the surface owners. State courts had repeatedly ruled that the right of the companies to extract their coal is more important than the rights of the surface owners to protect their lands.

In 1984, pushed by Akers and the other KFTC members, the state legislature overwhelmingly passed a law forbidding a company to strip mine without the surface owner's consent. This law would have protected Akers and hundreds of other landowners from the abuses of the broad-form deed. It was a great victory, but it had little immediate effect, as the state continued to issue strip mine permits to companies for areas covered by the new law.

KFTC sued the state, which in turn contended that the new law was unconstitutional. The state supreme court agreed, overturning the law in July 1987.

So in the 1988 legislative session (the Kentucky General Assembly meets for only sixty days every other year), KFTC supported passage of a constitutional amendment to limit mining under broad-form deeds to the types of mining in existence at the time the deeds were signed—underground mining. In effect, the amendment would provide the same protection to landowners as the derailed 1984 law. Because an amendment must receive a majority of the popular vote in the November general election, this approach would keep the matter out of the state courts and give the people of Kentucky the chance to express their view.

The bill sailed through the General Assembly, and then the real work began. The campaign for the amendment vote was made difficult by the fact that outside rural eastern Kentucky, few people had ever heard of broad-form deeds. A series of television and radio documentaries and advertisements produced by Appalshop, a nonprofit eastern Kentucky media cooperative, helped to spread the word. So did the network of KFTC members throughout the state.

Four women who had been "broad-formed" or were in danger of having their land destroyed by strip-mining toured the state the week before the election, holding twenty press conferences and telling everyone who would listen why they should vote yes on the constitutional amendment. Meanwhile, other KFTC members were holding press conferences and interviews throughout the state.

And Everett Akers, confined to the Veterans Hospital in Lexington for health problems, campaigned up and down its halls, telling his fellow patients, nurses, and doctors why they should vote yes on November 8.

"You tear the ground and water up and you're going against the teachings of the Bible," Akers said. "God didn't mean for you to tear up the land. When I see St. Peter at the golden gates, I want to make sure he knows that I've been working hard to right these wrongs."

The vote passed by an overwhelming margin—82 percent of the people across the state voted yes, despite a half-million-dollar media blitz by the coal industry.

Everett Akers died two months later on January 23, knowing that he had helped to make his state a better place.

Lawrence County Concerned Citizens

In Lawrence County, KFTC members worked for six years to keep a proposed hazardous-waste incineration plant from locating there. PyroChem, Inc., whose owner had been cited in at least four states for violations of toxic waste disposal laws, fought hard to convince the state that the plant would not endanger the local community, but residents were not so sure. They formed the Lawrence County Concerned Citizens and a chapter of KFTC to protest the plant. Meanwhile, members researched the company and its president and talked to residents of communities where he had operated before, several of which were now on the federal "superfund" list of contaminated sites.

They presented their findings to the state agency in charge of permitting such plants and pressured state officials to oppose PyroChem's plans for Lawrence County. At the same time, they persuaded their county government to adopt a county zoning plan that would prohibit the toxic plant.

As they worked on their local issue, members of the Lawrence County Concerned Citizens got involved in other KFTC issues, helping their neighbors work for fair taxation and land rights. They also led in the formation of a statewide network of citizens fighting for improved toxic-waste regulations, more local control over the location of hazardous-waste incinerators, and waste-reduction measures.

Two days before Thanksgiving in 1987, the state Division of Waste Management announced that it would not issue a permit to PyroChem, based on the poor management record of its president and on Lawrence County's zoning plan. The victory was sealed by the 1988 General Assembly, which passed a law allowing local governments to ban toxic-waste plants. Today, citizens of Lawrence County are still active in KFTC activities and have begun to work with a community in West Virginia where PyroChem now proposes to build its incinerator.

The victory over PyroChem was important not only to Lawrence County residents but to other eastern Kentuckians as well, says KFTC chairperson Patty Wallace, who was active in the fight against the plant. "If we had let a toxic-waste incinerator locate here, you know that the other industries that moved in would be ones that need a toxic-waste incinerator—producers of toxic wastes." Such a concentration of toxic-producing companies would discourage other employers from locating in the area, she said, leading in the long run to a poorer economy.

Working for the Future

The economic problems of eastern Kentucky are largely a result of the region's dependence on the mining industry and the control that industry has on the state government. Only when the state's citizens gain some measure of control over the decisions that affect them will the state's economy become more responsive to the needs of its people. And KFTC's training of citizen activists is preparing hundreds of people to claim that control.

The 1988 broad-form deed victory was an important step in breaking the power hold of the industry. The companies' ability to strip mine against a landowner's wishes had become a symbol of the ways the industry has traditionally pushed the people of Kentucky around—on the job, in the courts, in state and local government.

Kentuckians For The Commonwealth are coalminers and housewives, schoolteachers and retired military officers, with one thing in common: a vision of Kentucky's future, where their children and grandchildren can live in comfort.

In the fifth-anniversary issue of KFTC's newspaper, *balancing the scales* (December 1986), long-time member Joe Begley of Blackey, Kentucky, echoed the sentiments of its members: "The bottom line is that when we get what we are out for, the people of Kentucky will be far better off than we have ever been. We are heading in a straight line and we are not sidewinding either way. We are older and wiser, we are sincere and headed down the right road."

NOTES

1. For a bibliography of this literature, see Steve Fisher, "A Selective Bibliography for Appalachian Studies," *Appalachian Journal* (Winter–Spring 1982): 209–42.

2. A summary of this study may be found in Appalachian Land Ownership Task Force, *Who Owns Appalachia?* (Lexington: University Press of Kentucky, 1983).

CHAPTER

3

Voices from the Coalfields:
How Miners' Families Understand
the Crisis of Coal

Mike Yarrow

Millions of Americans have had to make major adjustments in their strategies for living because whole industries have gone into long-term decline. One of the most rapid declines has been in metallurgical coalmining. With the dismantling of the American steel industry and the increasing competition on the international market, demand and price have plummeted, followed by massive layoffs. Since miners, by achieving living wages, safer working conditions, pensions, and better health care for their families and communities, have inspired the efforts of others, the destruction of their gains is doubly tragic.

The miners' world has been changing drastically in the past decade. Since the long 1978 contract strike, the industry has lost domestic and export markets and the price of coal has declined. Coal companies have sought to defend profits in various ways. They have introduced mechanization, pushed for deregulation of mine safety and environmental protection, subleased their coal properties to small operators, introduced production bonuses and threatened layoffs to induce miners to work faster (productivity has doubled since 1977), and fought to deunionize their work force. United Mine Workers of America (UMWA) membership has fallen from 160,000 in 1978 to slightly more than 70,000 today. The coalmine labor force nationwide has shrunk from approximately 250,000 in 1978 to 150,000. In these and other ways, coal companies are coercing mining families and communities to subsidize their profits in the name of making the industry competitive.

A sizable portion of the job loss has been in the metallurgical coalfields of southern West Virginia and western Virginia. The union work force in that area has shrunk from approximately 58,000 in 1980 to 17,200 in 1987. This is where my wife Ruth and I talked to thirty-five working miners, twenty-five laid-off or retired miners, and thirty of their spouses between July 1986 and July 1987. Employment here has been particularly hard hit, shrinking by 83 percent in the past decade.[1] In this chapter miners and miners' wives talk about how they live this crisis, how they understand it, and what responses they are making and thinking about for the future.

To put their responses in perspective, it is essential to remember the historical context of Appalachian coalminers. In each generation there has been a major structural reduction in coal employment as well as minor layoffs with the normal business cycle. During the 1930s, the world depression, combined with the early stage of mechanization, led to layoffs and short weeks. Sectors of the coal work force, including disproportionate numbers of black and immigrant miners, left the coalfields even though there was little work elsewhere. Then during the 1950s and 1960s, while the rest of the economy was booming, two-thirds of the coalmining labor force was displaced by the next wave of mechanization. They migrated for the most part to the industrial cities of the Midwest. Now displaced miners find few opportunities for well-paid unionized employment in sectors where their skills are relevant. The crises that confronted current miners' parents and grandparents have provided both relevant and misleading lessons for the present generation.

Also important are the events of the decade immediately preceding the present decline. In the 1970s, rising oil prices and electricity consumption led to a short-lived coal boom, which attracted a new generation of miners to the high-paying jobs with health insurance and pensions included. The Appalachian coalfields in the 1970s also experienced one of the most militant rank-and-file mobilizations in the postwar American labor movement. Since the late 1960s, rank-and-file miners, miners' wives, pensioners, and widows have organized to get black-lung compensation and new, tougher mining health and safety laws, to depose an undemocratic union president, and to democratize the miners' union. At their union conventions in 1973 and 1976 they adopted negotiating demands, including the right to strike during the life of a contract and the improvement of community services in the coal towns. In the four years before 1978, rank-and-file miners, in opposition to their union leadership, participated in a wave of wildcat strikes, a number of which extended across the entire eastern coalfields. In the first eight months of 1977 the worker-days lost to strikes were 10.33 percent of available work days, compared with the 0.17 percent average for all industries:[2] more than sixty times the average rate! In 1977–1978 miners conducted a 111-day strike in which they tried to protect their union-controlled comprehensive health coverage, their right to strike, and workplace rights. They were eventually forced to settle for a contract in which they lost the right to strike, the union's own health plan, and their attempt to equalize pensions.

The contrast between the prosperous and militant 1970s and the current coal depression significantly affects the understandings and responses of coal families. Since I conducted interviews of miners during the 1978 strike, I am able to trace the shifts in their understandings that the present crisis has wrought.

Living the Crisis: The Workplace

In response to the profit squeeze, coal companies have adopted two strategies of mechanization. The large companies have rapidly introduced capital-intensive longwall technology from Europe, which is more productive than earlier methods. This has allowed them to increase production with smaller work forces. Miners tend to view the new machines as a threat to their jobs. As one miner in his sixties put it:

It's been less and less people working in the mines, all the time, 'cause the better machinery they make, the less people they have to have to do it. Now ploughs [mechanized longwall] is going to come in and they're going to cut off a lot more people because they run a lot more production per man. A lot gets down to push a button. After while might not be nobody left, the way it looks. These companies are looking for a way to get rid of people, cheaper cost, and I don't know where the end's going to come to. It ain't gonna be no good for the coalminers, I know.

At the same time there is a contradictory trend toward more primitive technology. While rapidly introducing the longwall, many companies are also subleasing portions of their properties to small, undercapitalized operators who lease second-hand equipment and try to become competitive by cutting corners on maintenance, labor costs, and safety precautions.

A laid-off miner in his late thirties would not go back to mining for a small operator because of his perception of the deterioration of working conditions:

Working conditions now are so severe that I couldn't tolerate it. I couldn't tolerate the stress of not reading a book to my son at night. These are things I really love doing. Seeing him just maybe on Sunday—nooo. You hear older miners talking about the old times. Miners came home. They just set their lunch buckets down. They were dirty. Some of them fell asleep right beside the fire. Got up and went back to work. That type of history is kind of repeating itself. They are coming in and catching a few hours' sleep and going back to work. You are also dealing with the technology of present-day mining. So you got the stresses of being a skilled worker on top of that. People working down in these hellholes are not going to live more than three or four years. Because if you work like that, I don't know how you can physically handle it and be a father and a husband, and hold your life together. I couldn't.

It is difficult to get an accurate assessment of what has happened to safety in the mines. The number of inspectors has been reduced, and miners charge that both federal and state inspectors are less rigorous. In 1987 the federal Mine Safety and Health Administration (MSHA) charged mine companies with covering up injuries and fatalities. At small and nonunion mines, safety regulations for which miners fought and sometimes died are often honored in the breech. As one miner pointed out, every regulation was written because of a fatality. Having to overlook safety considerations in order to keep a job leaves a bitter taste. A miner at "Shelden" explains what has happened to the job of fireboss. Firebosses inspect the mine for violations of mining law. They look for dangerous roof conditions and any buildup of gas. They file a signed report on any violations found, and they are liable for negligence.

Firebossing always fascinated me. It was an interesting job. I felt I was doing something. I was trying to protect my buddies. If I didn't do my job properly, they could be in trouble. Any dangerous conditions I found, I was supposed to report. I knowed what my job was then.

All right, I go to fireboss at Shelden. I got to run like a crazy man. Not get to do my job. Just go through the formality. Not write up any serious violations. Sign the book. Put my neck out on the block. Shelden buffaloed me from doing my job. It's a wonder they don't get somebody killed or blowed up, because we were running without proper air and that is a gassy mine. [Mine safety laws require a certain flow of air through a mine to take away gasses and dust.] It blowed up in 1982 and killed seven or eight people. But when I was a union fireboss I could do my job.

The president of a strong union local, which has experienced problems with subleasing operators, feels he must bend on safety:

We realize with these small contractors we got to run coal for them to make money. We overlook a lot of safety things and contractual things that we used to hold the company to. At some places we have worked unsafe. We did a lot of things illegal to try to run the company some coal.

But you can only go so far. Gracious! A man's got to look out for his health. Right now I am trying to get the company to get me a respirator. To only wear when I am up under the continuous miner loading the buggy. That's the only time I actually need it. And they keep saying, "Aw, you don't need one. You are not in that much dust."

All during our conversations, he coughed.

The trend toward subleasing has affected not only safety but also wages and benefits. As the following miner testifies, miners and their union have had major problems getting subcontractors to live up to their obligations:

Most of your big companies are going to subleasing. They're contracting all of their mines out to small operators. They [small operators] don't have no money when they go in business. If they do make money in the coal-mines, they take it and leave. Most times, they leave owing people money. These subcontractors have been the downfall of the union. They can't furnish the contractual benefits like a big company could. They don't want to furnish them. We'll jump on a small operator for hospitalization and he'll carry it for a month or two and then he'll drop it until we catch back up with him again.

They got this new law in West Virginia that companies have to be bonded when they go into business, and that has helped us a lot. But it takes a long time to collect from a bond. These small operators still don't pay after you win an arbitration or even take them to court.

I worked for four companies in one year and still only worked about seven months. I guess since 1981 I have probably worked for about ten companies. I'd say they have left owing me somewhere around $12,000.

A few times when a company left owing us money, we stopped them from taking out the equipment. When they tried to take their equipment, we just set up a picket line and said, "Until you pay us what you owe us, you are not leaving." That's worked a couple times but a couple times a sheriff come and moved us and let the people take their equipment, and there is nothing we can do about it.

Subleasing, combined with other tactics, has undercut the strength of the union and its ability to organize new mines. Subcontractors have been known to have a front man sign the UMWA contract and then deny that he was part of the company. Since jobs are so scarce, some miners have gone to work for small companies for $5 an hour with no benefits in hopes of getting a union job eventually; others work for nothing for a trial period of several weeks. By contrast, A. T. Massey and a few other major producers have been willing to pay above union rates to avoid the union.

The tragic irony of the crisis is that with thousands of miners laid off, those still working are often expected to work many hours of overtime a week because the employers wish to avoid taking on health insurance and pension commitments to additional employees. Miners lucky enough to have a job are faced with long hours in deteriorating working conditions and often a climate of fear. They prefer it to unemployment.

Living the Crisis: Families and Communities

This miner has a college degree, his wife has a job. Yet the fear of unemployment is very real.

During the last year before any mine blows out they usually try to get all the coal they can. So I was working six days a week, sometimes 10 and 12 hours a day. And I made about $35,000. It sounds like a lot but it's a lot of Saturdays. I was able to save a little bit of money. But I didn't think I'd be laid off, because I was working for a mine owned by a railroad. I knew they weren't making a lot of money on the coal, but I thought they was making their money on the haulage. But they shut her down. It's been flooded and it's not going back. It shocked me. I took all my savings and paid off every bill I had, Master Charge, car, and put away $2,000. We planned to get through to the end of August.

I thought by that time I would really find a job. I have been to 7–Eleven stores. I have been to every hotel applying for a night auditor job. And everything conceivable I applied for. I ended up mowing grass. When you don't have nothing, $10 is a lot of money.

January and February I really looked for work and there were thousands of others out there looking for the same thing. My major depression when I lost everything and became self-absorbed was in March and April. Rejection after rejection after rejection, and you are on the American slicky slide. You see yourself sliding down and you don't know where you are going to land when you get off the slicky slide. A lot of people land at the welfare office if they fit into a certain category which the government makes up. A lot of them don't even fit into a welfare category.

I was off for nine months one time and unemployment run out. You had to weigh the decision to buy a popsicle for your child. I was going to graduate school and I came home to find out I had been called back to work and had to quit school. I was so happy—the feeling of going back. . . . I remember getting the first paycheck and going to the store and buying food and coming home and crying. Crying because I was happy I could buy food. But at the same time all the other people at the store were on food stamps. Because West Virginia has been going down for a long time. I was watching how they weighed their decisions to buy this or that with their food stamps, decisions I was making just a week before. And I filled my cart up with steaks, with soda pop for the mines.

You got that paycheck to insulate you from poverty. Then once you get working again, you come into a new frequency and you deal with working problems and you less and less notice the poverty around you.

There is no political system for adjusting the unemployed person. People like myself are lost. There is no retraining. Skilled people can't be plugged in. I wish unions could get together and push on these things.

Unemployment puts you in a state of emotional tension because the means of survival are unknown. When you are poor, existence becomes a war. There comes a point when this is endless. These goddamn hard times!

The hardest part about getting involved again in society is having hope. Where do you get it from? The only source of hope I know is just carry on *every* individual day with love and caring and just see what you can learn from that.

Unemployment tends to cause strains and sometimes breaks in families. The unemployed miner quoted above alludes to the tensions that his depression caused in his family. One wife told of the strain that comes from grown children moving in with their parents and living off their pension and black-lung checks when unemployment benefits run out. Another miner's wife emphasized that the strains have been too much for many people and families in her coal county:

What is so bad around here is that men only know coalmines. I bet our divorce rate has gone up fifty percent since our mines have shut down in the past three years. When times get hard, some don't pull together. Wives, husbands have left. The security goes. Some women look at their husbands as a meal ticket. People panic, put too much value on money.

You see depression, you see aggravation, you see alcoholism, you see drug abuse, you see battered wives, you see mistreated children, you see abandoned children. I'm talking about the whole county. You see suicide. You see some of the women having to get work, and the men staying home and having to take care of the kids. They resent that.

The strain has also tested mine communities. Widespread unemployment means people are locking their doors for the first time. It also means a destruction of the economic future for the region's young people. Many turn to the military as a way out. Others find temporary escape in drugs or alcohol. In one remote coal camp I visited, adults complained about a group of young men who do drugs and get destructive. The miners talked of starting a vigilante group to keep them in check. Residents also complained that since miners who left could not sell their houses, they rented them to "low-lifes," long-term welfare clients who, they say, did not keep them up. It was rumored that two had brought AIDS to the community. And yet the community retained a strong support network that helped its residents cope with the crisis.

Considering the extent of the layoffs, the relative lack of other well-paid employment in the coal region, and the pattern of coalminers as sole breadwinners, the adaptability and resilience of mining families are amazing. The whole family must learn how to cut expenses. Miners, their wives, and older children may take on odd jobs. Flea markets or roadside retail operations may become a family project. One miner gathered moss with his children in the mountains and sold it for $200 a pickup load. A young father of two describes doing odd jobs:

> Your in-laws will help you, or your parents. If you don't want them to give it to you, you go up there and do a job for them, paint their house, help them with carpentry work. You work it out so you are not accepting charity. I painted one house that is like forty feet high. The yard is straight down toward the riverbank. I got paid darn good. I painted it once before during the strike in 1978. I told my wife then, "*Never* would I paint that house again." Well, there I was.

These strategies tend to bring families together, but other miners have been forced to leave their families to seek work outside the region:

> You got so many people in this area going out of state, young men, in their twenties, married with one or two kids. They are going five or six at a time up to Virginia earning just enough to survive. They are working in a brick company up there, nonunion. I think the top pay at the brick company is about $4 an hour. And this one boy, when he left here he weighed about 270. He was a horse! And I saw him the other day and I bet the boy don't weigh 140 pounds. They burned him up. He told me, "I don't know how much longer I am going to be able to survive." But he has a wife and kids. He has to go. He said where he worked it stayed better than 100 degrees all day. He sweated it off. I said, "Man, you better do something or you are going to blow away." That's that "right-to-work." [*laughs*] That's why if it ever gets here we are all going to be hurting.

For a significant number of families, survival involves wives getting jobs. A woman of forty with three children living at home describes the years she spent doing two jobs while her husband was laid off:

I don't see how I ever managed to do it. When he was laid off, I worked at the nursing home at night, from 11:00 to 7:00, came home in the morning, took a bath, fixed breakfast, changed clothes, and went out to work doing insurance inspections during the day. I did two jobs for sixteen months. But we had no other choice. Somebody had to do it. It was better for me, because it was easier for me to get a job than it was for my husband. And yet the pay was nothing.

When you're unemployed, there are a lot of things you want that you can't have, especially with children. Children think that you should have the same amount of money that you've always had, regardless. And that you have to give it to them. They want to go somewhere all the time. It's hard to explain to them. If they go somewhere, if their friends have $10, then they should have $10, too, because their friends ask them, "Well, how much do you have?" So you try to make cutbacks yourself so you don't deprive the kids. 'Course I need a new car; I'm driving an old 1973 car.

Faced with cutoff of their breadwinner, mine families struggle for survival with determined resourcefulness. The unit of economic struggle becomes the family rather than the union. The union has not been able to stop the job hemorrhage or to provide much assistance to its laid-off members. Parents, spouses, and other relatives are often there in the emergency. They remember their own hard times and typically can give without disapproval. The crisis survival strategies employed by mine families also involve changes in the division of work between husbands and wives. Since mine families are shaped by a subculture forged in hard times, flexibility is valuable for survival. Whether the changes in relationships between husbands and wives endure beyond the crisis remains to be seen.

Collective Struggles

Besides the struggles of mine families to survive the crisis, the union and some mine communities have fought deunionization and the deterioration of community services. The largest and most heated conflict to date involved the fourteen-month strike against the A. T. Massey mines in Mingo and Pike counties, which straddle the West Virginia–Kentucky border. Massey, owned by the Royal Dutch Shell and Fluor corporations, has a balkanized structure of subsidiary companies. The union argued that since some of these companies signed the 1984 contract, it was binding on all. Massey maintained that they were separate corporations and attempted to run several mines on a nonunion basis. A previously uninvolved young miner describes the struggle:

At the beginning of the strike we tried everything peaceful. We tried to set down in the road. We tried setting on the railroad tracks. We tried serpentines—parking cars in the road far enough apart to where an ambulance could get by but not a coal truck. All that is peaceful. When the first serpentine got run over by coal trucks, if the courts would have said— "That's enough, pickets go home, company shut down, negotiate"—you wouldn't have had the three men that got run over by a coal truck. You wouldn't have had $450 million damage against the company. You wouldn't have had that picket shot over on Sharondale's picket line. You wouldn't have had these houses shot at. We slept on the floor under the windows with blankets over the windows. All your court had to say was, "That's enough."

The activism generated by the strike spilled over into electoral politics:

The reason we ran the election campaign is because we saw that Massey controlled Mingo County. We started campaigning before the strike was over and the election was just after. We got two union men, Mike Whitt and Jim Reid, to run for the House of Delegates [in West Virginia], and the union interviewed the other people and put them on our slate, too. Six of us from my local went every day for six weeks door to door; of course some went from other locals, too. Our wives went door to door several times and they did a telephone poll several times. I hadn't done anything like that before. We had political rallies and [union president Rich] Trumka and [vice-president] Cecil Roberts would come down and speak.

When I went door to door to all these retired people, I'd start telling them, "I am with the UMWA." A lot of them, seven out of ten, would tell me, "I'll tell you one thing right now. I done got my letter from Rich Trumka and I'm a voting right down the line." That's why I said if all these unions would get together they could do something. They'll listen to you, especially retirees. And sure enough they must have voted right down the line because we had a 66 percent turnout and swept our slate to victory.

In the November 1988 elections the reform coalition involving the UMWA won all the Mingo County races. Shortly after the election Shell and the UMWA reached settlement of the remaining issues from the A. T. Massey strike. Massey agreed to recognize the union at the mines that had been struck and to rehire strikers for whom the U.S. Labor Department had issued unfair firing complaints. Approximately fifty miners on whom the company had evidence of strike related violence were not rehired but were given $40,000 in settlements. One union official was sorry to see the most courageous union miners fired but was hopeful that they could get jobs in new mines opening up in the area.

The UMWA has also opened an organizing office in Matewan (Mingo County); it is launching an energetic drive to educate union members and their families for political action and to organize the unorganized in eastern Kentucky and southern West Virginia. An innovation in the organizing is the plan to target workers other than miners in coal counties. This effort, which the organizers hope will involve union–community coalitions, may allow coal-miner families to exert a more powerful influence on the way their communities deal with the wrenching economic dislocation.

Understanding the Crisis

In attempting to understand the developments that have had such devastating effects on their lives, miners are presented with two competing interpretations, the corporate and the union. The corporate explanation is available from coalfield newspapers, coal company management, coal associations, and many coalfield politicians. It contends that American unions, especially the miners' union, have become too strong and have bargained up wages, benefits, and working conditions to the point that coal mined with union labor is not competitive on the world market. Unions, they assert, have protected lazy, unproductive workers and wasteful work practices that lead to massive inefficiencies. Their solution includes lowering taxes, weakening environmental and safety regulations, cutting labor costs by lowering wages and benefits, increasing managerial control, and destroying unions.

The miners' union tries to counter this explanation with one of its own. It argues that miners did not price themselves out of the market but that the market was fundamentally altered by forces beyond their control. They point out that as U.S. coal has been losing out to foreign coal, the labor costs of U.S. coal have decreased by almost 50 percent due to a doubling of productivity. They see a corporate plot to destroy domestic unions and reduce labor costs by producing in low-wage, low-tax countries with lax regulations. Their answer is protectionism: saving U.S. jobs by reducing imports and protecting the living standards of American workers.

Although varying in their analyses, miners and their spouses tend to combine elements from both the corporate and union explanations because each resonates with their experiences. From the perspective of the present crisis, they look back on the 1970s as a time when they did live "high on the hog" compared with their parents and grandparents and a time when they did exert considerable power over the labor process. They remember protecting unproductive workers and defending unproductive practices, and they now view the tighter discipline under which their parents worked as necessary. On the other hand, they see the corporate decisions to open nonunion mines and import coal as a plot to destroy their union. They experience this directly in the closing of large union mines and the subleasing of the coal rights to small nonunion operators and the investment in large, new, government-protected "scab" mines that pay above union scale. There is a strategic debate about contract concessions, with the strongest voices in favor coming from the unemployed and the most forceful opposition being articulated by union organizers who are having difficulty talking union to nonunion miners with above-union wages. But most miners are reluctant to give up the hard-won gains that are a measure of their collective achievements.

Beneath these analyses lie some important reassessments of basic social relationships. At the peak of rank-and-file mobilization during the 1978 strike, miners considered themselves powerful, able to win the strike and possibly to force more far-reaching structural changes on the UMWA president. The perceived loss of that strike caused them to reevaluate their position with respect to their corporate opponents. Ten years of gathering crisis have convinced most that the corporations are ruthless and practically invincible.

With this diminution in the perceived power of rank-and-file miners has come a reassessment of militance. The wildcat strikes of the 1970s, which were seen in 1978 primarily as a noble attempt by miners to fend off operator aggression, are now typically seen as foolish and often ignoble, the view the operators have had all along. Rank-and-file power is also questioned through increasing criticism of union democracy. Although not optimistic, miners hope that their union leaders will be able to find a way out of the present crisis. They perceive themselves as powerless to do it, so they want to give their leaders as much power as possible.

Perhaps most dramatic is the change in emphasis on the two criteria of manliness. While in 1978 the stress was on a miner's ability to face down the boss, now it is on how hard a worker one is. Thus the definition of masculinity has become less class-combative. This change has been accompanied by an alteration in the use of history. Whereas in 1978 the elders were cited for their struggle against operator oppression, they are now revered as hard workers. The new generation of miners hired in the 1970s, who were then lauded for their militance, are now seen by many as a cause of the downfall of the industry and union because they "were not interested in working or in their buddies' welfare." In times of crisis, harmony of interests with precarious operators becomes more plausible and hard work is stressed as a way to keep the company in business and protect jobs.

These perceptions of the balance of power affect miners' thoughts about appropriate strategies. Protectionism, which the union supports, is a common response to the international dimension of the crisis. Miners know that the energy corporations are operating globally, but they know little about miners and their unions in other countries. Thus it is difficult for most of them to imagine a transnational brotherhood of miners even though the logic of class conflict leads a number to recognize the necessity. Instead they feel very keenly the sapping of their strength by competition with "slave labor" and want protection from it.

Many accept the portrayal of U.S. foreign policy as international welfare and insist that charity begin at home. They are indignant that hungry mining families are losing their homes yet being taxed to give foreign aid to obscure and unappreciative people. A number of union militants supported President Reagan's aggressive foreign policy and military buildup for reasons of national pride. Few believe that U.S. foreign policy is designed to maintain the vast international low-wage labor pool that destroys their bargaining power. One who does is an unemployed miner who sees southern West Virginia becoming part of that labor pool:

> Many parts of Mingo County and McDowell County and even Raleigh County are as much a part of the Third World as the Third World is itself. You have a global economy that's going on now. And you are going to have peasants next door. They have to disperse the steel mills to Mexico. They have to give the Third World part of the capitalist enterprise to keep them from merging with communist aspirations. Capitalism can come to them. And part of the price of taking capitalism to them is that we have to become part of the Third World.
>
> If the real facts could get out there about how much of the land is out-of-state ownership—what is it running now, 70 percent? West Virginia is almost like a colony. I mean it is almost like South Africa or some foreign nation that this country owns. We are down to those issues of land ownership. We'll have to come back to the basic level of politics, to get a handle on the economic development of West Virginia. There is no land that these corporations are going to let go of to build plants on. I don't think West Virginia is really conscious of that.

Another would like to see the government control capital flight but sees corporate control of government preventing it:

> If the companies would put more of their effort into the United States instead of other countries, I think that could be a help. I think if the government would step in and, when these companies go to other countries, put some kind of tax on them so as to equalize them with the United States, I think that would help. But I don't think we'll ever see something like that. [Laughs] Because those big companies run the country.

A few miners, especially those who have been involved in recent collective struggles, remain hopeful about miners' collective power, especially when linked to the power of other workers. A striker from Matewan envisions a coalition of unions electing people who would represent workers' interests.

They holler "solidarity, solidarity, solidarity." We proved what we, the UMWA, could do in Mingo County. You take a big state like Kentucky, I mean [former] Governor Martha Layne is Kentucky's scab protector. You take the Mine Workers, the Steel Workers, telephone workers, railroaders. You have a mass meeting of the officials in one room and they would set down and evaluate each candidate. What can they do for solidarity, not what can they do for my union or my little group? They pick who they want. Each union gives their political arm the authority to endorse these people. Your presidents of the unions send letters to their members, to their retired members. It costs money but it is better to pay now than pay a whole lot more later. You have to stick to your guns each four years. That is the only way you are going to have labor represented. Divided we are too little. You have to get solidarity.

A miner whose community shut down a small nonunion operation at the head of their hollow imagines a general strike to force the government to work for the people:

If our union could ever get in with enough different unions, auto and all them, and put pressure on this country at one time, they would get something done. Stop this country still! It would be a heck of a thing to do to stop a whole country, but it's going to take something. It's going to take people with enough backbone to stand up and say, "OK, government, now you want to run it, you run it." Let them do your jobs. You could put a squeeze on any country. I think that's about what it's going to take. In other words, it's going to be a stinking war between the rich and the poor.

Miners' history of class conflict and periodic deprivation has fostered a resilience that has helped many survive the present crisis. At the same time, however, their perspective seems to limit their ability to develop new strategies for dealing with the crisis. Miners see their power as deriving from their position as wage laborers and to a lesser extent from their willingness to use violence to intimidate "scabs" and nonunion operators. When there is no demand for their labor and the courts have effectively enjoined their use of violence, most see themselves as powerless. They also perceive a gradual unraveling of the brotherhood, as miners with jobs try to amass a nest egg for their families rather than join unwinnable struggles for their buddies. Collective strategies that involve finding new sources of power and new allies, such as women and other male workers, are imaginable only for those who have been involved recently in bitter strikes such as those against A. T. Massey. They also reject visions of the future that detach them permanently from the underground brotherhood, the basis for their collective struggle survival strategy.

Yet crisis forces change, and change brings the possibility for effective new responses to the many problems confronting coalmine families in the metallurgical coalfields. To support their families, an increasing number of miners' wives has joined the labor force. This fosters adjustments of the relationships between husbands and wives, which may lead to a new solidarity of men and women for the survival of their families and communities. With the help and sometimes leadership of wives, coalmine families have found new ways to struggle in the 1980s, including election campaigns, bridge blockades by miners' wives, and injunctions against taking overloaded "scab" coal trucks across weak bridges. Despite the demoralizing conditions, mine families have demonstrated that if they can find tactics with a chance of success, they are willing to fight collectively with determination and courage.

The type of future that miners and their families are struggling to create, however, remains largely undefined. Since the coal industry has so visibly shaped their region for its purposes, they have great difficulty imagining a future to fight for if their coal is no longer in demand. Perhaps the material conditions for imagining such a future are increasing communication with communities that face similar crises in different regions, countries, or industries and have found some promising ways to proceed. The solidarity of coalmining communities, their survival skills, and tactical creativity provide mine families with the potential fulcrum to shape a positive future for their children. They need to borrow or create a vision of an economy to serve them.

NOTES

Acknowledgments: Research for this article was supported by a sabbatical leave from Ithaca College and an Appalachian Studies Fellowship. Ruth Yarrow interviewed miners' wives. Barbara Ellen Smith, Kristin Layng Szakos, and Ruth Yarrow provided helpful editorial advice.

1. Estimates from United Mine Workers of America officials in Districts 17, 28, and 29, presented at a meeting in Welch, W.Va., 1986, and in personal communications with the author.

2. Bituminous Coal Operators Association (BCOA) statement, presented at the first session of the National Bituminous Coal Wage Agreement negotiations, Washington, D.C., October 1977.

CHAPTER

4

Women Miners Can Dig It, Too!

Betty Jean Hall

Founded by women who grew up in the Appalachian coalfields, the Coal Employment Project (CEP) has been working since 1977 to help women claim their rightful place in the well-paid coal industry.[1] Today, its work extends from the coalfields of Utah to West Virginia. It has become a symbol for the proposition that there is no job some women can't do.

CEP was born when the staffs from two public-interest groups in Jacksboro, Tennessee—Save Our Cumberland Mountains (SOCM) and the now-defunct East Tennessee Research Corporation—wanted to go on a tour of an underground coalmine.

The staff members contacted a local operator, who also happened to be the local criminal court judge, to ask if he would make arrangements. He said, "Sure, no problem, but send me a list of the names so we can type up the waiver forms." The next day he called back. "Who's this woman on the list? Can't have no woman going underground. The men would walk out, the mine would shut down. Now if you fellas want to go, that's one thing, but if you insist on bringing her, forget the whole thing."

That got them thinking: If they wouldn't even let her go on a *tour* when the men were going, then they'd never consider hiring her. But weren't there federal laws requiring companies with federal contracts to recruit women and minorities if they were underrepresented in the work force? (Remember, this was 1977.) And didn't that apply to most coal operators in their area, who sold their coal to the Tennessee Valley Authority (TVA), a federal agency, about thirty miles down the road in Knoxville? And why did all these people living in the middle of the eastern Tennessee coalfields not know a single woman miner?

53

I had grown up in eastern Kentucky, had recently completed law school, was living in the Washington, D.C., area at the time, and had done volunteer work for a variety of mountain-based organizations over the years, including the two Jacksboro groups. Soon after the incident with the coal operator, I got a call from the director of one of those groups, Neil McBride.

He requested that I research the status of women in the coal industry. Within days, I had the answers: 99.8 percent of all miners were men and 98.7 percent of all *people* in the coal industry, including secretaries and file clerks, were men. The law was on our side, but clearly not much affirmative action was happening.

Within days, Neil had persuaded me to get on a train and meet him in New York so we could raise money to start a special project on the issue of "women in coal." So began the Coal Employment Project. We came home with a $5,000 grant from the Ms. Foundation to get us started.

Frankly, in these early days, I wasn't at all convinced that there actually were substantial numbers of women in the mountains who really wanted coalmining jobs. If not, what did it matter that we had a great legal case? But when I started tracking down the few women who had gotten mining jobs, there was no question that *lots* of women wanted them. When I asked the women miners if they were an exception or if there were other women who wanted the jobs, they would invariably say something like: "Honey, I could have fifty women here tonight that would *love* to get a mining job. It's the only good-paying job around. We know we can do the work. The problem is getting the job."

When I asked what had ever given *them* the idea to apply for a mining job, they said one of two things: "I read in the newspaper [or heard on the radio] that they were going to have to start hiring women" (90 percent of the time) or "My girlfriend got a mining job. I figured if she could do it, I could too" (10 percent).

Mavis's Story

I will always remember Mavis, the woman who convinced me that we were really on to something.

Mavis had grown up in eastern Kentucky, but by 1977, when I met her, she had married, lived away from home for many years, and had come back home a few years earlier as a single parent with four teenage and preteenage children. She knew she had to get a job, and found one operating a posting machine in a bank for the minimum wage.

Mavis soon realized that she could not support herself and raise her children on a minimum wage, especially considering the gas money involved in driving a considerable distance to work. One day, she heard on the radio, or maybe read in the paper, that the mines were going to have to start hiring women. Having grown up in a mining family, she knew what those jobs paid and figured, "Why not me?"

She did apply for mining jobs but, even though they were hiring inexperienced men all around her, she never got hired. Soon she confronted the person in charge of hiring at one of the mines and asked him why she hadn't been hired. "Well, Mavis," he told her, "mining is just too hard a job for a woman to do."

"You know, at first he made me mad, and then I had to smile," Mavis explains. "I mean, I thought back to when my two youngest were still in diapers and we lived on top of a hill with no running water. Every morning, even in the dead of winter, I had to bundle up those two babies and all their dirty diapers and carry them down the hill to wash out the diapers in the creek. And I had to carry those two babies, and all those wet diapers, back up the hill. I figured if I could do that, there wasn't any job in the mines I couldn't do."

When Mavis finally got called for a mining job, she was the first woman to work at that mine. On her first day of work, the atmosphere was tense. Soon she found out what the problem was: fearing that production would go down if there was a woman on the crew, none of the bosses wanted Mavis assigned to his crew. Finally, Mavis spotted a boss she had known in school many years earlier. "Look," she said, "you've got five kids you're trying to raise, and I've got four I'm trying to raise. If I can't do it, I'll get out. Just give me a chance." He asked to have her put on his crew, and soon Mavis was a productive miner.

Once she established her mining career, some changes developed in Mavis's extended family and in the community. For generations, the women had accepted that they couldn't possibly expect any help around the house from their hard-working coalminer husbands. Then the women saw Mavis, coalminer and mother of four, doing all the things they did *after* she put in her shift: washing clothes, getting supper on the table and dishes cleaned afterward, getting lunchboxes packed, homework done, and the house cleaned.

I wish I could report that Mavis is still working in the mines, but she got caught in the layoffs several years ago. Since women did not start working in the mines until the mid-1970s, they have less seniority and tend to be the first to go in layoffs.

However, there is a bright side to the story. After pioneering as a woman miner in her area and then being laid off, Mavis became the first female letter carrier in Cumberland, Kentucky, and is now blazing another trail for the benefit of women from the coalfields who want well-paid jobs.

Strategy and Program Development

The Coal Employment Project (CEP) started out as a "legal" project. But, after putting thousands of miles on our cars and talking to lots of people from eastern Kentucky, Tennessee, West Virginia, and southwestern Virginia, we became convinced that we had to develop a multifaceted strategy to help women gain and retain jobs in the coal industry. Attacking the problem from many sides simultaneously became, in my view, the key to our success.

The elements of our strategy evolved gradually out of the experiences and needs of women miners and those who wanted jobs in the mines. For example, women's consistent statements that they applied for mining jobs after learning about them through television, newspaper, or radio stories alerted us to the need for a media strategy. So we learned how to write press releases, hold press conferences, and attract attention to our cause. When we filed a major lawsuit against 153 coal companies and mines about a year after we got started, we were able to do so with great fanfare in the national press.

As a result of the successful media work, we were soon flooded with requests for help from women who were being turned down for mining jobs or were suffering harassment on the job. It soon became obvious that we could not respond effectively to every single call for help—and that even if we could, it wasn't a good idea: ultimately they were going to have to solve their own problems. We began telling women that, if they could get together a group of those who faced the same problem, we would help them figure out how to tackle it. That was the beginning of our support-group strategy.

The local support groups were by no means 100 percent successful: many flourished for a few months and then died out; others continued but had difficulty standing on their own feet and operating independently of CEP staff. Despite these problems, the groups became a very important part of our strategy. They helped a lot of women survive and develop a sense of community, and they gave CEP an organized, identifiable base among women miners. Today, there are active support groups of women miners in Utah (Lady Miners of Utah), Pennsylvania, Alabama, West Virginia, southwestern Virginia, and Illinois.

Out of the support groups developed a communications strategy. Women miners wanted to meet one another face to face and share their victories, problems, and stories. So we initiated a monthly newsletter and an annual conference. Both are great sources of support. One woman miner from Pennsylvania said of the conference, "That's my mental therapy for the year. When things are bad and I feel myself getting weak, I know that if I can just hang on until the next annual conference, I'll be OK."

The conference workshops became so popular that women began to ask for longer, more in-depth sessions on their favorite topic. That request became the basis for our leadership and empowerment programs, which offer week-end long workshops on such topics as "Using the Media," "Developing and Maintaining a Support Group," and "Organizing to Make Ourselves Count."

We also developed more technical workshops for women who wanted to become miners. We knew that the first women would either make it or break it for all those who followed them. Therefore, it was important to give them the best training possible—not only in the technical aspects of mining (including basic practical information such as "Tool Use and Identification"), but also on such subjects as "Communicating with Confidence," "Support Group Development," and "Legal and Contractual Rights That Protect You."

Finally, underlying all these activities have always been our litigation and legal support, the backbone of CEP. Because our numbers are small, our ability to respond swiftly and strongly when a major instance of sex discrimination is brought to our attention has given us the power we need to deal with the industry.

CEP Grows

To make a long story short, within a few years, we marked up some stunning successes, including these:

- The percentage of women hired as miners increased from 2.0 percent in 1976, the year before we started our work, to 11.4 percent in 1979. Since 1979, women have averaged a little better than 8 percent of the total hired in any given year.

- The number of women hired as underground coalminers soared from 0 in 1972 to 830 in 1978. In total, 3,871 women nationwide have started underground coalmining jobs since 1972, approximately one-third of them from West Virginia.

- There has been extensive national and international media coverage of women's success as coalminers: network television coverage, including a *Sixty Minutes* segment, on sexual harassment in the mines; national press coverage in publications such as the *New York Times;* business press coverage in publications such as *The Wall Street Journal* and *Business Week;* and even industry press coverage in publications like *Coal Age.* There was a "CBS Movie of the Week" about women miners starring Cheryl Ladd and Ned Beatty, a Kentucky native.

- Women miners have received the strong support of the major coalminers' trade union, the United Mine Workers of America (UMWA), even though they constitute only about 1 percent of the union membership.

- We have also earned the wary respect of the industry, whose company executives generally respond with concern when CEP or our women members bring a severe case of sex discrimination or sexual harassment to their attention.

- CEP's work has helped inspire other women's organizations to initiate similar programs. For example, the Southeast Women's Employment Coalition (SWEC), which emerged in part because of CEP, focused on hiring practices in the road-construction industry.

■ Women miners have also developed international ties and influence. Through visits to mining communities in Great Britain, Canada, and China, we have sparked interest in nontraditional jobs among women in other countries.

It is important to point out that women miners have had an impact on some of the nation's social issues far greater than their numbers. For example, consider the visual impact nationwide: if women can mine coal, what excuse is there for any other industry? For another example: women miners have spearheaded a national campaign for adequate family leave for all workers.

The Family Leave Campaign is geared toward giving workers job-secure, insurance-secure time off from work to deal with the birth and adoption of children and the serious health condition of children and other family members. What you might not know is that much of the spark and substance for this campaign came out of a weekend gathering of seventeen women miners from throughout the nation's coalfields in April 1983.

The original goal of the women miners was to get a good family-leave clause in the UMWA contract, and we have made significant progress toward that goal, including having strong support from the highest officials of the UMWA to make this a priority. Our work has now expanded to include other trade unions.

The language developed by women miners has become the basis for proposed federal legislation and proposed state legislation in approximately thirty states. In addition, several major corporations, including Champion International, have implemented corporate family-leave policies, based in large part on the same language.

After months of painstaking groundwork throughout the nation's coalfields, one of our proudest moments came at the December 1983 UMWA international convention in Pittsburgh, when, with only 20 women among about 1,500 delegates, the membership *unanimously* demanded that a family-leave clause become a priority for the next collective bargaining agreement.

Ties with the UMWA

Given the often hostile relationship between labor unions and women's employment organizations, especially those advocating nontraditional job access, CEP's ties with the United Mine Workers of America are quite unusual. We had the advantage of dealing with a union that does not have a direct role in the hiring process (as in the building trades); this arrangement typically generates an adversarial relationship from the start, since the union tends to perceive an outside advocacy group as a threat to its control over hiring. In the coal industry, however, the company was our common adversary on employment issues, rather than a collaborator with the union in keeping women off the job.

Moreover, many women who became miners were from coalmining families with a strong pro-union tradition. They needed no convincing of the importance of supporting and participating in the UMWA. Indeed, they instructed us from the start never to cross the union.

The development of a positive working relationship with the UMWA did not happen automatically, however. Early on, we sought for many months to obtain some sort of official endorsement from the union, not for CEP as an organization but for the concept of women miners. We got nowhere fast.

Finally, a sympathetic member of the international executive board was able to get a resolution passed unanimously, putting the union's governing body on record in support of women miners. We backed him up with a mailgram blitz to every executive board member and international officer in the union. That got our foot in the door.

The real turning point came a few years later, after the election of Richard Trumka as UMWA president. The women's support group in Pennsylvania worked very hard on his campaign; after the election, its members asked him to be the keynote speaker at the CEP annual conference (to be held in Pennsylvania) and sought his direct endorsement. About thirty women miners came out in force to an executive board meeting and put the question to him. He agreed. Since that time, the top leaders of the union have regularly attended the women miners' conferences. We are treated with respect by the union, and we've become strong allies.

Facing the Future

Since 1984, we have had to face the reality that coal is no longer a growth industry; what we are seeing today represents far more than the "bust" side of a boom-and-bust cycle. As recently hired miners, women have been among the first to be laid off. Since the high-water mark of 1979, the number of women employed in the mines has dropped each year. Remarkably, though, women's participation in CEP has not flagged, and attendance at our annual conferences has continued to grow.

The dramatic decline in employment has, of course, occurred at a time of political conservatism and retreat from the policy of affirmative action. This, too, has compromised our ability to advocate successfully and to expand women's employment in the industry.

Once the handwriting about layoffs was on the wall, women miners had to decide whether to seek superseniority or some other form of protection for their jobs and for affirmative action in the mines. As they had done with similar questions in the past, the women decided not to seek special treatment. They would stand with the men.

Indeed, instead of trying to insulate ourselves and protect past achievements (which in all likelihood would have been impossible anyway), CEP has started shifting energies into our Future Directions Project. This is a plan for expanding our work to include other industries that have traditionally discriminated against women. We have looked closely, for example, at the highway construction and maintenance industry, an area brought to our attention by SWEC. How many women are seen working on highway crews? And how many of them are doing something other than flagging?

The Future Directions work has been the subject of much discussion and disagreement within CEP. Some women have a deep-seated identification as coalminers and are reluctant to expand CEP's focus. Others believe that this expansion is the only way CEP can survive and remain dynamic over the long run. Whether the Future Directions Project will continue remains to be seen.

The unfavorable economic and political context has also fueled questions about our organizational structure. CEP was never a membership organization, though the annual conferences functioned in effect as membership meetings where priorities for the coming year were set. We staff members always saw ourselves as advocates who needed leeway to respond quickly and effectively to opportunities and new developments in the industry. However, as the potential for successful advocacy declined and the number of committed participants in CEP rose, the notion that we should become a membership organization spread. Finally, in February 1988, CEP was reorganized as a membership organization with new staff.

As CEP embarks on its second decade, the organization faces some of its toughest challenges to date. The employment crisis in coal persists and continues to diminish the ranks of women miners. The programmatic work of CEP, particularly the fate of the Future Directions Project, must be determined. The new organizational structure requires new processes for decision making, new relationships between board and staff, and many other adjustments. In the midst of these many changes and challenges, however, the traits that have upheld CEP in the past—the daring and resilience of women miners— remain as strong as ever. That is cause for great hope.

NOTE

1. Betty Jean Hall was director and general counsel of the Coal Employment Project from 1977 until March 1988. This article was written while she was still on the project's staff.

CHAPTER

5

Organizing Women for
Local Economic Development

Chris Weiss

For the last fifteen years, my family and I have lived on a 260-acre farm in rural Lincoln County, West Virginia. As many rural women do, I commute to the city of Charleston to earn my living. When I describe our family's farm to others, I usually explain that only about 30 of these acres are flat; the rest you can lean on. We do some farming, but it is mostly to supplement our family food budget. We can vegetables and fruit and raise our own beef, like many other families in our small community. I worked in the city for eight years as the executive director of an organization called Women and Employment, an organization that I helped form eight years ago.[1] It is a community-based organization working on issues of economic justice for West Virginia women. All my work history has been concerned with rural women and economic justice issues.

I also have a granddaughter named Naomi, and I often think about her and all the other six-year-old women in our collective lives who will inherit West Virginia's current economy. Judged by today's standards, their economic future in this state is not very bright. According to national predictions, female poverty is on the increase. Analysts of the "feminization of poverty" (as it has come to be called) predict that by the year 2000, if present trends continue, almost all families in poverty will be women and their children.[2]

But these are national predictions. What about here in West Virginia? Using national 1980 census data, the West Virginia Women's Commission, a state-supported agency for the improvement of the status of women, arrived at figures that are shocking. According to this study, more West Virginia women are heading families living in poverty than in 1970, and more of us are living in rural areas than women in the rest of the United States. Also, most of us are not being counted as part of the official labor force, because the participation rate includes only those who work for pay (or are looking for work); in fact, according to the study, we have the lowest rate in the country. Only 36 percent of West Virginia women work for someone else, a rate lower than that of some underdeveloped countries. In 1980, West Virginia women earned only 43 cents for every dollar men earned in wages; black women earned only 40 cents. One of the statistics that must be most galling to women facing student loan debt is that state men who had finished high school had incomes greater than those of women with seven or more years of college.[3]

As we read the poverty statistics and general bad news about ourselves and our families in West Virginia, we are apt to look around and ask how this happened. After all, we grow up with the assumption that we will get married and live happily ever after. However, the census data as well as our own experiences provide us with a more realistic assessment. Between 40 and 50 percent of West Virginia adult women live independent of a male partner. They are divorced, separated, single, or widowed.

Economists and sociologists who are in the business of providing answers to questions raised by these statistics are in general agreement on two reasons for the causes of poverty. One, the kinds of jobs that we are encouraged—sometimes forced—to take are occupationally segregated, a pattern that reserves for men jobs in technical and industrial fields that are well paid, unionized, and carry unemployment compensation when the going gets rough. "Women's jobs" are in the service sector and are likely to be dead end, low paying, and nonunionized. Many of these jobs are part time and seasonal, and the alternative is welfare.

The second reason is that women are the prime caretakers of children and the home. For those of us who do work outside the home, it is generally our responsibility to make sure that our children are cared for while we work. Because of our low wages, the cost of child care definitely makes many of us part of the working poor. *Finding* child care is also a problem, since twenty West Virginia counties have no licensed day-care centers "despite the increase in the number of mothers with children under 6, working outside the home," according to the study. The lack of affordable, subsidized day care is a major reason that women and their families are pushed into poverty. The United States is the only industrialized country that neglects to provide this service for its citizenry.

So what do we do about all this? The sociological implications of the commission study are vast, for they reflect the changing nature of the family in America. But for many women's organizations and other groups concerned with alleviating the pain of the economic bad news, the answer lies in economic development activities that produce jobs. Even though many women are not counted in the official labor-force participation rate, all women in West Virginia work very hard to maintain family survival. However, employment in the formal economy at a living wage, whether it be for someone else or for oneself, is the only answer to alleviating poverty for many women in this state.

Job Creation and Women

So, if the issue is jobs for women, we must next look around at how these jobs are produced. It is clear from talking to women through my organization and in my community that there are more women in West Virginia who want steady full-time employment than there are jobs. In 1984, Women and Employment, together with a group called the Roane/Calhoun Women's Resource Network, participated in a major study of women in the Southern economy, sponsored by the Southeast Women's Employment Coalition (SWEC). We surveyed more than 5 percent of the adult female population in Roane and Calhoun counties to make a significant statistical sample. We learned that 48 percent of those currently working want different jobs for higher wages, and 66 percent of those not working for pay want a job. I have no reason to believe that the statistics would be different for women in any rural county in West Virginia or anywhere in Appalachia or the rural South.

A report on this research by SWEC, issued about the same time as the Women's Commission study and titled *Women of the Rural South,* argued that in West Virginia, "Dependence on absentee-owned resource-based industries that were defined as male domains continues to limit very severely the availability of jobs for women—even 'women's jobs'!—and their economic potential to sustain themselves and their families." SWEC ends its report on West Virginia (one of three states profiled) with these comments: "Public investment in creative, far-sighted economic development that makes use of local resources and skills is urgently needed in West Virginia. Rural women, certainly no less than men, have a tremendous stake in that development." [4]

An example of economic development in Roane County illustrates the problem. Two years ago, the state economic planning division predicted that the town of Spencer, the county seat, could support new plants, and suggested recruiting manufacturers to the area's new industrial park. Their recommendations: a ball-bearing factory, a casting plant, industrial truck and trailer operations, and knitting factories. Only the knitting factories traditionally employ women. However, the largest group of unemployed people in Roane County were the women who had been displaced from the state hospital when it reduced its patient load. None of the recommendations from the state planners took this into account. They might, for example, have recommended a medical products manufacturer to utilize the skills of the unemployed work force.

In an attempt to evaluate current economic planning by government or the private sector and how it will benefit women, we look to information coming to us from beyond the state borders. Sara Gould, director of the Economic Development/Technical Assistance Project of the Ms. Foundation for Women, says, "Although states have been the leading economic development policy innovators in the last ten years, they have not yet begun to involve women as a matter of course in their overall economic development planning process. The state initiatives that have benefited women's economic status have come mainly from . . . within the executive branch, state social and human service agencies. We must participate in, and bring women's concerns to, the departments of commerce, development, and industry, because only then will we have access to overall economic development policy planning." [5]

Much of the response to poverty in this country has involved concentrating development activities toward job creation, relying on the trickle-down theory to take care of all jobless or underemployed people. State governments, which have taken the lead in economic planning and development in recent years, have relied on attracting large manufacturing plants and resource-based industries. There is some evidence that these schemes do not reach women, minorities, and the rural poor.

Studies in Kentucky and Colorado, for instance, show that women do not benefit equally from traditional economic development that simply aims to increase the number of jobs in an area. In fact, these studies indicated that women's net disposable income was actually reduced when jobs in manufacturing and mining were developed primarily for a white male constitutency. In Colorado, a 1980 study estimated that development in two coalmining towns reduced the percentage of women's wages compared to men's from 20 to 40 percent. High wages in the energy industries caused prices to rise locally, further reducing the buying power of women who worked in more traditional jobs. [6]

In the mid-1980s in Kentucky, the U.S. Department of Agriculture studied the trickle-down effect: is the alleviation of poverty and unemployment distributed evenly between men and women, young and old, in those counties where the number of jobs has increased? The answer is no. The study report, "Will Employment Growth Benefit All Households? A Case Study in Nine Nonmetro Kentucky Counties," noted, "Households headed by women had a limited benefit from the area's employment growth even though that growth increased the number of jobs available to women. . . . Households headed by women were more likely to be poor, and more households headed by women entered than escaped poverty over the study period." [7] Just increasing the aggregate number of jobs in a community did not improve conditions for women in rural Kentucky.

Without jobs, or decent-paying jobs above a poverty wage, women and their children are left to the not-so-tender mercies of the social welfare system that exists in the United States. This system was created with the goal of alleviating poverty and hunger. However, stereotypes about the role of women currently reinforce occupational segregation and prevent social service programs from taking bold steps to encourage nontraditional occupations or small-business development as a way out of poverty. A prime example of the perpetuation of one of these stereotypes involves Aid to Families with Dependent Children (AFDC) regulations that do not permit recipients to start small businesses or to become self-employed. Current federal welfare regulations do not allow them the traditional separation of personal and business income that is available to everyone else under various tax and business codes. Hence, if a woman starts a business she must be prepared to forgo all welfare assistance. For one thing, the $1,000 ceiling on personal resources that welfare clients may have effectively prohibits buying inventory, leasing a piece of equipment, or taking out a loan to capitalize a business. Second, *any return* to the business is considered personal income, regardless of the business expenses incurred, and, however small, is deducted from the welfare check.

Women make up 95 percent of the AFDC rolls, and these two provisions prevent them from becoming self-employed. The rules exist because those who develop policy view welfare recipients as incapable of small-business development or self-employment because of their presumed lack of education, training, or initiative. In fact, many programs started by women's organizations around the country, including Women and Employment, have illustrated that these women are quite capable.

For several reasons—not the least of which is that in rural areas and inner-city ghettos, there are generally more job-seekers than jobs—self-employment is an important option for many women trying to break the poverty cycle. As a way of surviving, many women operate in the little-recognized "informal economy." The informal sector is where people improvise when there are no jobs in the formal sector. It is largely unregulated, its practitioners are often highly entrepreneurial, and it is, especially for women, highly exploitative.

In rural areas, particularly in West Virginia, there is a vast informal economy mainly run by women. They raise produce for sale, sell goods by the side of the road, take care of children and old people, and generally provide a wide array of community services. Through barter, flea markets, and agricultural activity, women learn skills and uncover development possibilities for themselves. Since these activities exist outside the formal labor market, there is little recognition of their potential for generating growth through job development, tax collection, and entrepreneurial initiatives. Many of the successful programs run by women's organizations build on these activities.

A healthy economy cannot be maintained by those who have been raised in poverty, nor can it remain healthy, if it ignores the unused resources of half its labor force. Women and the organizations they create have defined the kind of planning that perpetuates poverty and discrimination for women as the problem. As an alternative, they have proposed a more holistic approach to economic development, looking at the needs of the whole community instead of at the aggregate number of jobs created. Day-care centers produce jobs as well as provide child care for working parents. Community reinvestment by banking institutions in local housing development and small businesses creates jobs and revitalizes a community. Combining an economic development agenda with social service initiatives could create a more equitable distribution of economic resources for women.

In the course of analyzing economic development and job-creation strategies that affect West Virginia women, I have done some research into international development that has targeted women in the Third World. I believe that here in West Virginia and in other areas in the nation, there are lessons to be learned by looking at development strategies that have benefited women in those countries. The similarities between the economies in Third World nations and the Appalachian states have been documented many times.

At the close of the United Nations Decade for Women in Nairobi in 1985, an international group called DAWN—Development Alternatives for Women in a New Era—presented an analysis of economic conditions for women around the world. They made the startling pronouncement that unless poor women's perspective is taken into account, no substantial gain can be achieved in efforts that seek to bring about macro changes in the global economy. In *Development, Crises, and Alternative Visions*, published in 1987, the authors, DAWN members, maintain that, "if the goals of development include improved standards of living, removal of poverty, access to dignified employment, and reduction in societal inequality, then it is quite natural to start with women. They constitute the majority of the poor, the underemployed, and the economically and socially disadvantaged in most societies."[8] The women scholars and activists who make up DAWN base much of their analysis on an understanding of the informal sector that I have observed to be active in West Virginia and that is present in every country of the world in varying degrees.

Where Do Jobs Come From?

Starting with women, then, let's look at four requirements for creating jobs in a local economy. The first is the presence of entrepreneurs. Entrepreneurs must be active and recognized in a community, and their activities must be encouraged as a strategy to create and multiply jobs. Figures from the U.S. Small Business Administration point to the track record that these risk takers have set in creating jobs in local communities. Women are becoming small-business owners faster than men in West Virginia and throughout the United States.

I would like, however, to expand the standard definition of entrepreneurs. Many entrepreneurs are women in the informal sector of the economy. Through their efforts at selling their goods and services, they have gained marketing, management of cash flow, and time-management skills. Women's organizations have recognized and valued these skills and have built on them when training female entrepreneurs to move into the formal business sector. Entrepreneurial activity is also found in cooperatives and other collective forms of business ownership. In West Virginia, women are joining together to form craft co-ops and other forms of business ownership to pool their resources collectively. These groups must learn business skills and develop leadership, but they often receive little help in doing so.

Entrepreneurial activity in this broader sense is also found in the non-profit, community-based groups such as community development corporations or women's advocacy organizations. These groups bring money to the region, hire staff, generate their own income through various activities, and pay taxes. They are mostly ignored by the private sector, but they fill an important role, not only in the number of jobs they create but in the education on economic issues they bring to the wider community. They add a much-needed "other" voice to the debate on economic development activity in questioning established policies and procedures. For example, Women and Employment has consistently faulted a West Virginia state economic policy of "smokestack chasing," recruiting out-of-state manufacturers to the state with promises of tax breaks and a nonunion work force, and the recruitment of additional contracts for the buildup of the U.S. military machine. Both these tactics have an adverse effect on jobs for women.

The second requirement is access to credit. Without adequate capital, a local economy may be unable to expand and thus unable to support its entrepreneurs. In West Virginia, especially in rural areas, banks, on average, have the lowest asset-to-lending ratios in the country, and recent attempts by the West Virginia Banking Commission have done little to address the matter. Not only do most rural banks not lend money, but very few banks anywhere lend money in small amounts. The experience at Women and Employment is that women need very small amounts of money to become self-employed. However, the informal sector does not produce a track record that would interest banks in lending money to these women. The formation in West Virginia of the first U.S. affiliate of Women's World Banking, an international loan-guarantee program, was a start toward providing for the credit needs of these women. Working with a Charleston bank that actually makes the loans, Women's World Banking, West Virginia, guarantees loans up to $10,000. One year after the first guarantee was made to a small rubber-stamp business, the owner had two full-time and one half-time employees (members of her family) earning wages and learning skills to support their families.

The third requirement is not so specific to women as it is to whole communities. People must have control over their land and natural resources. The experience in the Appalachians with land and mineral ownership patterns is that of colonial people everywhere. Outside ownership and control of natural resources prevent communities from having strong local economies. Local tax bases are affected. Without access to land, the small-business community cannot thrive. The effect on women has been mainly in the availability of jobs. Occupational segregation in the coal, oil, and gas industries, which define the majority of jobs in West Virginia, has prevented women from entering the formal labor force in any significant numbers. Without diversification of the West Virginia economy and without strategies to wrest control of the land, particularly in southern West Virginia, women will continue to be exploited in low-paying, part-time jobs and confined to the informal sector of the economy.

Fourth, the need is for partnerships between government and people in communities. In the United States, government on every level has turned its back on its responsibility to build local economies. Let's look at the record in other industrialized countries. In Canada, the Community Futures program has created local committees of citizens in areas of high unemployment and rural underdevelopment. On Cape Breton Island, a local committee is made up deliberately of equal numbers of men and women. After identifying local needs and developing a plan for implementation, the government has a grant and loan program to work in partnership with the local committee, businesses, and nonprofits to encourage entrepreneurs with loan programs, technical assistance, and business planning. In England and in France, people on public assistance can use their checks to support themselves while becoming self-employed. In Norway, the government, while mandating programs for women, has a policy of encouraging growth in rural areas and targets entrepreneurial development for support. In West Virginia, government continues to rely on the recruitment of outside industrial plants to take care of job creation and ignores the realities for women, except for services offered by various welfare agencies. Nonprofit local initiatives are sustained only by out-of-state foundations and, in some cases, churches.

The role of women's organizations thus becomes critical for raising public policy concerns and educating the public on economic justice issues for women. In West Virginia, in the Appalachian states, and in the South, women's voices are beginning to be heard through grassroots organizations that have organized women around issues of economic concern. Lobbying efforts of women in West Virginia produced a bill establishing a model program enabling women receiving AFDC benefits to become self-employed and start their own businesses. In Alabama, women forced the state to subsidize day-care centers through state tax revenues. In North Carolina and South Carolina, women have convened statewide meetings to discuss public policy issues and recommend legislative agendas.

Development of, by, and for Women

There is still much work to do. Affirmative action and equal employment hiring practices still need to be legislated, especially for our state agencies. Of particular importance are the highway and transportation departments in each of the southeastern states. With the failure of federal enforcement of current laws and regulations, state legislatures and administrations must address departments of transportation and their hiring practices in regard to women and minorities, occupational segregation, and political favoritism. In West Virginia, for example, the highway department is the largest state government employer and excludes women from all job categories except clerical.

All women must participate in the economic development planning process at local and state levels. This participation starts with local and state-level organizing to focus attention on women as a key constituency of economic development programs. Women must get appointed to local development authorities, task forces, planning committees, and advisory groups to question the costs and benefits of local and state industrial projects. Access to jobs, good wages, child care, and health benefits are all important considerations for working women. Women must question tax writeoffs and incentive programs because of their effect on community services that government should provide. They must evaluate federal and state job-training programs and determine whether women are being trained in all fields or just the clerical and service jobs. Women must look at placement rates and wage levels to determine if these programs are serving them well. In a 1986 report on the West Virginia Department of Vocational Rehabilitation, it was determined that more women than men have been served to the point of "successful closure," but many of the women have been rehabilitated into homemakers, definitely a nonpaying occupation.[9]

Women must recognize the potential entrepreneur in all women and advocate programs that will assist women and their families. Women receiving public assistance must be enabled to create jobs where none exists and receive benefits while they are becoming self-employed. Banks and financial institutions must begin to bear the responsibility of reinvesting in their communities, using the money that women and men deposit with them to build low-income housing and to develop small-business lending programs.

All this work is part of a public policy agenda that cannot be put off if my granddaughter and all the other granddaughters in West Virginia are to face a brighter economic future. Naomi must have choices—of nontraditional jobs, of being self-employed, of adequate housing and day-care centers for her children. Women's organizations must organize to make these changes, so that the next West Virginia Women's Commission report can document a happier picture of life in West Virginia for women. When we do this, we will join multitudes of women around the world who are forcing economic change in their communities. Only by working together can we assure the economic stability and growth of our West Virginia economy and economic justice for poor women and their families everywhere.

NOTES

1. Chris Weiss was director of Women and Employment at the time this article was written. She now works in West Virginia for Women's World Banking and the Ms. Foundation of New York City.

2. Diana Pearce and Harriette McAdoo, "Women and Children: Alone and in Poverty," National Advisory Council on Economic Opportunity, Washington, D.C., September 1981.

3. Nancy Matthews, ed., *West Virginia Women in Perspective: 1970–1985,* (Charleston: West Virginia Women's Commission, 1985).

4. Barbara Ellen Smith, *Women of the Rural South: Economic Status and Prospects* (Lexington, Ky.: Southeast Women's Employment Coalition, 1986), 51, 59.

5. Sara Gould, "Women and Economic Development: Creating a Strategy for the Future," Conference Report, 1985, Wisconsin Department of Development/Wisconsin Women's Council.

6. Elizabeth Moen, Elise Boulding, Jane Lillydahl, and Risa Plam, *Women and the Social Costs of Economic Development: Two Colorado Case Studies* (Boulder, Colo.: Westview Press, 1981). Donald Larson and Claudia White, "Will Employment Growth Benefit All Households? A Case Study in Nine Nonmetro Kentucky Counties," Rural Development Research Report no. 55, Agriculture and Rural Economics Division, Economic Research Service, U.S. Department of Agriculture (Washington, D.C.: U.S. Government Printing Office, 1986).

7. Larson and White, "Will Employment Growth Benefit All Households?" 14.

8. Gita Sen and Caren Grown, *Development, Crises, and Alternative Visions: Third World Women's Perspectives* (New York: Monthly Review Press, 1987), 8.

9. Judy Beatty, "The Occupational Distribution of Severely Disabled Women in West Virginia," unpublished report, Women and Employment, Charleston, W.Va., 1986.

Case Studies
from the Piedmont

S O U T H of the steepest mountains of the central Appalachian coalfields lie the Piedmont regions of North Carolina, Tennessee, Virginia, and Kentucky. Historically, they have relied on both manufacturing and agriculture for their development. As industry came to the Piedmont, attracted by community concessions and cheap labor, the area saw the development of the worker–farmer, who worked both on the land and in the factories to survive.

In the 1980s, with changes in the national and international economy, plant closings have swept through many communities of the region. Many companies have moved operations overseas or simply closed because of international competition. The pattern of industrial decline is uneven, for the region simultaneously continues to attract new industries. But as the case studies in this section remind us, economic development should not be confused with increased quality of life for workers and communities.

It has always taken grassroots organizing in this region for workers and communities to receive their fair share of the economic pie. Such struggles today are made difficult by the fear invoked by capital mobility, the ability of industries to move around from community to community, as we see in John Gaventa's study (Chapter 7) of the movement of a seat-belt plant from Michigan to Tennessee, to Alabama, to Mexico—all in search of cheaper labor. Such a climate creates labor and community concessions—trading jobs for dignity. Using interviews with workers around North Carolina, John Bookser-Feister and Leah Wise demonstrate (See Chapter 8) that new jobs in today's climate may also bring workplace harassment and ill health.

While times are hard in mill and manufacturing communities, Hal Hamilton's report (Chapter 6) reminds us that farming communities are also facing difficulties. Farmers in the South have a greater dependence on off-farm employment than farmers in any other region in the country. In many areas, such as Bluegrass Kentucky about which Hamilton writes, tobacco is the major cash crop for these worker–farmers. Now, facing a growing health lobby and the internationalization of tobacco

71

production, farmers are affected by declining prices. Like others around the region, they are caught in a double jeopardy: unemployed, they cannot make it off the land; without the land, they have difficulty surviving unemployment.

The hard economic times are spawning new struggles here, as in the other sub-regions of the South. In Kentucky, the Community Farm Alliance is organizing farmers to participate in shaping farm policy. In South Carolina, the Workers' Rights Project, a creative worker organization using community organizing approaches, is taking on policies that affect worker compensation and harassment. In North Carolina and Tennessee, new labor alliances are challenging plant closings. Community and labor organizations must work not just to get a fair share of the pie, but also to have their voices heard in fundamental decisions that shape economic development.

CHAPTER

6

Organizing Rural Tobacco Farmers: Central Kentucky in Global Context

Hal Hamilton

The predicament of the farmers of our region is indeed critical. Many of the farms are small or of moderate size. These farms depend for survival on the income from burley tobacco, which is now under severe threat. Because this tobacco-dependence is as old as the white people's occupation of this part of the country, the development of alternative sources of farm income will not be simple or easy. For the proposed, and greatly needed, transition to succeed, new crops and new markets will have to be brought into existence simultaneously— an achievement obviously beyond the reach of farmers individually or in small local groups. A regional effort is necessary, and such an effort is now being made by the Community Farm Alliance. . . . The agricultural economy of this region is not, for us, an abstract or a theoretical issue. We are trying to survive, as farmers, as a family, and as a community.

Wendell Berry

The South and Appalachia are rooted in the land. Farms and small towns permeate the region and its culture, and agriculture still underpins portions of the economy.

Across the United States, however, the family-farm system is undergoing its most sustained and profound crisis of the century. The farm crisis has also come to the upper South. The symptoms are many: foreclosures, boarded-up small-town businesses, soil erosion on unkept land. Economic transformation is wrecking rural agricultural communities just as certainly as the loss of mining or textile jobs has devastated other communities in the region. This chapter focuses on the farm crisis in Kentucky, where farmers have always depended on a single cash crop, tobacco. During the late 1970s and the 1980s the tobacco companies internationalized their operations, and influenced legislation that forced down prices for farmers, putting thousands of family farms out of business. Dairy, grain, and livestock farmers face similarly low prices and troubled futures.

As a result, farmers and other rural residents are organizing for their own survival. Kentucky farmers have formed the Community Farm Alliance and have united with similar grassroots rural organizations from across the country.

Farm policy, both state and federal, is the arena of struggle. Farmers seek better prices, controls on production, credit relief, and help with diversifying into new crops and markets. The Community Farm Alliance (CFA) provides its members opportunities for leadership development, community organizing, and legislative campaigns. CFA's goals include democratic ownership of land and stewardship of resources—issues that affect us all.

The Tobacco Program, Farmers, and Farm Communities

The upper South "Burley Belt," including Kentucky, is a region of small farms. Vital towns still dot the landscape. More than half of Kentucky's population lives in rural areas and in small towns, working on farms and also off the farm in other rural jobs. Even though Kentucky is the nation's premier coalmining state, agriculture remains the Commonwealth's largest industry, with revenues of $3.4 billion a year. Kentucky has the most agriculturally dependent counties of any state east of the Mississippi. The system of family farming, supported by a New Deal farm program, sustains rural communities and enables careful tending of the rolling land.

Nevertheless, storm clouds loom for Kentucky farmers and their communities. Kentucky's farm crisis started later than those in states to the north and west, but its crisis is nonetheless severe. According to the U.S. Department of Commerce, net farm income of Kentucky's farms fell 39.97 percent between 1981 and 1986.[1]

In Kentucky, as in many states of the upper South, farming, especially small family farming, is virtually synonymous with tobacco production. Burley tobacco, used primarily to flavor cigarettes, is grown on 80 percent of the farms in Kentucky, and half the state's farmers depend on the crop for at least half their gross farm income. Tobacco accounts for 8.9 percent of total employment in Kentucky, more than double that of coal. More than four-fifths of the labor on tobacco farms comes from family members, on family farms.[2]

This dependence on tobacco production is not unique to Kentucky. Tobacco is grown in parts of eight states, with the heaviest concentration in the upper South: Kentucky, Tennessee, western North Carolina, and southwestern Virginia. Current trends bode ill for tobacco farming communities, however. Consumption of cigarettes has steadily declined over the past decade, and tobacco companies have increased their imports of tobacco from less than 14 percent of domestic consumption in the 1970s to 35 percent in 1988.

In Kentucky alone gross income from tobacco fell almost $450 million, or almost 50 percent, between 1984 and 1986. The loss of income is devastating for rural farm families, already living at the margin of economic survival. Of Kentucky's 83,000 tobacco growers, 57 percent gross less than $15,000 annually. The average per capita income in six of every seven tobacco-producing counties is lower than the state average, which itself is the fifth lowest in the nation.[3]

Traditionally, many tobacco farm families have other sources of income, both on and off the farm. In Kentucky, 65 percent of farm families have at least one member working off the farm to supplement family income, perhaps at a retail store or a local textile factory. The farm may also support a dairy. Another very common pattern is raising a few acres of tobacco, keeping a herd of twenty or thirty beef cows, and growing a little corn and hay. Now, however, all these activities are increasingly problematic, except perhaps the minimum-wage jobs at the fast-food restaurant or retail outlet.

Why the crisis in tobacco communities? Part of the decline in the industry has to do, of course, with rising health concerns about smoking. Cigarette consumers may be only vaguely aware of the economic impact their choice not to smoke has on Southern tobacco communities. But there are also fundamental issues of power and policy at stake. While tobacco-growing communities are going broke, tobacco companies are not. And these thriving tobacco companies, like other parts of the agribusiness industry, have enormous resources to control policy and influence public opinion.

Before looking at the power of the tobacco industry, we must examine some of the policy issues at stake for the tobacco farmer.

How Does Federal Farm Policy Work?

Farm activists in Kentucky are not promoting the *smoking* of tobacco but rather a system of production controls and price supports that protects the growers from the power of the tobacco companies. If everyone were to quit smoking tomorrow morning, the world would be better off. But as long as anyone still smokes, the growers might as well be small family farmers with price supports. Keep in mind also that tobacco price supports do not cost the government *anything*. Compare the tobacco program with the corn program.

Price supports for tobacco cost taxpayers nothing because they are price floors rather than cash payments. If a farmer's tobacco fails to bring the support price at auction, that tobacco is put into storage by a cooperative association of farmers, and money is borrowed from the government to pay the farmer. Eventually, as inflation raises the market price of tobacco, the tobacco is sold out of storage, the government loan is repaid, and the farmer receives any additional profits.

The price-support system works because the production of tobacco is managed to keep supply balanced with demand. Each farmer has a production quota that is adjusted up or down each year. Production is dispersed among hundreds of thousands of small family farms because concentration is virtually impossible. And no tobacco farmer has ever received a subsidy check.

The corn program is the opposite. Like most grain programs, it combines three policy goals: (1) to help grain companies and processors purchase raw materials as cheaply as possible; (2) to enforce low raw-material prices on the rest of the world; and (3) to create enough subsidy checks for farm-state politicians to pass out to farmers so that they vote, survive, and buy fertilizer, chemicals, and tractors.

The result is a two-tiered price structure. The market price is kept very low. The target price, an arbitrary higher figure, determines the level of subsidy checks written directly to farmers from the U.S. Treasury. The biggest farmers get the biggest subsidy checks. Even with subsidies, most farmers still receive less than the cost of production.

Who Is Making Money on High Food Prices?

As farmers suffer from the low prices of the 1980s, the companies that buy farm products are doing fine. From 1981 to 1986, R. J. Reynolds averaged a 22.8 percent return on equity; Kellogg reported a five-year average of 33.4 percent, H. J. Heinz, 21.2 percent.[4] The average return for most farmers over the same period has been − 13 percent. Tobacco prices to farmers peaked in 1984 at $188.40 per hundred pounds, but by 1987 they had dropped 16.5 percent to $157.20. In 1988 Philip Morris acquired Kraft. According to an Associated Press story, "The immense profitability of cigarettes is what gives Philip Morris the muscle to try to buy Kraft."[5]

As agribusinesses conglomerate into larger and more profitable firms, they also internationalize their production. Five companies, for instance, essentially control the world's trade in grain. In a prospectus prepared by Merrill Lynch for Cargill, one of the five, Cargill reported a 66 percent increase in fiscal 1986 earnings over the previous year. According to the prospectus, Cargill's international grain-trading profits improved substantially, while record earnings were generated by corn milling, beef processing, cotton, coffee, salt, seed processing, international poultry, steel, and commodity brokerage operations.[6]

As corporate agribusiness profits have gone up, the farmer's share of the consumer food dollar has declined dramatically. Between 1981 and 1988 costs to consumers rose seven times faster than prices for farmers did. Many farm activists argue that the government is not subsidizing farmers; it is instead using farmers to launder money that subsidizes the agribusiness corporations. As Texas Agriculture Commissioner Jim Hightower says, "If you did to a 7–Eleven what these giant food-processing conglomerates and international grain shippers have done to American farmers, you'd be doing twenty years to life in a state prison."[7]

The tobacco industry, too, is dominated by a few corporate giants, including household names such as Philip Morris and R. J. Reynolds. Together six multinationals produce around 40 percent of the world's cigarettes.[8] In recent years, American tobacco companies have greatly increased their activity—and their earnings—internationally. During the early 1980s a large amount of tobacco was imported from overseas, much of it from Latin America, and this imported tobacco was used to "break the pool," the domestic, cooperatively controlled inventory of surplus tobacco that has served tobacco farmers for more than forty years.

Free Drinks on Philip Morris

In tobacco, as in other agribusiness, wealth is used to buy power and influence. Recently, for instance, twenty-five young tobacco farmers were wined and dined, along with many of Kentucky's other farm leaders, under the gilded chandeliers of the University of Kentucky's mansion, Spindletop Hall. Philip Morris had paid $250,000 for a two-year "leadership development" program for these young men, a program begun at the University of North Carolina.

The University of Kentucky accepts large grants from the tobacco companies, in this case to train farm leaders. Just what are they being trained for?

Fundamental issues are at stake. Can these young leaders be expected to ask tough questions about farm policy issues that divide farmers and companies? Over the past two years they had been treated to trips to Washington, Virginia, and, most recently, Argentina. At the "graduation" banquet, the guests enjoyed drinks and prime rib and, of course, there were many packs of cigarettes on the tables. University officials applauded the generosity and vision of Philip Morris. A vice-president of Philip Morris congratulated the dean on his wisdom and urged support for tobacco legislation in Congress.

The companies need the political support of farmers, but who really gains? Tobacco companies are extremely profitable operations these days. Tobacco farms are not.

Why have the tobacco companies financed the university development of mechanical tobacco harvesters, which will only be used by very large operators in very large operations? Why have university employees helped train tobacco-farm managers in Brazil? Why has British American Tobacco set up tobacco plantations in southern Africa? Acquisition of the cheapest possible raw materials is the goal that drives these investments and policies.

Tobacco lobbyists in Washington, financed by both companies and farmers, say they preach the "interests of the whole tobacco industry." Farmers, however, have their own distinct interests. Farmers are naturally interested in higher prices and import quotas. Farmers want to protect the progressive aspects of the tobacco program. At the same time, they need to diversify into other crops, especially if other crops can be organized with price supports.

Is the Family Farm Obsolete?

Conventional opinion may dismiss tales of greed and political power with an observation that the family farm is obsolete and inefficient. "Put those farmers in a museum, give them a welfare check if we have to, let the efficient producers take over," is an attitude one hears expressed. The loss of the family farm is rationalized as the natural progress of a free-market economy.

But farmers and other rural Americans know that they are efficient producers. They know that family-scale farms are necessary to steward the land, especially hilly land. They know that small towns still nurture seeds of cooperation, community, and democracy. They know that as land ownership passes into the hands of fewer and fewer people, we all lose one of the foundations of our pluralist democracy.

If current trends continue, land-ownership patterns in the United States will be similar to those in much of Latin America, where a large proportion of the productive land is in the hands of a small class of owners. Land reform will become the rallying cry.

But we are not there yet. Millions of U.S. farms still operate. For most commodities, the corporate elite would rather control the markets and let family farmers do the labor—how could they ever get employees to take all the risks, work eighty-hour weeks for less than the minimum wage, and bring the family out to work for free?

There are realistic solutions to the farm crisis. A farm movement, growing across the country, has developed price and supply-management policies to protect small farms.

Creating a New Vision, Organizing a Different Future

Farm financial crises of the past have always spawned new grassroots movements of rural people. The Farmers Alliance of the 1870s and 1880s began the largest mass movement in American history and spawned radical demands for a federal subtreasury and for abolition of unfair banking and railroad practices. The farm crisis of the 1920s and 1930s spurred the development of grassroots movements embodied in the National Farmers Union and Farm Holiday, whose political demands were in many respects realized in New Deal farm programs that brought relative prosperity to rural America into the early 1950s.

Today, a cohesive farm policy reform movement is again emerging. As in the past, the work is being done through a new set of grassroots organizations, such as Wisconsin Farm Unity Alliance, Missouri Rural Crisis Center, United Farmers Organization of North and South Carolina, and the Community Farm Alliance in Kentucky. These organizations are formed by farm families, church members, and community activists. They are pushing established farm organizations to new ground, and they are bringing into play broader elements of the rural community. They have focused the struggle on continued diversity in the ownership structure of American farming. Their federal policy goals have centered on two elements: mandatory production quotas sized to sustain family-scale operations and support prices that ensure farm income from the marketplace rather than from the taxpayers.

The Midwest has paced this fight for reform because the farm crisis has been especially deep there. The monocultural farming practices of the corn, soybean, and wheat belts were more susceptible to irrational expansion in the 1970s and then in the 1980s were subject to irrational contraction because export markets collapsed.

The same scenario now appears in the upper South, because the region's agricultural linchpin, the burley tobacco program, is threatened. Ironically, what the Midwest seeks in farm policy reform is inherent in the failing burley program, a hard-won gain of earlier farmers' movements. In that program, production is regulated by a strict allotment or supply-management system that allocates most production to small family farms. The tobacco program distributes the right to market tobacco to areas of historic production and not to the areas most topographically suited to intense mechanization. Burley tobacco has a support-price loan rate that is pegged to production costs. Taxpayers pay nothing to support tobacco prices; all expenses are paid by growers or buyers of tobacco.

The Community Farm Alliance

In Kentucky, the Community Farm Alliance (CFA) is working to sustain policies won in the 1930s and to rebuild the rural economy according to principles of community accountability. CFA is a membership organization, with county chapters that elect representatives to a state board of directors. CFA leaders are farm people learning to speak out on their own behalf, learning to run an organization, and learning to promote policies and visions to revitalize their communities. Here are some examples.

Joan Mattingly works for the Community Farm Alliance. She lives in Marion County, not far from where she grew up, and her family farms there. Joan has raised seven children (she says that makes her a natural organizer). In her words, "My boys would like to farm the worst in the world." Why can't they? Because making a living from farming has become nearly impossible. There's a local joke: "Do you know how to make a small fortune farming? Start with a large fortune."

Dickie Nally is a member of the board of directors of the Community Farm Alliance. He raises hogs, milks cows, and drives a half-day mail route. Dickie chairs CFA's statewide credit committee, which represents county chapters in an effort to find policy solutions to the farm debt crisis. Dickie wrote in the CFA newsletter: "It used to be all a farmer had to do was produce a good crop and everything else would take care of itself, but that is no longer true. As much effort should be put into the marketing and political aspect of it as in producing it."

Kathy Aman is a CFA member from Nelson County. She and her husband have grown market vegetables on their farm for several years. Because of Kathy's efforts through CFA, with help from the Louisville Legal Aid Society, farmers in Nelson, Washington, and Marion counties can now sell fruits and vegetables in bulk to community centers in Louisville, which will market the fresh produce in poor neighborhoods.

Duane and Glenda Parker are dairy farmers and CFA leaders in Fleming County. In the spring of 1988, Duane arranged for the donation of more than

3,500 bushels of free seed corn to needy neighbors. Duane and Glenda enthusiastically recruit their neighbors as members of the Fleming County chapter because CFA helped them save their farm from impending foreclosure by the Farmers Home Administration. CFA staff person Deborah Webb runs the only statewide hotline in Kentucky for farm families with credit problems. In addition to valuable assistance to individual families, Deborah has trained dozens of farmers and attorneys in the intricacies of farm credit law.

Bob Shanklin is the CFA field staff person in southwestern Kentucky. He is black, a Baptist minister, and an experienced organizer from the Southern Christian Leadership Conference. Bob is organizing CFA chapters and helping black farmers to become leaders of CFA. If current trends in agriculture continue, black people will have lost their entire land base by the end of another decade. CFA, whose membership is about 15 percent black, would like to contribute toward reversing those trends.

Leadership development is CFA's central method, and its main purpose. CFA has representatives on national coalitions, in Washington, D.C., and in Frankfort, the state capital. Many of them had never been to such places or participated in such meetings, but they are learning to understand farm legislation, to develop state policies, to chair meetings and hold press conferences, to have confidence in their own abilities.

Making the Transition from Tobacco

Local CFA leaders have a vision of rural revitalization, agricultural development, and environmental sustainability that serves the needs of their communities. During 1987 Deborah Webb and Kathy Aman spent a week at the Texas Department of Agriculture studying programs to help state farmers diversify. CFA then began developing similar policies for state government in Kentucky.

While at the federal level the most important question is how to provide a support system for the small farmer, at the state level it is how to diversify agricultural production to relieve small farmers' dependence on tobacco. But the strategy of diversification raises further questions. Who will do the diversifying, and who will benefit from it?

State-level politicians usually conclude that the way to diversify the farm economy is to lure agribusiness corporations into the state to process vegetables, poultry, or other resources. CFA believes that cooperative, smaller-scale, farmer-controlled enterprises are best, and that farmers need state government to help make these smaller developments emerge.

During 1987, the problems created by luring in outside industry were starkly illuminated. Georgia Vegetable Company, a multimillion-dollar corporation, began its relationship with Kentucky agriculture in 1985 as a broker for the green peppers produced by farmers in the Kentucky Agriculture Marketing Cooperative in Clark County. As broker, Georgia Vegetable took 12 percent of the farmers' sales.

In 1987 Georgia Vegetable leased 1,000 acres of prime land and became the largest grower in the co-op. The co-op's bylaws do not protect smaller growers from the intrusion of out-of-state corporations. A professor of agriculture at the University of Kentucky pointed out that the presence of Georgia Vegetable as both broker and major grower in the co-op presents a danger of "the tail wagging the dog."

The foundation for Georgia Vegetable's operation in Clark County was laid by a variety of taxpayer-supported agencies: the University of Kentucky, the Department of Agriculture, and the city of Lexington. They all claim that the project is "vital to laying the groundwork" for large-scale vegetable production in Kentucky. As broker and largest grower (the next-largest grower has fewer than fifty acres), Georgia Vegetable is the major beneficiary of the co-op and its facilities.

The co-op was originally funded by a $615,000 community development block grant, which was intended to help small- to medium-sized farmers. However, the Georgia Vegetable operation in Clark County represents the development of corporate farming, not family farming; its profits flow primarily out of state, not into the local community. Labor income goes primarily to migrant laborers from out of state, not to Kentuckians. Production methods, including the use of migrant labor, are those of industrial agriculture rather than family-scale agriculture. Water used for irrigation may deplete the local water table or decrease water pressure from municipal sources. Chemical use is highly concentrated. Soil erosion and pesticide runoff are potential problems that worry local citizens.

Some state farm experts asserted that Georgia Vegetable will "teach Kentucky farmers how to grow vegetables." CFA argues that, with help from the Extension Service, the average Kentucky farmer can learn to grow *any* crop that promises to return a decent income. What farmers need are markets and the bargaining power in those markets to get a fair price.

State-level policymakers are inclined to believe that economic development can be accomplished only by large corporations, corporations that must be lured into the state with tax breaks and subsidies. "Don't stand in the way of progress," they warn. "Progress for whom?" we ask. After a dry season in 1988, Georgia Vegetable pulled out of the Clark County vegetable co-op. The co-op now finds itself discredited in the eyes of farmers and near bankruptcy.

Long-Term Implications

The farm movement now consists of many state organizations like CFA linked in national coalitions. The focus is on building effective and democratic organizations capable of winning better policies in each state and in Congress. As CFA member Dickie Nally puts it:

One farmer's voice is like a snowflake. It is a very fragile thing, but if farmers would speak in one voice they could be heard in Frankfort and Washington. The industries that the farmer deals with (lenders, processors, wholesalers, retailers) all do their homework in Frankfort and Washington and get the laws made to benefit themselves. CFA offers the farmer the same opportunity to do this.

Our opposition consists of corporate processors and traders, buttressed by the ideology of "survival of the fittest," when "fittest" means writing the rules. This is the ideology supported by the Farm Bureau (a huge insurance company that requires its policyholders to become members), chambers of commerce, and other business organizations.

The movement to unseat these powerful few is profoundly important to the future of our democracy. That is why most of Capitol Hill reacts with astonishment when farmers demand higher prices, but then votes for more subsidy payments to keep the farmers quiet, while incidentally continuing to supply the corporations with cheap raw materials.

Farm policy has congruent purposes. Farm prices in the United States, legislated by Congress, set the pattern for agricultural commodity prices worldwide. Large companies like Cargill benefit doubly: they can buy Kansas wheat for $2.40 a bushel and Argentine wheat for a little less. If U.S. farmers succeed in raising support prices, farmers all over the world will benefit. If U.S. farmers succeed in instituting production control policies, Third World nations will be more likely to achieve food self-sufficiency.

Politicians often set farmers in one country against farmers in another. The Reagan administration tried to blame the Europeans for the farm crisis, and Reagan's first Secretary of Agriculture, John Block, vowed to bankrupt the European Economic Community with cheap U.S. farm exports. "Food is a weapon." Cheap food, that is. Higher commodity prices and managed production will help all producers of basic raw materials. The farm movement has important implications for justice around the world, and for this reason American farmers have begun to establish links with those in Europe, Japan, and Latin America.

Tobacco farmers, dairy farmers, steel workers in Pittsburgh, auto workers in Detroit, textile workers in South Carolina—what do we all have in common? Our ability to see the big picture, to organize, to renew pride in our strengths, to rebuild community, and to wrest control over the political process. We can do it. We *are* doing it.

NOTES

1. U.S. Department of Commerce, Regional Economic Information System, Bureau of Economic Analysis (April 1988) as analyzed by Ben Poage in an unpublished paper, "Farm Income in Kentucky, 1980–1986" (Berea, Ky.: Kentucky Appalachian Ministry, n.d.).

2. Report of Tobacco Task Force of Kentucky General Assembly (Frankfort, Ky.: Legislative Research Commission, 1986).

3. Ibid.

4. *Forbes,* January 12, 1987.

5. (Lexington) *Herald-Leader,* October 19, 1988.

6. *The Wall Street Journal,* February 25, 1987.

7. Texas Department of Agriculture press release, March 2, 1987.

8. See Peter Taylor, "The Smoke Ring: Politics and Tobacco in the Third World," *Southern Exposure* (September–October 1984): 43.

CHAPTER

7

From the Mountains to the *Maquiladoras*: A Case Study of Capital Flight and Its Impact on Workers

John Gaventa

Ⅰn recent years the U.S. economy has lost hundreds of thousands of jobs in manufacturing. According to a study by the Office of Technology Assessment, in the years between 1979 and 1985, 11.5 million workers lost their jobs as companies decided to shut down or relocate manufacturing plants, increase productivity, or shrink output. These plant closings and layoffs have prompted warnings of the "deindustrialization of America," and have caused major disruptions in workers' lives, ranging from long- and short-term unemployment, underemployment, foreclosures, and associated family stress.[1]

Until recently, the South was often thought to be exempt from these trends. In fact, for decades deindustrialization of the Frost Belt North meant the growth of the Sun Belt South. The South was on the receiving end of capital mobility, as runaway shops from the North came south in search of a "favorable business climate"—meaning low-wage labor, cheap resources, and community subsidies. But by the early 1980s, the trend began changing, and the industries that had once moved to the South also began to close or relocate overseas. As Southern economic historian James Cobb writes, "Industries fleeing the South are purchasing one-way tickets to Taiwan and other exotic destinations just as readily as they used to depart Akron, Ohio for Opelika, Alabama."[2]

An example of the impact of deindustrialization may be seen in Tennessee. At one level, economic development in the state has been successful.

85

The South has lured dozens of factories within its borders and has received national attention for its recruitment of mega-manufacturing plants such as Saturn (see Chapter 14). But like other Southern states overly preoccupied with industrial recruitment, Tennessee has failed to keep many of its traditional manufacturing plants. Between 1980 and 1985, 2,844 manufacturing plants closed; 605 of them employed more than fifty workers each. Between April 1986 and the end of 1987, some 10,000 workers lost jobs as sixty plants, each with fifty or more workers, closed or made permanent layoffs. These layoffs were in all sectors of the manufacturing economy—textiles, apparel, paper, chemicals, furniture, machinery, and transportation.[3]

Despite the trends, plant closings in the South have received little public attention. The region has heralded its success in recruiting industries from the North; closings are a threat to the Sun Belt image. Moreover, where closings have occurred, they have often been more invisible—in smaller, more rural industries, with less unionized and less powerful workers—than have closings in the auto plants or steel industries of the urbanized North.

Until now, few studies have described the process of capital flight or analyzed its impact on the workers and communities affected. Why are plants leaving, and where are they going? Do workers in the Sun Belt experience problems of dislocation similar to those of other regions? The following case study provides a classic story of the movement of capital from the North, to the South, to the Third World, in constant search of cheaper labor and a more favorable business climate.

The Move to the Appalachian South

The Jim Robbins Seat Belt Company was originally based in Michigan and first considered Knoxville, Tennessee, as a plant site in the early 1960s. The mood of the time encouraged industrial growth and expansion. Demand for seat belts was also growing, and the company moved rapidly to meet it.

Early one morning in November 1965, Robbins's chief executive officer telephoned the industrial development executive of the Knoxville Chamber of Commerce about possible sites for a new plant. That same afternoon, corporate officials arrived in Knoxville in an executive jet, piloted by the company owner, Jim Robbins. A lease on an abandoned Du Pont facility was signed. The following Monday the company began hiring about 50 workers. Within two weeks employment was up to 100, with two shifts daily producing 50,000 belts a week—all under contract with Ford and General Motors.

By 1967 local employment had risen to 1,200 people, and production to 60,000 assembled seat belts a day—enough to meet 60 percent of Ford's requirements and a large percentage of GM's. Local papers heralded the operation as the largest seat-belt manufacturing company in the world, producing more than 19 million belts a year.

The company heads cited Knoxville's favorable business atmosphere and the attitude of the workers as playing a big part in their decision to locate in the city. In 1967 the company president, Bill Johnson, praised Knoxville's "progressive local government," which was "interested in the requirements of industrial development." The city government had helped the company acquire land, cut through red tape for installation of utilities, and in general displayed a "cooperative spirit." "The workforce has a progressive attitude and a desire to work which is essential for industrial growth," Johnson said. "They're good workers and they're intelligent too. Your labor force here trains very quickly." Moreover, he stated bluntly, "The future of our expansion in Knoxville depends on the business atmosphere."[4]

The business atmosphere was also affected, of course, by wage differentials between Michigan and Tennessee. In 1972, according to the U.S. Census of Manufacturers, the average wage for production workers in the industry in Knoxville was $2.58 an hour, about half the $5.04 an hour that similar workers received in the Detroit area. And the company did what it could to ensure that the favorable "business atmosphere" continued. By 1973, only eight years after the location of the initial plant, the Jim Robbins Seat Belt Company had become the largest manufacturing contributor to the local chamber of commerce. One company official led a chamber of commerce project to produce a film that would document local industry's impact on the area's economy. The company made donations to the United Way, to a local black college, to the YMCA.

By 1979 the company employed almost 3,000 workers and ranked, with two other textile firms, Levi Strauss and Standard Knitting Mills, among the city's largest industrial employers.[5]

The Bubble Bursts: From Tennessee to Alabama

The atmosphere of industrial growth began to change very quickly in the 1980s. In an eight-month period during late 1979 and early 1980, the company laid off 1,500 employees. This was followed by a further series of layoffs, bringing employment down to between 300 and 400 workers by 1983.

At first, in 1981, company officials publicly attributed the layoffs to the deepening effects of the recession on the automotive industry. By 1983, as the country climbed out of the recession, the company blamed the slump in new U.S. car sales and increased imports.

However, at the same time the company was saying it could not afford to reinvest in Knoxville, it *was* investing handsomely in a new facility in Greenville, Alabama, a rural, nonunion area anxious to acquire new industry. Between 1980 and 1985 the company carried out three expansions there, and increased its Alabama work force threefold, from 300 in 1980 to 960 in 1985.

In Alabama, the company echoed the story that Knoxville officials had heard fifteen years before. The company needed room to expand. Greenville offered a "large and motivated workforce, most easily trainable and many already seasoned in industrial sewing, thanks to the area's history of textile and carpet production." Moreover, the strong work ethic of the local labor force was complemented by the "upbeat, co-operative ready-to-serve attitude of local officials and business leaders." [6]

As Knoxville had fifteen years earlier, Greenville responded quickly. The mayor's office, the Industrial Development Board, and local banks provided revenue-bond financing for the purchase of the first building in 1980, and another in 1982. The Alabama Development Office helped the company by providing a training program in sewing and assembly, and by handling all employee recruiting and prescreening. [7]

As in the move to Tennessee, differences in wages were also a factor. Butler County, where Greenville is located, is more rural than Knoxville, with fewer unions and fewer industrial competitors. In 1982, wages for manufacturing workers in Butler County were approximately 60 percent of those for similar workers in Knoxville. [8]

Economic Blackmail

Rather than reinvest in equipment and retraining in Knoxville, then, the company moved to a new area that offered cheaper, nonunion labor and favorable state subsidies. Moreover, as the company increased its facilities in Alabama, it used the threat of further layoffs and movement of capital to exact concessions from the Knoxville work force. By the 1980s "the company increasingly used job blackmail against us, playing the Knoxville workers off against the Alabama employees," said one local union official.

In 1983, the company offered to bring some of the jobs back to Knoxville, but only if workers there would reduce job classifications and accept pay cuts. Desperate for jobs, the union members accepted the offer, returning to work for wages lower than those rejected three years before. "We're hoping it will be a start of a major turnaround," the union official said at the time. "It's definitely a trend going in the right direction." [9]

The optimism did not last long. Not long after a few jobs returned to Knoxville from Alabama, they were transferred again—this time to new plants in Mexico. In August 1985 more than 200 workers were laid off, leaving employment at slightly above 200 in an area that only six years before had been declared the seat-belt capital of the world.

From the Mountains to the *Maquiladora* Zone

For its new seat-belt facility, the company chose the town of Aqua Prieta, one of the smaller and newer *maquiladora* border towns. Freely translated, the word *maquilar* means "to assemble." The *maquiladoras* are companies located along the Mexican border that assemble products with Mexican labor for re-export back to the United States or other countries.[10] The *maquiladora* zone is now growing at a phenomenal rate, as hundreds of U.S. plants move across the border for lower-wage labor.

Located in the state of Sonora, directly across the border from Douglas, Arizona, the town of Aqua Prieta is typical.[11] In recent years more than twenty manufacturing plants have located in the town, almost all of them sewing, electronic, automotive part, or other labor-intensive operations from the United States. With factory work abundant, the population has more than tripled in ten years, from 18,000 in the mid 1970s to more than 60,000 people by the mid 1980s. Growth has outstripped services and infrastructure. Plants sprawl in unfinished industrial parks. Mexican workers, attracted from miles around, find housing and services in short supply.

The new seat-belt plant opened on January 1, 1986. According to sources in the plant, the company employs about 500 people, and is growing. There, in repetitive, noisy assembly-line work, the workers cut the webbing and assemble the seat-belts for shipment back to Greenville for U.S. distribution.

The wages are minuscule, compared to those in the United States. Workers in this plant, as in others along the Mexican border, work 9½-hour days for about $3.50 a day, or 37 cents an hour, one-sixteenth of the wages workers received for comparable work in Knoxville.

Although the wages seem low to the U.S. visitor, the jobs are on the whole welcomed by local workers. Bumper stickers on cars parked near the plant claim in Spanish, "I love Bendix." (By then the seat-belt company was the Bendix division of a large conglomerate.) Local merchants are glad of the revenues. Even the local union, which is tied into the official national union, does little to question the arrangement. In short, the business climate is very, very favorable. As one U.S. resident along the border told me, "If you think economic boosterism is big in your part of the world, you haven't seen anything until you come here."

It may be more intense, but this pro-business climate arises out of a very familiar development policy: recruit industry from the North. In Mexico, the *maquiladora* zone has emerged as the official solution to regional underdevelopment. But to large multinational businesses like the seat-belt company, it is simply one more area in the world economy that, desperate for development at any price, will provide cheaper labor and a more favorable business climate.

The Growth of the Multinational: Mergers and Conglomeration

As the seat-belt company moved from the North to the urban South, then to the rural nonunion South, then to Mexico, it also was becoming integrated into a larger multinational corporate empire. When the company came to Knoxville in 1965, it was a private venture owned by Jim Robbins, a self-made Michigan millionaire, with holdings ranging from banana and cotton plantations in Venezuela to seat-belt and plastics factories in the Detroit area. Shortly after the move to Knoxville, Robbins was killed while flying his private jet near his buffalo and pheasant ranch in Platte, South Dakota. A year later the firm was bought by the Allied Chemical Corporation, a vast chemical and manufacturing firm. In 1982, Allied took over the Bendix Corporation, and in 1983 the seat-belt operation became the Bendix Safety Restraints Division.

In 1985, Allied merged with the Signal Corporation to form Allied Signal, now one of the largest manufacturing holding firms in the world. As workers in Knoxville were being laid off as a result of the movement of their jobs to Mexico, top officials of Allied and Signal were receiving at least $50 million in cash, stock giveaways, options, and other benefits in what *The Wall Street Journal* marked as one of the largest windfalls for corporate executives in merger history.[12]

The Impact on Workers

With a climate of competition between workers and communities in different locations for scarce jobs, large corporations can use the threat—and the reality—of massive plant closings and layoffs as a tool for "economic blackmail" and bargaining for labor concessions. Allied used the movement of jobs to Alabama as a tool to exact concessions from workers in Knoxville. Even when the concessions were made, the company still laid off workers in Tennessee in order to gain yet cheaper labor and more favorable conditions in Mexico.

Conventional economists, of course, might argue that such industrial location and relocation are a natural process of economic development and that they ultimately serve to produce jobs and economic growth for workers and communities. However, Allied Signal workers have not fared well in this process of economic transition. Interviews with 170 workers laid off in 1985 show that:

- Some fifteen months after being laid off, 44 percent of the workers remain unemployed.

- Of those workers who have been able to find new jobs, less than half (47 percent) have been able to get full-time work; 53 percent are working at part-time jobs.

- Of the workers who have been able to find new jobs, average wages have dropped from $5.76 an hour to $3.70 an hour.

- While they worked at Allied, none of the workers earned less than $5 an hour. For those who have obtained new jobs, 91 percent are earning less than $5 an hour; three-quarters now make less than $4 an hour.

- The jobs the workers lost were union jobs. For 91 percent of them there is no union at their new jobs.

- Ninety-five percent of the workers lost their health insurance when they were laid off. Only 48 percent are covered under a new plan.

- The impact of layoffs has been especially severe on older workers, women, and families with only one primary earner in the household.

Workers in Knoxville have suffered this decline in wages and quality of life despite the fact that overall, Knoxville enjoys a *growth* economy; the loss of manufacturing jobs has been far outpaced by the gain of jobs in the non-manufacturing sectors, especially services and wholesale and retail trade. However, seat-belt workers have fallen through the cracks of economic transition. When those laid-off workers have gotten new jobs, the largest percentage have been in the service sector, where they have lower wages, fewer hours, and no union representation.

The Allied case is representative. National studies have also found that the increasing number of service jobs may be accompanied by a *declining* standard of living for many workers.[13] In fact, the seat-belt workers seem to have fared worse than dislocated workers nationally. Only 47 percent were able to obtain new full-time jobs, compared to 60 percent nationally. Some fifteen months after being laid off, almost 60 percent of the workers reported an average household income of less than $10,400 a year (the poverty line for a family of four).

To survive such poverty, most of the workers (93 percent) drew unemployment compensation after the layoff, and about half did so for the full twenty-six week period for which they were eligible. Once their unemployment benefits ran out, these workers were faced with major problems of survival. Remarkably few used food stamps—only 18 percent of the total. Most people turned to more informal means of survival, made possible in part by the somewhat rural culture of the area: 22 percent reported they gardened or farmed, 22 percent did odd jobs, and 21 percent borrowed money, often from friends and relatives.

But for many workers, this informal system has not provided protection against severe hardship. For instance, almost a quarter of the workers have faced large medical expenses while laid off. One woman, aged thirty-seven, has three teenagers, all of whom had medical emergencies: one son broke his arm; the other two were involved in car and motorcycle accidents. Facing a debt of $18,000, she had to declare bankruptcy. For her, a woman who had worked all her life, starting at fifteen, such a decision has a high psychological cost.

Another woman faces $16,000 in medical bills. She is relatively lucky: her husband has a job as a government meat inspector. But even so, she works two jobs to try to pay off her debts—by day at a photography shop for $4.50 an hour, by night at a pizza parlor for minimum wage.

Loss of income has also had an impact on housing. Over a third of the workers interviewed had a mortgage on their home, and almost a quarter faced monthly rent payments. No cases of actual foreclosure were reported, but some had to sell their homes and rent apartments or move in with relatives.

And they are not alone. Many workers with large medical bills or housing costs have gone into debt, used up their savings, worked extra jobs, or depended on relatives' help to meet their expenses. Many cut back on basic needs for themselves and their children—clothing, food, transportation, and electricity. Others have dipped into savings that were intended to provide their security in the future. The uncertainties of unemployment or of working minimum-wage jobs take their toll in countless other ways as well. Almost half (48 percent) of the workers reported psychological problems such as stress and depression.

Lack of Job Training

It is precisely this type of economic "skidding" that job-training programs are designed to ameliorate. Theoretically, the laid-off Allied workers were eligible for retraining benefits under Title III of the Job Training and Partnership Act of 1982 (designed for displaced workers) and under the Trade Adjustment Assistance Act (TAA), designed for workers losing their jobs because of imports. In fact, both programs failed to meet the retraining needs. Even though at least 236 of the workers laid off in 1985 were found to be eligible for retraining programs, almost two years later only two had actually enrolled in the retraining, under TAA sponsorship. One state department of labor official described the problem this way: "We don't have programs for 200 people who are refugees from the garment industry. . . . If we got 10 of these folks into job training programs, we'd be lucky." The government attitude toward these workers was described more bluntly by another federal official: "Their skill level is such that you can't do anything with them." [14]

Toward New Strategies

In sum, then, capital mobility and economic transition have created severe hardship for workers in Knoxville, Tennessee, with problems ranging from unemployment to mental stress, from loss of income to loss of health benefits and housing. This case supports the thesis that problems related to plant closings and worker dislocation occur even as new service jobs are being created, and they happen in the South as well as the North.

These problems present new challenges for economic development policy. Traditionally the South has concentrated on industrial recruitment as its strategy for economic development, yet trends show that industries, once recruited, are leaving and that new industries are less likely to come. The jobs that are being created are not necessarily bringing increased economic well-being for working people; many are trapped in a spiral of low-wage and part-time underemployment or even unemployment. Programs designed to help train workers for the better jobs in the "new economy" are failing to assist those most in need of them. As James Cobb points out, "There is a grim irony in the fact that the South, having worked so diligently to create a business climate attractive to footloose industries, should now find its economic future threatened by an increase in industrial mobility." [15]

But so far, Tennessee, like most Southern states, has paid little attention to countering deindustrialization. Policies and programs on job dislocation must be added to those that concentrate on job creation. Community stability must become as important as capital mobility.

The labor movement must also confront deindustrialization trends, or it will see many of its hard-won gains eroded. The situation calls for new strategies by labor: continue to represent workers in existing jobs (made increasingly difficult by the climate of economic blackmail and concession bargaining), fight to save the manufacturing jobs at risk, and organize new service-sector jobs to obtain improved wages and benefits.

In other parts of the country workers have met these challenges by joining with community coalition groups and policymakers to support legislation to require early warnings of plant closings; taking over ailing plants and running them as worker- or community-owned enterprises; getting more involved in the economic development process by participating in local industrial boards, state development agencies, and economic development initiatives; establishing coalitions with workers and communities in other parts of the country and in other countries to counter economic blackmail. [16]

If the case of the seat-belt workers is indicative of broader trends—and I believe it is—then policymakers, labor unions, and community groups throughout the South must explore new strategies to counter the effects of capital flight and worker dislocation. We must learn to measure development potential not only by the business climate, but also by the climate for workers and communities.

NOTES

Acknowledgments: This chapter is based on a longer report by John Gaventa, *From the Mountains to the Maquiladoras: A Case Study of Capital Flight and Its Impact on Workers* (1988), available from the Highlander Research and Education Center, Route 3, Box 370, New Market, TN 37820. Special thanks to Mark Pitt and Doug Gamble of the Georgia-Tennessee-Alabama Joint Board of the Amalgamated Clothing and Textile Workers Union (ACTWU) for assistance provided, and to ACTWU Local 1742 for its cooperation.

1. U.S. Congress, Joint Economic Committee, *The Great American Job Machine: The Proliferation of Low-Wage Employment in the U.S. Economy,* study prepared by Barry Bluestone and Bennett Harrison, December 1986. U.S. Congress, Office of Technology Assessment, *Technology and Structural Unemployment: Reemploying Displaced Adults,* OTA-ITE 250 (Washington, D.C.: U.S. Government Printing Office, 1986), 5. For effects of layoffs, see Barry Bluestone and Bennett Harrison, *The Deindustrialization of America: Plant Closings, Community Abandonment and the Dismantling of Basic Industry* (New York: Basic Books, 1982), and Robert B. Reich, "The Hollow Corporation," *Business Week,* March 3, 1986.

2. James C. Cobb, "The Southern Business Climate: A Historical Perspective," *Forum for Applied Research and Public Policy* 1, no. 2 (Summer 1986): 98.

3. See William F. Fox et al., *Entries and Exits of Firms in the Tennessee Economy* (Knoxville, Tenn.: Center for Business and Economic Research, 1987); additional data from the Tennessee Department of Economic Security.

4. *Knoxville News Sentinel,* November 29, 1967. Text of speech by Mr. Johnson, "The Decision to Locate in Knoxville and Resulting Success," November 30, 1967.

5. In the summer of 1988, both Levi's and Standard announced that they were closing down their Knoxville operations.

6. *Nation's Business,* May 1985, 40J.

7. Ibid.

8. Based on U.S. Department of Commerce, Bureau of the Census, Census of Manufacturers, 1982. Data on wages of textile and apparel workers in Butler County were not available.

9. Quoted in *Knoxville News Sentinel,* November 23, 1983. Information about Knoxville worker concessions derived from interviews with local union officials and from a comparison of "Agreements between Allied Corporation . . . and Amalgamated Clothing and Textile Workers Union," December 1, 1980, with agreements dated March 15, 1982, and December 1, 1985.

10. In Mexico, the companies are exempt from certain laws, such as those governing foreign investment, and do not have to pay import duties on materials to be as-

sembled for export. The process is also encouraged by the U.S. Tariff Code, Sections 806.30 and 807.00, which reduce tariff duties on imports assembled abroad using components in the United States.

11. Observations about Aqua Prieta are based on personal visit and interviews, September 24–26, 1987.

12. *The Wall Street Journal,* August 12, 1985.

13. See, for instance, Bluestone and Harrison, "Great American Job Machine."

14. Correspondence, U.S. Department of Labor and Senator Albert Gore, April 24, 1987; and Senator Gore to Mark Pitt, ACTWU, May 13, 1987. Quotations are from telephone interviews with the author.

15. Cobb, "The Southern Business Climate."

16. See, for example, Gilda Haas, *Plant Closures: Myths, Realities, and Responses* (Boston: South End Press, 1985).

8

Betrayal of Trust:
The Impact of Economic Development Policy
upon Working Citizens

John Bookser-Feister and Leah Wise

When these companies tell you that everything's o.k., get somebody from the inside to give you the straight facts. That's working there; that knows what it's like. Because I'm not the only one. There's a whole lot of them. There's a lady there now, her hands—she's a darker complexion than I am—all the pigment in her hand and this is eaten away. Her hands are raw. But she's still got to work because she's got children. They don't care. All that they want is their dollar.

Not only did it affect me, it affected my family. My children, they had bad headaches. We didn't know what they was comin' from. But because of the clothes that I was working in, I'd come home in 'em, wash my children's clothes in 'em, they was having headaches. All up my nose, my throat, all of this was burnt, due to the chemical. They call it "lung fungus."

Alright, while I was out sick I thought I had insurance, which I didn't have. They was taking out of my paycheck $7.55 a week, but the clinic notified me that I didn't have any insurance, which was over $2,800 of doctor bills. Alright, I filed workman's compensation. When I did, this company terminated me.

So, the companies tell you one thing, but they do another. And, as long as you can do their work, you're doing fine.

And it's dangerous, very dangerous. Because it don't only affect the person that's in it. It affects the whole household, your whole family.

—Mattie Brown, disabled machinist
Wilson, North Carolina[1]

In an era when most regions of the United States are undergoing major economic transition, we might look to the South for ideas on how *not* to pursue regional economic development. Contrary to some popular myths outside our region, economic development practices in the "New South" have had mixed results: jobs have been imported from other areas, but mostly they have been low-wage and often physically dangerous. Regressive economic development policies mean that state governments are unashamedly pro-business, and local government leaders are either acquiescent or just plain ignorant. Working people—the vast majority of Southerners—are left without protection from corporate leaders who publicly express more responsibility to stockholders than to communities.

A major avenue for protection—organizing labor unions—has been effectively blocked for most Southerners. The two Carolinas, for example, vie for the honor of being the least unionized state in the United States. Roughly 95 percent of the labor force in both states is unorganized. Other Southern states are not far behind. Hoping to attract industry with a "good business climate," state and local governments have aggressively nurtured an anti-union climate, with tactics ranging from universally enacting right-to-work laws to interfering with organizing campaigns. Rather than being the guardians of the citizens, local, county, and state governments have become suppliants at the altar of economic development.

It is often considered heretical in the South to utter these facts. People will acknowledge that jobs brought to the South were not always the best jobs, but at least they were jobs. People seem to be saying, "We know that we need better-quality jobs, and let's do what we can to *get* better jobs, but in the meantime, let's take what we can get. Jobs are jobs." As a region then, we are in a blackmail situation—we tolerate destructive work situations for the appearance of progress. Any hint of scrutiny is quickly silenced for fear of losing jobs.

There is a dynamic of desperation afoot in the South today, as families, communities, and states compete for a shrinking economic pie. The resultant stress on families and entire communities is tremendous. There is a climate of fear in workplaces as increasing numbers of unemployed people compete for the same jobs. The stage is set for the most irresponsible corporate behavior: profits are maximized essentially at the expense of desperate employees and communities. As companies "tighten up" to increase profits, more tax abatements are demanded, payrolls are cut back, production lines are accelerated to unsafe rates, and safety measures are ignored. (Federal agencies such as the Occupational Safety and Health Administration [OSHA] offered little protection during the Reagan years.) Perhaps the harshest dimension of this tightening up is the widespread practice of terminating employees to avoid paying workers' compensation claims or unemployment benefits.

Impact on Citizens: Two Stories

Southerners for Economic Justice (SEJ) is a nonprofit advocacy and organizing group founded in 1976 to develop community support for workplace organizing. The organization is based in North Carolina, but also serves as a regional resource on economic justice issues. In 1984 SEJ staff received requests for help from two women whose situations pointed to a widespread problem for working North Carolinians.[2]

One of them was Mattie Brown, whose testimony introduced this chapter. At the age of forty-four, Mattie, a black woman, entered an on-the-job training program at a community college in Wilson, North Carolina. She had raised her family and wanted to become a skilled machinist. She was placed in a ball-bearing plant on the outskirts of town. She worked days and took evening classes.

Inside the plant, which was deceptively clean and trim on the outside, Mattie breathed kerosene fog so thick she could not see the person at the next work station. The ball-bearing tracks that she microscopically inspected were coated with a toxic chemical, Exxon Rust-Ban. Despite warning labels on the delivery containers Mattie was required to work near a large open vat of Rust-Ban and to handle coated parts. She breathed the noxious substance from a few inches' distance as she inspected the tracks for defects. She was provided no protective equipment.

Mattie so badly needed work that she endured this environment for about eighteen months, until she became too sick to continue. Along the way she developed a serious intolerance to the rustproofing chemical. When she first reported lightheadedness and nausea, her floor supervisor told her that she was imagining them. "If you can't take the heat, get out of the kitchen!" he told her. When she persisted, she was labeled "crazy" by management—and by co-workers who didn't want to risk association with a trouble maker.

Mattie became so sensitive to the chemical that she collapsed on the job and was hospitalized. When she returned to the plant she requested a new job but was still required to handle the same chemicals with no protective equipment. Her requests to leave early on days when she became ill were ignored, and she was removed unconscious from the plant *six times* by the rescue squad.

During her last sick leave, Mattie was fired. Management had asked her to take a medical leave of absence, but that would have terminated her health benefits, so she refused. She later discovered that the company had not been making payments on her health insurance policy, even though deductions were taken from her payroll.

In the end she was left without medical coverage, and was denied workers' compensation and unemployment benefits because she had been fired. She attempted to appeal the workers' compensation ruling, but never received benefits. As we interviewed her, the gas company was removing her heating oil tank because Mattie had run out of money. Her telephone already had been removed.

SEJ was also called by a pastor to assist Angela Summers, a young black woman who worked for Hanes Hosiery in Winston-Salem, North Carolina. Hanes at the time was a subsidiary of Consolidated Foods Corporation (known now as the Sara Lee Corporation). Angela acquired tendonitis while sewing T-shirts. She was paid a piece rate, a system that encourages a very rapid and injurious work pace.

Angela was a model worker. She worked fast enough to average $7 to $8 an hour, sometimes even $10, instead of the base rate of $4.87. She had received commendations for perfect attendance. But in her fifth year at Hanes, 1983, the strain of rapid, repetitive wrist motions caught up with her.

During training for a new assignment at the plant, a trainer advised her to use a particular series of movements to feed garments to the sewing machine. Angela heard a "pop" inside her wrist and felt soreness. She told her trainer, only to be accused of faking.

Angela tells the rest of her story:

The next day I went to the company nurse. She treated me and told me not to go to a doctor for forty-eight hours. That night I hurt so bad that I went to the emergency room. They told me I had mild tendonitis.

That year I was off a total of six weeks with tendonitis. I kept working because I had bills to pay. I made it through the week by working real fast on Monday, Tuesday, and Wednesday, because those last two days my wrist got real sore. I saved tickets from my work bundles on fast days, and turned them in on Thursday and Friday when I needed to work slower. A lot of the girls saved tickets instead of turning them in right away, because, you know, some days you might not be feeling good or something and not be able to work so fast.

The last time I went to the doctor he said I would have to get a double shot of cortisone next time, and be casted up again. Early in 1984 my wrist started bothering me again. I didn't want to get that shot, but it got so bad that I went to the nurse. That was on a Monday. I told her what the doctor had said. They made an appointment for me for that Wednesday.

Wednesday I came in to work before my doctor's appointment and they made all the girls watch a movie about tendonitis, telling you things you shouldn't be doing at home and stuff like that. On my way back to my machine they called me in and told me I was fired for stealing two dollars' worth of tickets. I never stole no tickets. I told them they framed me.

Angela, with help from Legal Services, requested a hearing at the state unemployment office. She would be eligible for unemployment insurance only if she could disprove the charges of misconduct. Hanes brought to the hearing a management team, from the divison manager on down to a trainer, to testify against Angela. The referee ruled in favor of Hanes, and Angela was unable to receive unemployment insurance or workers' compensation. Her wrist was still in a sling at the unemployment hearing.

Betrayal of Trust: Gathering Workers' Stories

After hearing about people like Mattie and Angela, in November 1984 Southerners for Economic Justice set out to gather testimony from other North Carolinians who have been unjustly fired. We saw it as an initial step toward developing a dislocated workers' organization in North Carolina to push for statewide policy changes in areas where workers are least protected: "at-will" terminations, the policies of the state industrial commission, unemployment and workers' compensation benefits, and the general character of the state's economic development program.

Through various sources—a statewide survey of attorneys, referrals from local grassroots organizations, and word of mouth—SEJ interviewer Barbara Taylor began to locate workers. Eventually more than eighty people were interviewed within a ten-month period. Barbara describes what she found:

From the very first interview it became increasingly clear that the issue of workplace injury and firing was complex and deadly serious. It was deeply rooted in the state's industrial policy and legislation; and it affected not only injured workers but also their families and communities. As I drove around the state, observing manufacturing sites—some enclosed with barbed wire atop tall fences with padlocked gates that look so much like prisons, some sitting in the midst of acres of manicured landscapes, some ghost-like fortresses of companies long gone, leaving behind broken windows and broken promises—I remembered a line I had read in an official state policy manual that North Carolina's industrial recruitment policy was to provide more jobs for the citizens of the state and to improve the quality of life. I wondered if anyone had ever bothered to ask the people who worked in those places just how much their lives had improved.

Being a novice at this task, the cold reality I faced was sobering. I met

Doris, Eula, John, William, and all the others. They graciously allowed me into their homes and into their lives and, one after the other, sat for hours and talked about how much they liked their jobs and were looking to stay within their companies, some having been long-time workers. They told me how, after they were injured, they were harshly treated—by the companies for which they had worked, by doctors, by insurance companies, by OSHA, by EEOC, by the Labor Department, and all the other agencies and people they thought would be there in their time of need. They spoke of harassment and intimidation from the agencies and people who should have been their advocates, but who dismissed their plight, who ignored, and in several cases blocked, their attempts to gain compensation. They told me of strife within their families and communities due to their attempt to deal with their problems and caused by fear of losing even more jobs.

SEJ also found that racism and sexism are not receding, but are being practiced blatantly and openly in the workplace. It is no coincidence that the resurrected white supremacist movement is enjoying its greatest success in the most economically depressed areas of North Carolina. Economic stress is nurturing an atmosphere of finger pointing and aggression. White men are by no means excluded from the ranks of injured and abused, but women and people of color, who tend to work the lowest-paying jobs, are bearing the brunt. For the majority of them, the state of North Carolina is an economic development disaster.

If those words seem strong, consider the following cases:

Ida Hooper

Ida Hooper, who won a major civil rights judgment against Hanes Corporation in the mid-1970s, eventually sought work at the Myrtle Desk Furniture Company in High Point. The plant where she worked employed about 600 people, mostly black women. She started there in 1983 for a wage of about $4.00 per hour; a year later as a desk finisher her hourly wage was $4.51.

At the Myrtle plant Ida was stricken with tendonitis, then suffered sexual harassment. "I first started having problems probably about March of 1984," said Ida. "I had never worked in that kind of plant and doing that kind of work. My shoulders just started to hurting and pains would run up and down the back of my neck," she said. She also complained of pains in her arm.

When tendonitis was first diagnosed, Ida was assigned a daily work load that included a variety of tasks, and her condition improved. But then she was transferred to a finishing job that required day-long repetitive motion. "When they transferred me, they put me in sanding all day. Eight hours a day. Everything on the line, and I am just constantly going all day long," she described.

With the new work, the tendonitis returned. "It really started acting up again when I was sanding. I was sanding and crying and sanding and crying," she said. Doctors advised Ida that her arm would not heal as long as she continued to work. Finally, she agreed to a six-week sick leave, and secured a note from the doctor explaining it. The doctor also called Ida's manager. Before Ida delivered the note, a friend who worked in the manager's office told Ida what she had overheard: Ida would never return to work at that plant. The manager suggested to Ida that she may have gotten tendonitis from washing dishes.

During 1984, Ida had begun to suffer sexual harassment from this manager. She tells what happened.

He tried to get fresh with me and I wasn't paying him no attention. I went by his office, and he gave me some little books in an envelope and told me not to let anyone see them. I showed them to the girl I rode home with after work. He told me that he didn't want to give me that job up front because I was looking so good and so clean. I told the man I needed to work. He told me, "When you read this you can come in my office and I know just what your body needs." He told me I was the prettiest black thing he had ever seen.

Then he started worrying me to bring the books back. I knew he was going to be out of town, so I took the books and gave them to the lady that worked in his office. He didn't mention those books to me since. But I felt like this was a buildup of him going on to get rid of me right then.

When I finally took him a note from my doctor, I asked him, "What is the status of my position?" He said, "As long as you are out of work, you got a job." I knew exactly what that meant: when I go back down there, I ain't got no job.

While out on leave Ida applied for workers' compensation, but her claim was denied. Aetna, which provided Myrtle's workers' compensation policy, insisted that her injury did not fall within the guidelines of the law. Ida's attorney asked for an appeal hearing in Winston-Salem, but before a date was set, Ida was terminated.

"The doctor gave me a little statement to go back to work on the 29th of July, prescribing 'light work.'" When she got to see the personnel manager, he told her that her position was no longer available. "He said that it is our policy to fill a position when somebody is out. I knew that was a lie," said Ida. "I said, 'Just what are you telling me? That I don't have a job and that I'm terminated?' He said, 'Yes, as of the 29th.'"

Ida also described problems with toxic chemical exposure in the plant. "A lot of people down there are suffering," she said, "a lot of 'em suffering. Scared of them little jobs. I would tell them in a minute that I didn't have to work under those conditions because I would call OSHA. One girl quit. She sprayed. The whole room would be sent up with spray. It got to the point where she couldn't get her breath."

The Abbott Workers

Abbott Laboratories is a pharmaceutical company, one of the "more attractive" industries that have been brought to the state in recent years. A newspaper series on workplace injury in the Rocky Mount *Evening Telegraph* in January 1985 spelled out the stories of three former employees, all disabled by their work at the plant.[3] Alerted by the series, SEJ conducted follow-up interviews with the workers.

Mildred Jones operated a machine that seals plastic bags with a hot bar. Part of the job was clearing plastic scraps from the hot bar as it cycled between bags. A machine malfunction pinned Mildred's right hand under the bar during the heating cycle. Mildred braced herself and pulled her hand from the machine. She was taken to the hospital, where she received treatment for second-degree burns and contusions. Then her hand was immersed in a therapeutic solution to soak for hours. "At 6 P.M.," according to the *Telegraph* story, "a representative from Abbott called the hospital and asked Mildred to return to the plant that night. She did."

Mildred worked the next day, but subsequently began to experience intense pain in the right side of her body from what she later learned was severe nerve injury in her right arm. Mildred was assigned to different jobs at the plant, and experienced resentment from other employees who switched tasks to accommodate her. She was accused of faking when she failed to perform some jobs adequately and, like many other injured workers, was eventually labeled a trouble maker. She was advised to leave the plant and "go out on compensation," and finally, the next year, she did. She was in too much pain to work.

Mildred received some benefits for two years from a company benefit called the extended disability plan, which Mildred says serves the purpose of lulling employees into a false sense of security. Workers must use company doctors to receive the benefit. Mildred discovered that the plan contained a number of loopholes that allowed Abbott to terminate her benefits after only two years.

The worst was a clause that excludes disability "caused or contributed to by mental illness or functional nervous disorder." Abbott's doctor said that Mildred suffered from reactive depression resulting from her accident. Reactive depression is a functional nervous disorder, so Abbott was within its legal rights to deny benefits.

Before the benefit termination, Mildred had signed a one-time settlement on her workers' compensation claim with the Industrial Commission, the state agency responsible for workers' compensation. She told the *Telegraph* that was an action she didn't fully understand, and one that she regrets. She lives with constant pain, and by her doctor's account is completely disabled. She told SEJ's interviewer:

> When it comes down to it, you don't have any rights. The government will go to big companies and listen to their plans for expansion, but no law official will ever go to these people and hear them as to what's really fair. They [Abbott] dodged their moral obligation to me as a worker and left me without a job, disabled and with unjust compensation for the injury. . . . I say it is time for our legislative branch of North Carolina to reevaluate the law and at least to give injured parties a 50–50 chance instead of the now 98 percent favoritism the law offers big companies.

Two other Abbott workers, Robert Garriss and Edith Hart, echo Mildred's sentiments of anger and betrayal. Robert injured his back when he slipped on a grease spill that was not cleaned up in spite of his requests. He returned to work after back surgery, but his pain persisted. One day when he went to the first aid room to get aspirin, he was told, "Either get back to work or go home and get a disability note." A few days later, while Robert was waiting for a doctor's note to arrive by mail, he was told to either return to work or take a personal—not medical—leave of absence. He took a personal leave with the understanding that it would become a medical leave when the doctor's note was received. When he brought the letter to Abbott, they refused to change his leave status, and his workers' compensation benefits were terminated.

Robert is illiterate, and he believes that Abbott took advantage of that. He remained on personal leave while he tried to change the situation, but when he failed to file an extension request he was terminated from his job.

Eventually Robert settled his claim with Abbott out of court, but he says the accident "tore my life all to pieces. . . . They wouldn't give me another chance. I was devastated." For the thirteen months that he received no pay or benefits, his family suffered severe financial hardship and emotional stress. There were no children's Christmas presents for two years.

"A lot of people get hurt in the plant," Robert told the *Telegraph,* but the plant tries to "look good" for the home office in Chicago by not reporting injuries. Abbott, in fact, boasts of a no-lost-time accident record, a record that affects both insurance rates and public relations. To preserve that record, companies go to great lengths to keep injured employees on the premises until their shift is completed or, as it did to Mildred Jones and Mattie Brown, to call them to work from the hospital to complete a shift. Robert is bitter: "Companies ought to be forced to change their tactics and forced to do something for the people they injure." He echoed Mattie Brown almost to the word: "You are all right until you get hurt. Then they don't want you no more."

Edith Hart was seriously injured on *three* separate occasions at Abbott, yet received only partial compensation. She, too, was placed on a personal rather than medical leave as she recuperated. A year after the third injury, while she was still on leave, she was terminated. Before the first accident she had a perfect attendance record.

Edith, like many injured workers, found that local doctors in a company-dominated town are unwilling to counter a company doctor's opinion, and it is no secret that company doctors work for the company: "The doctors around here aren't going to stand up against Abbott," the *Telegraph* reported. "When it came time for a showdown no one would support me."

Conclusion

The testimony from these workers is an indictment of the state of North Carolina and other Southern states that continue to pursue the "jobs at any cost" strategy. SEJ investigators had no trouble finding injured and abandoned workers. The fact that there are so many in so many counties points to a very serious issue of public policy. What is the wisdom of the industrial recruitment strategy? Who really benefits? Why are people who have entrusted their economic well-being to the state suffering so much? Putting all the competitive posturing aside, is the state's economic development plan really working?

North Carolina has been portrayed as a model for Southern economic development. The model perhaps looks better from corporate boardrooms than it does from the living rooms of many citizens. The model desperately needs to be changed, in ways that will vitalize existing communities. Effective reform should include both implementing protection in the current scheme and developing alternative programs for economic renewal.

Several alternative economic renewal programs are emerging in the wake of the 1980s' economic crisis. A report published by SEJ and the Institute for Southern Studies in 1986 highlights a number of ideas: a regional support network for worker-owned businesses; an eastern North Carolina rural day-care network to provide jobs, training, and a critical service; an aggressive affirmative-action monitoring program to find work for women; and a state-sponsored agricultural marketing program to link farmers directly with local grocery-store chains.[4] Each of these, given adequate state backing, could boost local economies. They would not be "here today, gone tomorrow," as so many recruited industries are.

Shifting the state's emphasis from industrial recruiting to local projects would yield a far higher return for the taxpayer's dollar. Locally owned ventures have the effect of pumping money into a local economy, in contrast to the extraction of capital to corporate headquarters elsewhere. Developing capital to support these ventures is an appropriate use of state money.

Alternative strategies are only one part of a solution. The state must also move to protect its citizens from the current epidemic of injury and community abandonment. The state's anti-union posture, which has done so much to recruit irresponsible industries, must be reconsidered. Locally, people who have experience working inside the plants should become members of county development boards. Industrial revenue bonds could require decent wages, health and safety provisions, and protection of the community from toxic waste. During the recruiting phase, agreements for early warning of a plant closing could ensure that communities will have time to plan how to cope with a shutdown.

State agencies whose jurisdiction includes workers' compensation and unemployment insurance need to have representation from working people. Occupational health and safety laws already on the books need to be vigorously enforced. Public education should include curricula that educate students about their rights and about health and safety issues, so that they can take steps to protect themselves as workers. Tax laws can be examined to see where they encourage corporate mergers that distance companies from local accountability. Indeed, there may be an endless list of potential reforms in the current system; it is completely slanted against communities and individual citizens.

The issue of how communities deal with plant closings is one of the toughest. In Rocky Mount, North Carolina, several groups are forming to combat the effects of Ingersoll-Rand's decision to move the Schlage Lock factory to Mexico. In 1988 workers from the plant started a high-visibility picketing campaign to alert the community to unfair treatment of workers, especially around severance and retirement pay, to widespread respiratory ailments among the workers, and to toxic dumping on the plant site. A vanload of North Carolina workers went to Ingersoll-Rand's annual stockholders' meeting in New Jersey to voice their protest. After several months of daily picketing in front of the plant (which was in its final months of operation) and City Hall, Schlage Lock began to negotiate some of the workers' demands. In the meantime, a panel of community leaders has formed to find ways to combat plant closings in the area. Almost immediately, that group began to look at methods to monitor local industries. A grassroots reponse to a plant closing may not be able to stop the plant from closing, but it can mobilize the community around economic issues.

And therein lies the seed of long-term change. To move state governments to the point where there is more on the bargaining table than jobs and maximum profit, to stop the abuse and injury that is occurring daily, the state's citizens must become actors in the economic development debate, from the county courthouse to the statehouse.

NOTES

1. Public testimony at an economic hearing held at the Catholic Center in Raleigh, N.C., February 2, 1985. Included in the videotape "Option for the Poor: The Southern Hearings" (Rockhill, S.C.: Connective Ministries, 1985).

2. The following accounts of workers' stories are condensed from *Betrayal of Trust: Stories of Working North Carolinians* (Durham, N.C.: Southerners for Economic Justice, 1989). Mattie's and Angela's stories appeared in similar form in John Bookser-Feister, "The Struggle for Work-Place Justice," *The Other Side* (April–May 1985): 46f.

3. Parts of this section are condensed from the four-part series by Kathy Harrelson, Rocky Mount (N.C.) *Evening Telegraph*, January 27–30, 1985.

4. *Everybody's Business: A People's Guide to Economic Development*, a special edition of *Southern Exposure* 14, no. 5–6 (September/October and November/December 1986).

CHAPTER

9

Worker Organizing in South Carolina:
A Community-Based Approach

Charles D. M. Taylor

Southern workers are facing immense challenges brought on by rapid technological change and an increasingly global economy. Unfortunately, they are
in a weak position to respond to these challenges because of the South's
unique history of economic oppression. South Carolina, for example, has
consistently ranked near the bottom in per capita income, and dead last in the
percentage of nonagricultural workers in unions and in voter participation. A
dismal working climate is maintained by anti-union industry groups such as
the South Carolina Chamber of Commerce, which has been called the state's
fourth branch of government.

One unanticipated consequence of the region's virulent anti-unionism,
however, has been the birth of nontraditional attempts by workers to take
more control over their lives. The Workers' Rights Project (now WRP, Inc.) is
an alternative workers' group in South Carolina that has begun organizing on
the basis of where employees live rather than where they work. Residing in a
state where there is little access to unions, WRP members are turning to state
courts, the state legislature, and the power of organization to advance their
interests.

WRP: A New Approach

In the mid-1970s, a group of civil rights activists joined to form Southerners for Economic Justice (SEJ). Concerned that newly won civil rights were
not being extended into Southern workplaces, SEJ first worked on unionization. During this period, a campaign by the Amalgamated Clothing and Tex-

tile Workers Union (ACTWU) to organize J. P. Stevens & Co. was in full swing, and SEJ committed most of its resources to supporting this effort. SEJ's support took the form of trying to soften middle-class resistance to union organizing efforts. SEJ sponsored public presentations in target areas, worked through local churches, held regional conferences to stimulate balanced discussions about unionization, participated in leafleting textile mills and in meeting with workers, and produced supportive articles in regional and national magazines, in local newspapers, and in its own regional newsletter, *Fair Measure.*

During the mid-1970s, J. P. Stevens was one of the largest employers in Greenville County, which is located in northwestern South Carolina. The mills in Greenville were targeted by ACTWU for intensive organizing efforts, and SEJ opened an office in Greenville to support the local drive.

SEJ maintained a staff of two in Greenville during the late 1970s, and they received many calls from workers not involved in the Stevens campaign. Some of the callers inquired about getting a union drive going at their places of work, but most simply had questions about employee rights or complaints about unfair treatment on the job.

The ACTWU campaign in Greenville ended shortly after a national settlement between the union and Stevens was reached in 1980. The union had been unable to organize any of the Greenville mills—even though the agreement stipulated that any of the Greenville plants that voted in union representation would automatically fall under contracts in effect at other Stevens plants.

An ACTWU organizer commented that the union targeted Stevens plants but ended up fighting the town of Greenville—the self-styled "textile capital of the world"—and the entire state. The union drive in Greenville was actively opposed by Stevens's management, a well-financed anti-union employees' group, daily newspapers across the state, local and state chambers of commerce, the South Carolina Textile Manufacturers Association, and anti-union law firms based in Greenville that have regional and national clientele. Other textile companies with headquarters nearby—Milliken & Company, Dan River, Springs Industries, and Greenwood Mills—also joined the union opposition.

A single mother who worked as a weaver at a local Stevens mill describes what it was like to be an active union supporter during the organizing drive:

It was hard because fellow workers, the ones who weren't for the union, wouldn't have anything to do with you. Your friends, the people you'd worked beside for years, just wouldn't have nothing to do with you. It was a real challenge for me, a time of mental turmoil is what it was.

Workers who were against the union would circle me in the hall and call me a nigger lover and say that I was trying to destroy the company. I got letters with no names or return addresses on them threatening me or my kids, saying my home would be bombed or my car would blow up the next time I tried to crank it.

If you were for the union, you were constantly watched and you knew you had to run your job better than the people around you. You couldn't give them a reason to fire you. Supervisors would harass us and we'd file charges with the NLRB [National Labor Relations Board]. They'd have to post notices on the bulletin boards promising not to do it again.

My daughter worked there, too. She was an oiler in the weave room. When they saw I wasn't going to take harassment, they started in on her. They watched her and clocked her and tried to make her do extra things that other oilers didn't have to do. When she refused, they fired her. We filed NLRB charges, but the judge ruled that it was insubordination and the firing stuck.

I have no doubt in my mind—I'll carry it to my grave—that they wanted momma and not her. The company figured they'd get me through her. My daughter was blackballed for a good while. Finally got a waitress job paying minimum wage.

The company way of getting to me made me stronger and more determined. I really got wrapped up in ACTWU then—went to their schools, read up on union history. Deep inside it made me a stronger person. It made me more patient.

When the ACTWU campaign ended, SEJ staff member Michael Russell was free to follow up on calls from unorganized workers. Russell and interested local workers began brainstorming about a new type of organization that could bridge the huge gap between worker disorganization and unionization.

The Workers' Rights Project was formally launched as a project of SEJ in 1980, under a grant from the Campaign for Human Development of the U.S. Catholic Church. WRP sought to answer tough questions: How can workers be empowered when they have little or no access to unions? What can a minority of workers in a plant do to win better pay and working conditions? How can worker activists protect themselves against company retaliation as they seek improved treatment?

The Start-Up Phase, 1980–1982

The period of 1980–1982 was spent on start-up activities: opening an office, acquiring equipment, developing a board, conducting outreach, hiring staff, and developing strategy options. Perhaps the biggest outreach project during this period was a mailer sent out to 10,000 residents in Greenville

County. The mailer got a predictably low response but did help to build a local mailing list of around 200 people by 1982.

The Greenville staff grew to four members during this time. Mike Russell served as WRP director. Sylane ("Syl") Sampson, SEJ's associate director, worked on community issues out of the WRP office. Attorney Stephen Henry, former deputy public defender for Greenville County, was hired as WRP counsel. I became a staff organizer. I had been a shift supervisor in the weave rooms of two Milliken textile mills, but I resigned in protest against the company's treatment of hourly employees, "defecting" to WRP as a full-time volunteer before coming on staff.

In addition to outreach, membership meetings, and some SEJ-related activities, the WRP staff focused on the issue of how a minority of employees in a given business location can safely win improvements in working conditions. We discovered that the National Labor Relations Act provided a major strategy option. The NLRA, passed in 1935, is the federal law that gives unions the legal right to organize and to bargain collectively. Section VII gives employees the right to join together for purposes of mutual aid and protection outside the union context. The NLRA is enforced by the National Labor Relations Board (NLRB), which has the power to order companies to remove disciplinary warnings from personnel records and to reinstate workers who are fired or suspended because of their group activity. Promoting "concerted, protected activity" among nonunion workers under Section VII of the NLRA became WRP's chief strategy during this period.

That strategy was tested in 1982, when a WRP member who had worked at a local textile mill for many years was fired. On her behalf, WRP filed a NLRB unfair labor practice charge against the company. After several weeks, the company reinstated her, ostensibly through an internal grievance procedure based on a letter she had written to a top manager. We all believed that her rehiring showed the potential of a concerted-action strategy in Greenville County workplaces.

WRP in 1982–1984: Change and Experimentation

While WRP was becoming more focused on concerted-action strategies and the creation of a new model of worker organization, SEJ was going through a period of reassessment. It was agreed that WRP would spin off and become an independent organization, and an amicable separation took place in 1982.[1]

Major staff changes also took place in 1982. Mike Russell wanted to become an Episcopal priest, and it was clear that it would be difficult to obtain the necessary church backing in South Carolina because of his "controversial" WRP work. Syl Sampson, who had led a successful grassroots campaign to obtain federal funding for public transportation in Greenville, in addition to numerous other SEJ duties, indicated that she needed a break from organizing. Both left in the first part of 1982. By mutual agreement of board members and remaining staff, I became WRP director and Steve Henry assumed additional duties while continuing to serve as WRP counsel.

The organizational challenges we faced were tremendous. WRP had to file for incorporation and for tax exemption on the state and federal levels. We were totally dependent on Campaign for Human Development (CHD) funding, and the final year of its grant ran from summer 1982 to summer 1983. We had little experience in foundation fundraising, and local fundraising efforts had been sporadic. A $50 annual dues requirement had reduced the mailing list from 200 to 20. The board met regularly but had not developed real leadership.

The annual WRP budget had averaged over $70,000 in the first two years, so an early act in 1982 was to cut this in half, mainly by reducing staff salary levels. A further cut became necessary in 1983, when each staff member was paid $8,400 for the year. Annual membership dues were cut from $50 to $25 to $15, the amount that local workers seemed willing to pay.

Several foundations stepped in and helped WRP survive, including the CHD (WRP as an independent organization was eligible for a new three-year grant), the Self-Development of People of the Presbyterian Church U.S.A., the Southern Office of the Youth Project, and the Fund for Southern Communities. Board election procedures were revised, and board development assumed a higher priority. A formal local fundraising system created by the board and staff in 1984 is still in use today.

Despite its rocky situation in 1982–1984, WRP's program blossomed as the group experimented with a variety of strategies. The concerted-action strategy, the centerpiece of WRP's organizing philosophy, was carried to its logical end in two campaigns during this period.

The first campaign involved local salespeople working for a national snack-food company. The company had four sales and distribution centers under the same management within a sixty-mile radius of Greenville. Every day the workers picked up boxes of potato chips and cookies and distributed them on assigned routes.

The workers were extremely dissatisfied with their jobs. Their pay was being docked for missing merchandise over which they had no control. One particular supervisor was abusive. There was no internal promotion system. With at least eight valid issues, workers came to WRP for assistance. Within a short period, more than half of the local company workers became WRP members.

A group letter complaining about working conditions was signed by the WRP members and was delivered to the company. The WRP staff was prepared to file an unfair labor practice charge if any member was harassed or fired. What ensued instead was more like a game of chess.

The workers were ordered to attend special meetings with managers to discuss complaints raised in the group letter. The meetings were scheduled after work in different locations in an apparent attempt to divide the group. The workers maintained solidarity by preparing and copying a group statement that was read by members at the different meetings.

Fearful that a union organizing campaign was starting, management began taking steps to appease the employees. Workers began receiving additional checks for pay that had been unfairly docked. Written warnings were removed from records. The contentious supervisor was fired, and a regional vice-president was transferred. A likable new manager promoted a spirit of cooperation. The workers had taken concerted action as far as it could go.

In the meantime, we learned that most other locations within this company were operating under Teamsters contracts, and Teamsters officials in Greenville were very interested in mounting an organizing drive. WRP set up a meeting between the workers and a Teamsters official from Washington. To the dismay of WRP staff, who supported collective bargaining as the logical next step, the workers voted not to pursue unionization. The workers said they wanted to give the new manager a chance to work things out, but a traditional distrust of unions among the workers was the real barrier that could not be overcome.

The second concerted-action campaign stemmed from the initial WRP vision of creating worker committees in local plants. The committees would use concerted action to win improvements in working conditions, and at the same time serve as bases of membership that could be brought together for larger WRP projects in the future. This particular idea was being tested at the textile plant mentioned earlier, where the rehiring of the unjustly fired WRP member had created growing interest in our organization.

By 1983, a group of around twenty-five mill workers was meeting on a regular basis. Their major project was an in-plant newsletter. Articles on job problems and safety hazards were written by WRP supporters, and WRP staff printed the newsletter and handed it out at plant gates at shift changes. Management addressed many problems raised in the newsletter, and the newsletter was popular among the workers. Two-thirds of the workers in the plant wore WRP buttons on a day designated for this show of support.

Alarmed by this display, managers abruptly changed tactics and began harassing key WRP supporters. When supporters received unjustified written warnings or other disciplinary action, WRP countered by filing unfair labor practice charges with the NLRB and succeeded in getting the warnings removed from personnel records. This was a practical, as well as a symbolic, victory: after three written warnings, an employee could be fired. As long as members could take the heat without quitting or doing something for which they could be fired automatically, the concerted-action strategy was extremely effective.

Then a woman who was only marginally involved in WRP activities at the plant quit under duress, against staff advice, and her irate husband demanded that NLRB charges be filed on her behalf. It was the first NLRB case that WRP lost, and management responded with a harassment campaign against key WRP supporters who had testified on the woman's behalf, long-term employees with excellent work records. The company fired a key WRP supporter and made it stick. Co-workers started backing off from WRP when they saw what was happening.

It was clear that raising serious employment issues where they work was putting members at maximum risk. At the same time, WRP's closed membership meetings had gotten stale, and the concerted-action projects were a major drain on staff time. Disillusioned with the strategy, the WRP board and staff began experimenting with other means of advancing workers' rights. The board decided that WRP would shift from concerted job actions and closed membership meetings to sponsorship of public presentations on employment issues.

In 1984, WRP held public presentations on polygraph testing, sex discrimination, and the rights of public employees. The sessions attracted an average of thirty-five participants, including workers that WRP would have missed in other forms of outreach. Each of the sessions attracted good media coverage that helped to increase WRP's visibility and name recognition. Most important, workers could attend, educate themselves on issues of interest to them, and speak out with a greatly reduced fear of retaliation. The meeting on polygraphs, for example, provided a public forum for worker complaints about being fired or refused a job on the basis of unreliable tests. The workers who attended learned how to file complaints against polygraph examiners.

There was also a growing interest among WRP members in working to create new job protections. Steve Henry, WRP counsel, was educating the organization about the employment-at-will doctrine, a century-old common-law doctrine that essentially says that a company can fire a worker at any time and a worker can quit at any time. A worker could be fired at will in South Carolina, except where the firing violated a union contract or antidiscrimination laws.

Henry explained that other states were carving out exceptions to this "fire at will" rule. State courts were taking the lead in chipping away at the outmoded doctrine, and state legislatures were creating antifiring laws in other parts of the country. The board and staff felt there was a better chance of changing the law through the courts than through the legislature in South Carolina, given the lobbying power of industry forces in the state.

WRP's Special Litigation Fund was established in 1984 through a grant from the Public Interest Law Foundation at Columbia University. The WRP fund paid the costs in two types of legal cases: (1) those with the potential for creating favorable state employment law precedents, and (2) those in which a person had a winable employment case under an existing law but was financially unable to pursue the case. Eight cases were initiated in 1984–1985. The six cases that sought to create new antifiring laws through court precedent were unsuccessful; two cases brought under existing law were won.

The litigation project was important for several reasons. It led WRP leaders to think seriously about policy change on the state level, and it was the first organized attempt to create new employment law through the state's courts. In recent years, two antifiring precedents have been won through similar lawsuits brought by other employees. The South Carolina Supreme Court has ruled that it is illegal to fire an employee who answers a subpoena to testify in court, or to fire a worker contrary to the procedures set forth in employee handbooks.[2]

The litigation project also pointed out that a grassroots organization cannot be built on litigation strategies alone. Trials are held during the day, which often precludes attendance by workers. The litigation timeline is not controlled by members and can be lengthy. The role that members can play is extremely limited, so a litigation project does not facilitate leadership development. It is difficult to recruit members around legal cases for these reasons, which means it is difficult to build the power of the organization. Legal cases can stimulate public discussion about employment issues and change public employment policy, but they will never empower workers in the sense that building an organization can.

The activity with perhaps the largest impact on WRP's development came in the summer of 1984. WRP was approached by more than fifty workers who had been fired from a local company that had been taken over by another firm; more than 100 workers in all had been laid off and told not to reapply. What made this situation unusual is that the new company was simultaneously applying to the city of Greenville for an $8.3 million industrial development bond.

WRP and the workers decided to try to block approval of the bond to leverage rehiring rights for the discharged workers. WRP organized a series of bond protests before the city council; about sixty workers participated. It was too late to stop the bond, but the group kept showing up and eventually won a major policy change. The council adopted a new set of bond guidelines: companies must submit detailed information on projected employment and wage levels in order to be eligible for bonds. If funded, they must also submit reports to ensure compliance with the plans submitted to the council.

Other activities during 1982–1984 included organizing a local coalition that sent more than fifty representatives to the 1983 March on Washington, which commemorated the historic civil rights march of 1963. The coalition consisted of eighteen organizations, and it followed the Washington event with three political education sessions: a mock precinct meeting, a "meet the candidates" forum, and a session on how to make government accountable. WRP members capitalized on this experience by moving an antipolygraph resolution from local precincts to adoption by the state's largest political party in 1984.

Testing State Waters: 1985–1987

By early 1985, calls for help had come from workers in more than fifty cities and towns across South Carolina. It was clear from these conversations and from local organizing activities that there was great confusion among workers about existing job rights and procedures for enforcement.

At the same time, many of the complaints made by workers dealt with statewide problems such as polygraph testing, being denied access to personnel records, and certain types of unjust firings. Many of these job problems could be prevented through passage of state legislation, and we monitored the growing number of state employment laws being passed across the country, particularly in northeastern states and in California.

With the experiences of 1982–1984 under its belt, in 1985 the WRP board launched the Job Rights Campaign, the organization's single major project through 1987. Primary foundation support for the campaign came from the Abelard and Buttenwieser Foundations (on the recommendation of Joint Foundation Support), the Pearl River Fund, the Youth Project, and the Norman Foundation.

The Job Rights Campaign (JRC) was an attempt by WRP to test the waters on the state level, since it was clear that a coordinated statewide effort was needed to win the type of employment reform that WRP was seeking. One cornerstone of the JRC was a series of job rights workshops, led by WRP counsel Henry, intended to inform employees about existing rights and how to get them enforced. To attract working-class participants, the workshops were held at night and cost only $5.

Cities were targeted for workshops based on their size and location within the state. Workshops were held in Greenville, Anderson, and Spartanburg in the upper part of the state; in Columbia and Aiken in the middle part of the state; and in Charleston and Conway along the coast. The sessions attracted an average of fifty participants, and served as "door openers" in cities where WRP hoped eventually to establish bases.

The second major cornerstone of the JRC was an attempt to determine whether an employment reform issue could be moved on the state level. Using a set of formal criteria for picking an issue, the board decided to seek to increase public awareness about the firing of injured workers. Although there has been a state workers' compensation system to compensate injured workers for more than fifty years, there was no prohibition against firing workers who exercised their compensation rights. Workers had been telling us horror stories about firings, denial of workers' and unemployment compensation, difficulties in finding new employment, and the resulting loss of housing, cars, and family stability.

Responding to an invitation from a legislative committee that had been formed to study workers' compensation issues, WRP promoted the testimony of retaliatory-firing victims at four public hearings held around the state from November 1985 to February 1986. The testimony of victims dominated media coverage of the hearings, and more than 600 workers attended the hearings in a dramatic display of support. Following the hearings, WRP members wrote and telephoned lawmakers and made a group visit to the state capital in support of an antifiring bill that had been introduced.

WRP consciously engaged in biracial organizing for the hearings. Outreach was done in both black and white communities through contact with established local groups such as NAACP chapters, unions, churches, women's organizations, civic groups, and neighborhood associations. WRP also ensured that black and white witnesses had the opportunity to testify. The South Carolina AFL-CIO and a claimants' attorney group were active and formidable allies in the antifiring campaign.

Thanks in large part to WRP's success in increasing public awareness on the issue, a bill outlawing the retaliatory firing of injured workers was passed in May 1986.[3] Though weaker than desired, the measure provides historic antifiring protection to more than 1.3 million workers in South Carolina. As important as this legislative precedent was the level of worker participation in shaping public policy. Many workers attended public hearings for the first time, testified at hearings for the first time, and observed a legislative session in person for the first time.

Industry forces countered in the 1987 legislative session by launching a frontal assault on the rights of injured workers. WRP conducted a new statewide campaign to increase public awareness about a package of antiworker bills that had been introduced, and none of these bills was passed into law.

WRP learned two primary lessons in these statewide campaigns. First, the campaigns were won by 200 WRP members and around 400 supporters, which shows that employment reform can be won in South Carolina by a relatively small but committed group. Second, issue supporters did not readily become WRP members, which means that an alternative (or at least parallel) approach was needed to increase the size of the membership and the power of the organization.

Constituency Building, 1988 and Beyond

Having established small membership bases in six cities through the workshop series, and confident that significant employment reform can indeed be won on the state level, WRP is taking its next major organizational step through its Carolina Alliance for Fair Employment (CAFE) project, launched in 1988. The primary activity under CAFE will be constituency building through local organizing, and the Needmor Fund is a key foundation partner in this project.

WRP is seeking through CAFE to establish chapters in Anderson, Greenville, Spartanburg, Columbia, Aiken, Charleston and Florence. We believe that CAFE/WRP will become a force to be reckoned with if the organization can increase to a level of 1,000 members located strategically across the state. Successful implementation of the project will create a permanent statewide structure and provide an in-state funding base that will enable WRP to decrease its dependency on foundation support.

The CAFE project entails structural changes for WRP, such as moving from a local to a state board, developing twin fundraising systems for chapters and the central operation, establishing chapter structures, and intensifying leadership development programs. Although perceived as unexciting by some, these nuts-and-bolts activities are crucial to organizational development.

At the same time, CAFE/WRP leaders expect reform efforts to continue on both the local and state levels. In Aiken County, for example, members are having great success working on a pollution issue affecting a working-class neighborhood. The Aiken campaign reflects a more holistic view of workers that has been developing within WRP. Chapters are free to tackle issues affecting workers off the job as well as on, taking our community-based approach to worker organizing to a new level. Meanwhile, chapters will work together on statewide issues of common concern.

Lessons Learned at the Grassroots

Groups engaging in nontraditional worker organizing must define their relationship with unions. WRP moved from trying to serve as a stepping stone to unionization, to trying to reinvent the wheel (in-plant committees are a poor substitute for unions), to working in partnership with unions on specific campaigns while maintaining an independent education and reform agenda.

Both foundation funders and Southern workers have an obligation to help finance organizing efforts. The foundations noted in this article are the exception rather than the rule in their willingness to support Southern worker organizing projects. At the same time, workers themselves must contribute financially if they are to retain ownership of grassroots groups. WRP members are proud that more than $15,000 was raised within the state in 1987, and $20,000 in 1988, higher than any individual grant received during those years.

Organization is the only way that workers can win the power to bring about employment reform. WRP has engaged in litigation and in coalition projects, but organizing—getting increasing numbers of workers into progressive organizations—remains the largest and most crucial challenge for us all.

There must be expanded opportunities for worker participation in the larger community life. The systematic exclusion of working people from public boards and commissions and elected offices must stop if we are to achieve a healthier employment climate. It is ironic that workers are faced today with the same issue that ignited the American Revolution—taxation without representation.

At a time when racism and sexism continue to be dominant issues in Southern politics, worker organizations can provide a useful forum for breaking down these barriers. A law prohibiting the discharge of injured workers benefits all employees. The process of fighting for such a law can be unifying when the organization is committed to maintaining a membership and leadership group that reflects, in terms of race and gender, the community it serves. Of the nine members of the 1987–1988 WRP board, four are black and eight are women.

In light of the alternative organizing going on, Southern business leaders with multistate operations may be forced to rethink their position on unions. A patchwork of varying laws is developing, thanks to new state court decisions and state legislation. A master union contract stipulating uniform rules for multistate operations may begin to make more business sense. At any rate, stomping unions is not going to stop the fight for workers' rights.

Two mottos have helped bring WRP to this point:
Have faith and work your ass off.
We could be wrong.

NOTES

1. For more information on past and current activities of Southerners for Economic Justice, write to SEJ at P.O. Box 240, Durham, NC 27702.

2. *Ludwick* v. *This Minute of Carolina, Inc.*, 337 S.E. 2d 213, SC, 1985. *Small* v. *Springs Industries, Inc.*, 357 S.E. 2d 452, SC, 1987. Section 41-1-80, S.C. Code of Laws.

3. It should be noted that, as required by the law limiting nonprofit organizations such as WRP, foundation funds were not used to influence public opinion during any of these campaigns.

Appalachian coal camp community. (EARL DOTTER)

Closed mine, Kanawha County, West Virginia. Mine closings
in the 1980s have left thousands of workers unemployed. (EARL
DOTTER)

Unemployed miner and son
receiving food assistance in West
Virginia. (EARL DOTTER)

Miners strike against the Massey
Coal Company in 1985 (see Chapter
3). (MARAT MOORE)

Detroit auto workers support
the Massey miners, 1985.
(MARAT MOORE)

Small nonunion or
"doghole" mine in eastern
Kentucky. (EARL DOTTER)

Strip mining in eastern Kentucky. (EARL DOTTER)

Citizens demand more equitable taxation of corporate coal land (see Chapter 2). (KENTUCKIANS FOR THE COMMONWEALTH)

Women miners organized in the 1970s for jobs in the coal mines (see Chapter 4). (EARL DOTTER)

Women arrested on the picket line in the Massey strike, 1985. (MARAT MOORE)

I'VE BEEN SHELDENIZED

Arranged from an interview with a West Virginia miner by Mike Yarrow

The guys will tell you in a minute,
if you don't do something, or
you don't do it fast enough.
They'll say, "You ain't been Sheldenized son."
I worked at Affinity mines for sixteen years.
I didn't take no shit for sixteen years.
Pardon the french.
I didn't let Affinity run nothing down my throat.
In three years I have took more off of Shelden
than I had even thought of taking off of Affinity.

We use the old phrase, "Kissing hind-end to hold a job."
I've worked so sick I couldn't hold my head up
knowing if I am off two or three days
and I am not over in the hospital
I don't have no job.

They tell you what you have to do to survive.
They'll tell you either do it or else.
They'll tell you in a heartbeat there's 10,000 men out there
waiting on your job.
And never bat an eye when they say it.

I have heard the guy that is president of Shelden Coal say
he would not work for Shelden.

Well back then you had 100,000 coal miners.
It's down to nothing now.
The ones that's working is barely holding on.
They are not going to say nothing that will jeopardize their job.
Because you can't run out here and picket a mine
that's got 500 people to back you, like it was in the '70s.

At one time I liked mining coal.
I liked going to work.
The men stayed "up" all the time.
They would joke and carry on. . . .

I hate to even go to work now.
At Shelden everybody is as serious as a heartbeat.
I said, "Fellas we can't keep working like this.
If we don't start kidding, and joking and carrying on,

we are going to go crazy."
Everybody was just scared and keeping their mouths shut.
Shelden keeps dogging their people.

My buddy Dan's not Sheldenized.
He gives me a lot of crap for letting them do it to me.
But if it comes down to it, Dan would get Sheldenized.
And . . . and he would love it because he won't eat if he don't.
He says, "Well, we're union down there."
The only reason they are union is because
it is a big company and a big mine.
You let Peabody close her down, sublease her out,
and he'll get Sheldenized right quick.

Boss told us to put "I've been Sheldenized" bumper stickers
on our cars.
Yeah I got one on the back window.
I didn't stick it on the bumper.

If you work for them you might as well be Sheldenized,
because you're not going to work for them if you're not.
Being Sheldenized is you give them your life.

I have worked seven days a week for three years.

I had a sixteen-year-old boy before he passed away.
He said, "Hey dad take me hunting."
"Hey dad do this with me."
"No son. I've got to work."

They took all of my self-esteem away,
you know—everything.
You are just like a robot to them.

There was no stronger union man than me.

Sometimes you have to eat crow to survive.

TRUCK ON THE TRACKS

Arranged from an interview with a UMWA organizer by Mike Yarrow

I just went down one day and pulled my truck
Crossways on the railroad track.
I got my sleeping bag
Got on the bank
And said I'm going to stay here till they do whatever.
It was time for the train to come in.
And all at once coming up the tracks,
Straddling the tracks was a woman in a four wheel drive.
So she got up close to my truck

And she just pulled hers across the track too.
And I had never seen her before.
So she got out and sat down on the bank.
So I watched her a few minutes
I went over there and said, "Lady who are you?"
She said, "I work for Massey or did."
I said, "Well, I'm going to leave my truck
Setting there until they pull it away.
And I am going to sleep here until they come."
She said, "Well I am too."

Tobacco farming has been a mainstay for Southern farmers (see Chapter 6). (JOHN BOOKSER-FEISTER)

North Carolina farmer. Blacks in the South have been especially hard-hit by land loss and foreclosures. (JOHN BOOKSER-FEISTER)

Industrial recruitment brochure, South Carolina Development
Board (SCDB)

Mexican industrial recruitment advertisement in the *Wall
Street Journal* (see Chapter 13).

Spring Hill, Tennessee, resident smiles at the news of the Saturn plant site. (ROBERT JOHNSON © *THE TENNESSEAN*)

A sign in Spring Hill shows how some residents view GM. Others are not so sure (see Chapter 14). (ROBERT JOHNSON © *THE TENNESSEAN*)

This sign in Roanoke Rapids tells another story of the jobs that are coming to the South. (EARL DOTTER)

Unemployed workers in Halifax County, North Carolina. (EARL DOTTER)

Toxic chemical plant in Virginia. Hazardous industries tend to locate in the poorest areas (see Chapters 12, 15). (EARL DOTTER)

A sign at a plant in North Carolina proclaims its accident-free work record (see Chapter 8). (JOHN BOOKSER-FEISTER/SEJ)

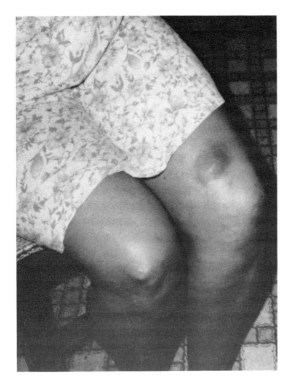

A North Carolina worker displays skin problems due to chemicals in the workplace (see Chapter 8). (JOHN BOOKSER-FEISTER/SEJ)

Lumbee Indians in Robeson County, North Carolina, protest "environmental racism" (see Chapter 12). (RICHARD REGAN)

In Bogalusa, Louisiana, blacks march past Ku Klux Klan
supporters guarded by state troopers (see Chapter 11). (© 1965
AP/WIDE WORLD PHOTOS)

A Klan family at a march in Forsythe County, Georgia, 1987.
Economic change in the South has been accompanied by a
resurgence of racial violence. (JOHN BOOKSER-FEISTER)

Maxine Waller of the Ivanhoe Civic League confronts local
industrial development officials (see Chapter 1). (HELEN M. LEWIS)

Federation of Southern Cooperatives 1977 meeting, Epes,
Alabama. Throughout the South grassroots groups are exploring
new paths of economic development. (JIM ALEXANDER)

Case Studies
from the Deep South

THE SOLID SOUTH has never been as solid as some have made it out to be. Within the South itself, there are differences even on the importance of race—the central issue in regional history. Areas in the Deep South have more of an emotional and political stake in white-supremacist attitudes and in the range of symbols associated with the "Lost Cause," as the Civil War Confederacy came to be known. South Carolina, Georgia, Alabama, Mississippi, and Louisiana are normally viewed as the Deep South. Other states in the region ("border" or "peripheral" states), while experiencing racial segregation and a defensive attitude toward white Southern history, show more diversity, less defiance, and swifter change.

Historically, the economy of the Deep South was extensively entangled with plantation slavery, the slave trade, and the production of cotton and other agricultural products. The Southern economy has been challenged to find alternative crops and industries as agriculture has failed to produce benefits comparable to those enjoyed in the remainder of the country.

The Deep South has been marked by declining population and uneven economic growth. In the long years of segregation, its black population was an excuse to avoid industrialization, either because industrialization would invite hated unionism or because it would remove cheap labor from the whim of the powerful plantation farmers. This essentially feudal arrangement persisted in sharp contrast to an expanding national industrial sector, which sought full access to all labor and a free market to distribute commodities without having to develop specialized racial appeals. The success of the civil rights movement lay in its ability to capture the politics of this thrust. The elimination of racial barriers was a precondition for the reintegration of the region on terms favorable to the consolidating institutions of market capitalism.

The Deep South now enjoys widespread black participation in government and development. Indigenous organizations, such as the voters' leagues discussed here, were early vehicles for community involvement as barriers were removed. There are some statewide groups organized, like the Alabama Democratic Conference, to pur-

121

sue a range of political, economic, and cultural goals. Some of the organizations, such as the Free Southern Theater (FST) in Louisiana, the Federation of Southern Cooperatives (FSC) in Alabama, or the Foundation for Community Development (FCD) in North Carolina, trace their origins directly to civil rights protests. The FSC and FCD focus primarily on minority economic development.

Deep South communities also have access to regional and local chapters of national organizations, including civil rights groups such as the NAACP, Urban League, and SCLC as well as advocacy groups such as the American Friends Service Committee, Clergy and Laity Concerned, and the Fellowship of Reconciliation. Federal programs aimed at low-income populations have spurred participation in such agencies as the Client Councils to the Legal Services program and Head Start advisory committees. Groups specializing in litigation have been active in the Deep South; these include the Southern Poverty Law Center, American Civil Liberties Union, Christic Institute, Lawyers' Committee for Civil Rights Under Law, Center for Constitutional Rights, and NAACP Legal Defense Fund.

Community activism filters through groups such as these in an effort to make some concrete community gains. Yet, as stories included here show, resistance has been intense. The Free Southern Theater and the Foundation for Community Development have been unable to survive. The Federation of Southern Cooperatives still exists but has suffered extraordinary persecution by government officials. These events show the continuing hold of the old New South ideology, in which it is assumed that the Deep South can develop without its black citizens.

Today the states of the Deep South, and their constituent local governments, dutifully set up industrial recruitment programs. But they face a large residual of untrained citizens historically victimized by neglect and discrimination. These citizens must now compete in an international labor market where low-skill work is more cheaply done abroad. The opportunities that do open at home often require credentials that they lack or involve hazardous industries that more prosperous areas can resist. These conditions give rise to new community-based activities, such as the triracial coalition we see in Robeson County, or the indigenous economic development project we see in south Georgia. But in general, the consequence of the new pro-growth attitude has been uneven growth characterized by expansion in the metropolitan areas, decline in the countryside, and a circle of poverty around people of color in the inner city. In this respect, the Deep South is becoming more and more like the rest of the nation.

10

Voting Rights and Community Empowerment: Political Struggle in the Georgia Black Belt

Alex Willingham

T he American Black Belt historically has been characterized by a classic dilemma: a biracial population with a black majority dominated in all social institutions by the white minority.[1] The mode of domination has been under intense pressure since midcentury from a civil rights movement designed to reclaim the citizenship rights of the black population. School segregation, unequal and segregated public accommodations, and denial of voting rights—key props in the system of Black Belt domination—have been eliminated. The social system that long held the black population in menial status is being transformed.

Change is occurring in towns and rural areas determined to carry through reforms already apparent in the larger cities—places such as Albany, Georgia; Selma, Alabama; Amite County, Mississippi; Bogalusa, Louisiana; or Fayette County, Tennessee.[2] These areas represent the soul of the resistance to biracial governance, and once typified the racial hatred that often controlled statewide policies (and regionwide attitudes) on the place of blacks in community life.

This chapter focuses on the efforts of black citizens in one county to address these conditions. Their story covers the range of grassroots development strategies attempted in the Black Belt, ranging from self-help, to community organization, to the use of litigation to ensure voting rights and political participation for black people.[3] These political gains are assessed in light of the current shifts in the economic base of the county.

123

Burke County, Georgia

Burke County, with a population of 19,000, is located in the east Georgia Black Belt just south of Augusta, on the South Carolina line. Burke County exhibits the key features of the Black Belt. In 1880, the first census after the overthrow of Reconstruction, blacks were 80 percent of the population. This basic pattern prevails today, although both the overall population and the percentage of blacks have declined.

The Subject Status

For most of the twentieth century, the black population in Burke County has been a subject population. Despite their majority, blacks have not been participants in political decision making until recently. In 1965, when the federal Voting Rights Act was enacted, a government study found that only 427 (6 percent) of Burke County's blacks were registered to vote, although some 6,600 were old enough. By contrast, 3,664 (84 percent) of Burke County's whites were on the registration books.[4]

The absence of a voting constituency ensured that no black would hold public office or influence policy decisions. Indeed, no black ran for office between 1868, when three blacks (John Warren, Malcolm Claiburne, and John Hall) were elected to the Georgia House of Representatives, and 1968, when Charles Francis and James Reynolds, Sr., ran unsuccessfully for superintendent of education and county commissioner.

As in most rural counties in the South, the key policymaking bodies and positions are the county commission, board of education, municipal council seats, probate judge, sheriff, and superintendent of education. Together these offices directly touch people's lives in the basic areas of education, the administration of justice, public works, social services, zoning, and commerce. Yet not one of the forty positions was held by a black in 1965. Furthermore, elected whites refused to appoint blacks to other authoritative offices or to employ them in the bureaucracy.

Though black and white citizens lived side by side in a community, they essentially occupied two separate worlds in matters of public life. A clique of whites enjoyed political monopoly based on low voter participation generally and on no significant black voting at all. Their outlook was insular and self-preservationist. Low property taxes, in-group decision making, and respect for racial place were the hallmarks of their views. Expansion of the electorate, especially to blacks, was seen as a threat to a way of life.

The separation in public life was also reflected in private relations in community affairs, leisure, social rites, and religion. Neighborhoods reflected a typical racial division. The schools were segregated.[5] White elected officials lacked contact with black citizens.

Disparities

Race segregation in Burke County was not benign, however. It required the majority black population to concede power and authority to the minority whites, to undervalue the responsibility of public officials and the role of the individual as citizen. Separation of races in social matters was key to the larger ideological and structural imperative of subordination. The separation bred unfamiliarity, excessively formalized contacts, and stereotypes. Such conflicts as did occur were grounded in private relations or personal misunderstandings, the resolutions of which were considered to exhaust the claims of blacks in the commonweal.

The administration of the public schools provides a dramatic illustration of the one-sided impact of the white monopoly on policymaking. At midcentury, the all-white county board of education provided four secondary schools for the education of the white minority, but only one for the much larger population of black children. Before 1950, blacks who wanted to continue beyond elementary school found it necessary to travel to Waynesboro, the county seat, and set up lodging for several months at a time.

The consequence was predictable. Differential educational opportunities for whites and blacks resulted in differential achievement. Fewer Burke County blacks were able to complete secondary training at the very time in American history when the high school became the key place for skill training and the diploma the key credential for decent employment. In 1960, 17 percent of the adults in the county had a high school diploma, but only 5 percent of the blacks. In 1980, the differences remained marked. While 39 percent of the total population had completed high school, whites were two-and-a-half times more likely to have a high school degree than blacks.

Employment patterns in Burke reflect the educational disparities. Given the historical predominance of the agricultural economy and the resistance to other forms of development, employment options have been few. For instance, the 1970 census shows that work in private households (as domestics) was still a significant occupation in the county; all these workers were black, and 97 percent were women.

Limited education and restricted job opportunities also resulted in disparities in income. The 1980 census shows that per capita income for whites ($6,223) was twice that of blacks ($3,027). Nearly 40 percent of black households were beneath the poverty line, compared to 10 percent of white households.

Other data suggest that these disparities will not be easily overcome and may reproduce themselves in future years.[6] Female-headed families count for more than a third of black families with children, compared to just eight percent of white families with children. Census data also show that, in the crucial young adult years (eighteen to twenty-four), the white minority is more likely to be enrolled in postsecondary schools generally, and one-and-a-half times more likely to be attending a college.

Leadership Development

Such a polarized socioeconomic situation has discouraged natural leadership development within the black community. The few blacks who did have education were public schoolteachers, and they avoided leadership. They were not active as founders of the local branch of the National Association for the Advancement of Colored People or aggressive in voter registration (even though Georgia's longstanding provision for the registration of eighteen-year-olds heightened the role of senior high educators). Nor did community leadership emerge from the approximately 100 county churches, plagued as they were by absentee ministers and submissive theology. Burke never attracted the outsiders we saw in other places, where "freedom riders" often stayed behind to encourage local leadership development. Indeed, in 1970 Burke had a "homegrown" population. The census reported that a mere 6 percent were born outside Georgia and, of these, 77 percent were born in other parts of the South.

There were no commercial ventures in the black community to serve the leadership recruitment role that local banks, for instance, played among whites. There are no labor unions in the county. No blacks were members of the Democratic Party, and Burke never developed the independent political movements, seen in other Southern states, that competed against the Democratic monopoly. There has never been a black lawyer in the county. There were no black First Families.

Over the years, the best and the brightest blacks have migrated away. The problem of leadership was as difficult an issue as the social problems brought on by the larger system of segregation.

Strategies for Change

Despite the array of forces working to preserve the system of racial subordination, there have been impressive grassroots efforts for change. From 1960 to 1975, men and women in Burke's black community engaged in organizational efforts that brought forth a new leadership cadre. Generally speaking, these efforts evolved from self-help, designed to accommodate blacks to the racist social processes, to demands that blacks share fully in the exercise of public authority.

Self-Help Strategies

Self-help covers those remedial activities that assume the absence of power and authority in the subordinate black citizenry. It is an effort to call up resources of the community to promote race advancement; to take advantage of racial isolation and the institutions of segregation.[7] This strategy applies traditional accommodationist thought, which assumed that black racial advancement could occur under segregated institutions. The key assumptions were that whites were interested merely in separation (and not special advantages) and that poor, disfranchised communities would be able to make such self-help strategies work in isolation.

The strategy usually has several components. One is the formation of an all-purpose civic group broadly designed to take action on conditions. Another is some formal interracial cooperation designed to increase contacts and communication among private individuals. A third is petition and public protest. Although these methods may be deployed with varying degrees of militancy, they are essentially accommodative and will generally avoid political demands that question the legitimacy of governing officials or the allocation of power.

In Burke County, the self-help agenda was put in place in the 1960–1970 period. In June 1961, a group of local black leaders formed the Burke County Improvement Association, which became the main instrument for action. A local chapter of the NAACP was also formed to petition officials for improvements in policies. The initial officers of the Improvement Association and the NAACP became the core leadership group in other ventures.

An interracial component was also present. This effort was helped along by people such as Frances Pauley, a white Atlanta woman who was a trouble shooter for the state human relations department. Under her encouragement, an interracial group met at an Episcopal church to address the issue of communication across the gap set by segregation. These meetings reflected an attitude, present in some sectors of Burke's white community, that favored change. The meetings were not merely token gestures: Roy Chalker, Jr., scion of a Burke First Family, was instrumental in a settlement that later brought blacks to the city council in Waynesboro; a prominent white medical doctor refused to follow the local custom of segregating his patients and actively supported empowerment of the black community.

One major initiative of the self-help phase in Burke County was the formation of the East Georgia Farmers' Cooperative for purposes of economic development. The co-op engaged in programs designed to help black farmers produce earnings through better market capacity. Co-op members developed a cannery to process vegetables and fruits, a meat-processing plant designed to expand the capacity of local farmers, and a credit union to expand the availability of cash.

Another strategy was to use outside resources from national philanthropic foundations and the federal government to ameliorate living conditions. Frances Pauley was an important source of information about available funds. One successful initiative was the formation in 1979 of Burke County Housing Improvement, Inc., a project designed to undertake new construction of housing for senior citizens. Ten housing units were eventually built with a $255,000 loan from the U.S. Department of Housing and Urban Development.

But the movement for self-help began to encounter obstacles from those in power, especially public officials who considered themselves the guardians of white racial privilege. For instance, the all-white county commissioners refused an offer of funds from a private foundation to address problems of infant mortality—even though the county had the highest infant mortality rate in the country. Another example concerned the Head Start program. In Burke the program was initially run by the private Burke County Improvement Association. It was set up in four communities in all-black schools and enrolled mainly black children. When the federal government required that the program be conducted in a school facility open to both races, the all-white board of education refused to allow the association to use public school facilities. The program was suspended for a year while the blacks searched for a suitable place to meet.

In another case, the city of Waynesboro, fearing the integration of the public swimming pool, negotiated a deal to give the pool to a private white group, which then ruled that blacks could not use it. In this incident, the town of Waynesboro realized that failure to take action would result in integration—which it feared. But in the other incidents the local governments did not even have that justification; they were fully aware that the programs benefited primarily low-income blacks. Yet they refused to cooperate. These incidents became dramatic illustrations of the power of government authority to affect even self-help programs based at the community level.

The formal efforts at interracial communication also fell short. On several occasions it was necessary to mount protests and economic boycotts to deal with problems that could have been solved through better understanding and basic courtesy. One such incident, in 1961, may be seen as the pivotal event in the move for empowerment. In a breach of Southern racial etiquette, a black teenager reproached a white female grocery-store clerk for a discourteous act toward him. She responded by having the boy arrested and jailed. Blacks meeting in response to this incident became convinced of the need for sustained organizational action.

The episode occurred as the new activists in the black community were also facing growing frustration in their attempts to negotiate policy changes regarding the desegregation of the county school system. The county school board refused to dismantle the dual school system. Like many Southern systems, Burke then operated under the "freedom of choice" concept, designed to limit school integration through a system of voluntary transfers by individual students. Blacks and their allies argued that compliance with the law sustained systemwide school segregation. The strategy had been to carry on negotiations through appeals by prominent community residents to the good sense of the authorities. The strategy was unproductive. As Herman Lodge, now a county commissioner, was to explain: "We discovered that it didn't work that way. The only way it works is that somebody had to gain some power. You can beat on their desks all you want to and they won't listen to you." The grocery-store incident was further proof that something more was needed.

The school issue finally was solved by calling on the federal government. Beginning in February 1969, eight years after the grocery-store incident, local blacks filed a series of federal lawsuits to abolish the freedom of choice plan in the schools. These suits were decided favorably in 1970, bringing an end to the dual education system in Burke County.[8]

Toward Political Power

As the limits of the self-help strategy became apparent, systematic community mobilizing became increasingly important. The priority of the black community shifted from negotiating to placing people of their choice in decision-making positions. The new strategy was designed both to acquire influence and to gain certain immediate policy changes. There was a focus on voter-registration and -education drives, with the help of outside voter-education groups.

This kind of activity was not entirely new. Community organization had always been a basic part of self-help activity. The decision to direct organizational energies into electoral involvement had come gradually, really in the 1970s, as activists reached beyond the constraints of self-help ideology. The turn to electoral politics was less difficult, for a new leadership cadre had already been developed through the self-help activities.

The voter-participation work gradually evolved into a sophisticated operation involving candidate evaluation, strategic endorsement, and a process for candidates to communicate with their constituency. Key features included the creation of a separate endorsing group (Citizens for Better Government) and a full range of election-day activity where the constituency was exhorted to vote, provided with mock ballots, and transported to and from the polls.

An immediate consequence was a move by some white candidates to seek out the support of black leaders. This was a halting move, however; each side was cautious, not sure exactly how to respond. Blacks had to avoid true public endorsements, for that would hamper their candidate's credibility among whites. Perhaps the most dramatic use of the vote involved a white principal who had been dismissed from the school system, but who subsequently won black support in a successful campaign for school superintendent.

As they developed organization, blacks also ran for office. Between 1968 and 1976, when a major federal lawsuit challenging the election system was filed (see below), eight blacks ran for office in nine elections. Before the Supreme Court finally decided the case in 1981, another fifteen had run in twenty-three contests. In those 14 years, twenty-three blacks ran for office in thirty-two elections, including those for county commissioner, mayor or council in the municipalities, and school superintendent.

But blacks were more successful in mobilizing and targeting white candidates than in actually winning office. Only three of the black candidates won office: J. C. Griggs won a seat on the Waynesboro City Council in 1975, and Dorothy Latimore won a City Council seat in 1978. Sammie Cummings won a seat on the Midville City Council in 1981. With their reelections, they account for nine election victories. None of the other twenty-three elections was won by blacks.

Coming as they did after extensive community organization, special voter-registration drives, and election-day mobilization, these meager results were sobering. The new tactics were exhausted in marginal increases, mainly in voter participation, that were still insufficient to open up the policymaking processes.

The economic dependency of the larger black population, and the resulting state of mind, restricted the black electoral constituency. Years of out-migration and differential birth rates had left a black population disproportionately young by comparison to whites. Politically astute whites, long active in the business of racial politics, responded deftly to exploit these differences. A token black was placed on the city council; creditors were prominent at the voting precincts on election day; white bloc voting persisted as a component of county elections.

The Place of the Voting Rights Movement

Self-help and community organization for political gain contributed in their own way to the advancement of social justice in Burke County. But the pivotal action was the use of litigation by the local black community, with the help of outside civil rights groups. This came in two phases. First, lawsuits were filed to improve policy, such as the school integration suits mentioned above. Second, as part of the voting rights movement, other lawsuits were directed at issues of full participation.[9] One suit in 1975 challenged the method of election in Waynesboro, the county seat. Another, in 1976, challenged the county commission system.[10]

The first suit, *Sullivan* v. *DeLouch,* was filed to challenge the at-large election system in Waynesboro. Drawing on their electoral experiences, the new black leadership concluded that election at large gave advantages to whites. Changing to a system of single-member districts would enable blacks to compete on more even terms. Response to the suit was an interesting indication of the way things change in traditional Southern communities. On one hand, the white political establishment made a swift defensive move, engineering the election of a black person to the city council. This was designed to render the lawsuit moot while keeping the old power relations intact, but it didn't work. The lawsuit was continued. It was resolved when Roy Chalker, a member of one of the powerful white families in the county, led the effort to bring negotiations to a settlement.

The crowning achievement of the Burke County group's struggle was a monumental lawsuit, *Rogers* v. *Lodge,* which set out to change the method of electing the county commission, the main governmental body. When filed, this lawsuit was understood to be a basic challenge to the old county power structure, and it was met with appropriate defiance. It was a tough situation, a perfect test case. A majority-black jurisdiction had a growing record of community leadership. There was no direct evidence that the at-large method was created with the intent to discriminate. White leaders in the county claimed they were being victimized by a band of militant blacks, mere malcontents among a population uninterested in politics. If a federal court wanted to find a rationale to limit the reach of voting rights law, here was a perfect scenario.

Filed in 1976, the suit was not finally settled until a U.S. Supreme Court decision five years later. Activity around the lawsuit was intense. The county appealed unfavorable court decisions, using the state's most prominent pro-segregation attorney. Thirty citizens from Burke's black community, together with the county commissioners, went to Washington for arguments before the Supreme Court. *Rogers* v. *Lodge* required massive legal investment. Conservative estimates are that the county paid nearly $400,000 in legal fees to plaintiff lawyers and special outside counsel—an amount equal to a third of Burke's 1987 budget of $1.2 million. (This does not include time put in by other county officials, including the county attorney.)

In 1981, the U.S. Supreme Court ruled against the at-large system in Burke, requiring the use of single-member districts. The decision dealt a major blow to white supremacy politics. In a special election ordered by the court in 1982, blacks ran for office in each of the new districts. Two—Woodrow Harvey and Herman Lodge—were elected. At the next regular election a third black was elected, giving blacks a majority on the commission. For the first time in the county's history, the black majority in the county was reflected in the county's policymaking body. The litigation had proved a pivotal resource in the struggle for empowerment, and, in contrast to the more restricted notions of the original self-help strategy, represented a major leap toward full citizenship.

The New Politics in Burke: What Really Changed?

The racial change in the makeup of county bodies was followed by a change in policies. For instance, where the previous all-white commission had rejected a private foundation grant to address infant mortality, the new commission revived the idea and accepted the money. This was matched with a $600,000 federal community development grant to build a new health facility.

Some longstanding black community grievances have been addressed, including the change to an elected school board, the creation of an affirmative voter-registration policy, and the holding of commission meetings at an evening hour. The commission created a human relations committee headed by a black to work on communication, another longstanding concern. Taxing and spending have seen the levy of a sales tax and new capital spending for health facilities, including a county health department serving the poor and a new hospital. A county-appointed industrial office has been charged with diversifying the local economy. In social services, the county now funds a full-time year-round recreation program and a full-time senior citizens' coordinator. Between 1982 and 1987, Burke spent $5.5 million to build a new hospital, $9 million on a new comprehensive high school, and $1.4 million to renovate the county courthouse.

In Burke County the process of community empowerment continues in a positive direction. Public policy is now more responsive to the needs of the community than at any time before. Commissioner Herman Lodge says the cooperative attitude of the black leadership is having a positive effect on white attitudes. "We're beginning to convince whites that we are not going to destroy the county, not going to run anybody off; we will be progressive."

Why have they been successful? Lodge says, "In order to be [effective] you have to have leadership within. It is real difficult for people from the outside to come in and help you." He says this is why the commission was able to work so well together despite six years of adversarial proceedings in the lawsuit.

Nevertheless, outside help was crucial. There had been a long history of outside involvement in Burke County going back to the Volunteer Emergency Food and Medical Program under the U.S. Department of Agriculture. Expertise in legal action, for example, was provided by outside lawyers. Financial support came from the NAACP Legal Defense and Education Fund, Georgia Legal Services, and the American Civil Liberties Union. Technical assistance in other areas was provided by the Southern Regional Council and the Voter Education Project.[11]

The outside help was important in yet another way. Even though the leaders of the Burke County Improvement Association were local blacks, many of them were economically "independent," meaning they were employed outside the county or in nonlocally owned companies or owned their farming land. The growth of major public and corporate employers in the surrounding areas, such as Fort Gordon, Continental Can, and the medical complex in Augusta, relieved the dependence of blacks on the local, politically dominated economy. These larger companies had little stake in local government conflicts.

The acquisition of political power presented new problems. Today the biracial Burke County commission routinely splits over personality and policy issues. The behavior there is similar to that in other Black Belt jurisdictions where recently acquired political empowerment has been accompanied by severe tensions. In the regular elections of 1988, for example, only one of the five Burke commissioners avoided serious opposition. Campaign expenditures reached new heights, but only half of those registered turned out to vote. Woodrow Harvey, who had been in the struggle from the very beginning, barely survived: he was unable to muster a majority in a four-person first primary and escaped with just 53 percent of the vote in the runoff.[12]

There has been small change in certain key social and political areas. One group of whites maintains a system of private segregated schools. All the single-seat countywide offices, including sheriff, are held by whites, and only one black has been elected to the county board of education, the same as under the old appointed system.

The county was back in the news—and the court system—again in the 1985–1989 period when citizens in the small black-majority town of Keysville attempted to reinstitute the municipal government. When elections were held, Emma Gresham and a slate of black candidates were elected over a white slate that preferred to keep the government dormant. The action required a hearing before the U.S. Supreme Court and conflict persists within the community over the operation of the new government.[13]

Finally, while there is a consensus within Burke on the need for industrial development, there is tension over the terms of that development. Nuclear power plant construction brought a spurt of employment activity and the operation of those plants secures the tax digest, but the construction winddown means a loss of jobs, and county officials are left to manage a county that is tax-rich but job-poor. And when a conflict developed between the Amalgamated Clothing and Textile Workers Union (ACTWU) and management at Samsons, a local apparel manufacturing company, it was the officers of the Burke County Improvement Association, including Commissioner Lodge, who warned of the perils of labor unions, saying, "We are convinced that the presence of the union has had and will have a negative impact on the economic well-being of all citizens of Burke County." The association's alliance with the management of a textile company with a virtually all-black work force is a signal of the predicament of the new black leadership and the nature of the new economic constraints.[14]

Future Prospects

Political change is coming to the American Black Belt at a pace that was unthinkable just fifteen years ago. Serious obstacles remain, however, including widespread poverty and limited economic opportunities. Nor have the old Black Belt elites given up on the search for new devices to regain their political monopoly. Private all-white academies dot the region. Powerful adversaries in the west Alabama Black Belt fanned allegations of improper use of federal funds and eventually secured a grand jury indictment against the Federation of Southern Cooperatives. No trial was held, but the action severely hampered the federation's work among a largely black and poor constituency that relies on cooperative ventures in farming, handicrafts, and credit unions.[15] State and federal voter-fraud prosecutions in Alabama and "ballot security" measures in Louisiana illustrate other rear-guard tactics. These areas still have the nation's most restrictive voter-registration procedures.[16]

Behind these political changes is a deeper crisis based in the economies of these areas. The new biracial governments no longer resist nonagricultural development. Their main theme is labor-intensive industrial development. Such development would make possible the stabilization of the population and a decent standard of living in areas that have never enjoyed industrial-level pay standards.

But years of neglect of human resources have left the Black Belt ill-prepared. Historically, companies that came south were low-wage, low-skilled ones that avoided the Black Belt for the Piedmont. Today, better-paying companies settle in the growth-oriented metropolises. The Black Belt rural areas are left with the less desirable industries—hazardous waste disposal and nuclear energy production. Georgia Power Corporation's location of major new nuclear facilities in Burke County illustrates the trend. Estimates are that, once completed, these nuclear power operations will provide 75 percent of the tax digest of the county.

Cash-strapped local governments in these areas are asked to grant significant concessions to low-wage or dangerous industries—to buckle under to economic blackmail. Black political empowerment, which often empowers the most desperate part of the community, too often means a better chance that those concessions will be made. But the new international environment provides alternative prospects for these companies. When they do settle in the Black Belt, they have no permanent commitment to the community.

The promise was that revolution in the Black Belt would bring the benefits of the American life to these citizens and lift a burden from the nation at large. Now some changes are occurring, but the promised development seems less likely. Continued underdevelopment may be required today, mandated less by the racial bigotry of a narrow ruling elite than by the imperatives of a consolidating national economy operating under international market rules. The circumstances pose a set of concerns about the larger economy and force us to recast the question of where fundamental change is needed.

NOTES

1. The Black Belt has been the object of romance, social science, and political controversy ever since the period of chattel slavery. All the South became dependent on the white-supremacy institutions created by the Black Belt elites: one-party systems, all-white nominating primaries, majority vote and runoff requirements, rigid social segregation, and race-conscious application of civil sanctions. V. O. Key, seeing the pivotal role of the Black Belt whites in the region's life, traced the range of peculiar practices to white people's fear of the exercise of democratic rights by their colored neighbors (*Southern Politics in State and Nation* [New York: Knopf, 1949]).

2. Scholars are beginning to shake their preoccupation with the themes of domination in urban settings and pay more attention to racial change in the towns and rural areas of the South. See K. C. Morrison, "Pre-Conditions for Afro-American Leadership in the South," *Polity* 17 (Spring 1985): 504–29, and *Black Political Mobilization: Leadership Power and Mass Behavior* (Albany: State University of New York Press, 1987); Margaret Edds, *Free at Last: What Really Happened When Civil Rights Came to Southern Politics* (Bethesda, Md.: Adler and Adler, 1987); Lawrence J. Hanks, *The Struggle for Black Political Empowerment in Three Georgia Counties* (Knoxville: University of Tennessee Press, 1987).

3. Bill Cutler, "The Faces of Burke County," *Brown's Guide to Georgia* 6 (November 1978): 18–34; Christena Bledsoe, "Burke County Today: The Coming of Power to Blacks in Burke County," *Georgia Poverty Journal* 1 (Fall 1986): 6–22; Marcia Kunstel, "A Trial of Wills and Wiles in Burke County," (Atlanta) *Journal and Constitution*, August 16, 1981; "Report of Voter Participation Project—Burke County" (n.d.); and three U.S. court decisions: *Rogers* v. *Lodge* 458 U.S. 613(1982); *Lodge* v. *Buxton*, 639 F 2d 1358 (1981); and the trial decision in *Lodge* v. *Buxton*, CA 176-55 (S. D. Ga. October 26, 1978).

4. U.S. Commission on Civil Rights, *Political Participation* (Washington, D.C.: U.S. Government Printing Office, 1968).

5. Burke County also had a historically black private school, to which youngsters from around the county came. This private school merely reinforced race separation in this context.

6. I present these data on family and children with a caution to the reader to be realistic about the problems facing children of color from poor families with a single head of household. No stigma is implied except against a society that refuses to recognize the capabilities of these individuals. Current social science research on family life and racism is extensive. See William J. Wilson, *The Truly Disadvantaged* (Chicago: University of Chicago Press, 1987), and questions raised about this sort of work by Adolph Reed, Jr., "The Liberal Technocrat," *The Nation*, February 6, 1988, 167–70.

7. Self-help has a long and controversial history as a form of political thought within the African-American population. For a classic statement see W. E. B. Du Bois, "A Negro Nation Without the Nation," *Current History*, June 1935. For contrasting views in the recent period, see comments in the *Report of the National Advisory Committee on Civil Disorders* (New York: Dutton, 1968), and untitled remarks by Eddie N. Williams presented to the Xavier University/SEF Public Affairs Project, New Orleans, La., August 9, 1987 (Washington, D.C.: Joint Center for Political Studies, 1987).

8. *Bennett* v. *Burke County Board of Education*, and *Bennett* v. *Evans*.

9. "Voting rights movement" refers to the campaign to bring about election reforms under the Voting Rights Act. It included the use of lawsuits as well as federal administrative review. These reforms were designed to eliminate discriminatory election methods. The key reform was the use of the single-member election district to replace at-large or multimember election methods. Communities in the Black Belt had other options during this period. In some cases, such as Greene County, Alabama, Hancock County, Georgia, or in the large cities, increased voter participation in areas with large black majorities enabled blacks to take over the political structure. Another approach, tried in numerous places, was the use of service-equalization lawsuits to force all-white government agencies to provide equal services to both races. A variant used the compliance processes in the federal government, for example, the Office of Revenue Sharing, to coerce local white officials to behave. Accounting for the exact place of these reforms is proving difficult for those studying the region. Compare Edds, *Free at Last;* Merle Black and Earl Black, *Politics and Society in the South* (Cambridge, Mass.: Harvard University Press, 1987); and Abigail M. Thernstrom, *Whose Votes Count? Affirmative Action and Minority Voting Rights* (Cambridge, Mass.: Harvard University Press, 1987).

10. Other suits included *Sapp* v. *Rowland*, which was filed in 1977 against the all-white jury commission. Another lawsuit challenged the exclusion of blacks from the Democratic Party (*Burke County Improvement Association* v. *Burke County Democratic Committee*).

11. The litigation in Burke saw the involvement of a number of lawyers. John Ruffin, an NAACP Legal Defense and Education Fund lawyer in Augusta, Georgia, handled the school cases. The protracted *Rogers* case involved lawyers David Walbert, who argued the case before the U.S. Supreme Court, Robert Cullen, of Georgia Legal Services, and Laughlin McDonald of the American Civil Liberties Union.

12. (Waynesboro) *True-Citizen*, August 24, 31, 1988.
13. *Poole* v. *Gresham*, 109 S. Ct. 523 (1988), was supported by the American Civil Liberties Union and the Christic Institute. See also "Vote Puts Small-Town Blacks on Top," *New York Times*, January 6, 1988; "Keysville: To Be A City or Not to Be?" (Atlanta) *Constitution*, October 19, 1988; and "Keysville Water Woes Escalating," (Waynesboro) *True-Citizen*, November 16, 1988.
14. See open letter, (Waynesboro) *True-Citizen*, April 26, 1989.
15. Thomas N. Bethell, *Sumter County Blues: The Ordeal of the Federation of Southern Cooperatives* (Washington, D.C.: National Committee in Support of Community Based Organizations, 1982).
16. U.S. Commission on Civil Rights, *Political Participation;* Frances Fox Piven and Richard Cloward, *Why Americans Don't Vote* (New York: Pantheon, 1988); Citizens Commission on Civil Rights, *Barriers to Registration and Voting: An Agenda for Reform* (Washington, D.C.: National Center for Policy Alternatives, 1988).

CHAPTER

11

Race, Development, and the Character of Black Political Life in Bogalusa, Louisiana

Rickey Hill

In recent years, the transformation of race relations has been the most dramatic change in the social conditions of small towns in the Deep South. Black citizens in these communities have acted purposefully to end segregation and racial domination. Hope among all rural Southerners has been fueled by the removal of race as a deterrent to overall economic development. In Bogalusa, Louisiana, a small Pearl River town of 20,000, significant change has occurred, allowing us to rethink the impact of changing race relations on larger strategies for social development.

Civil rights action in Bogalusa captured the attention of the nation during the 1960s. Black people there made a decisive effort to challenge their own subordination, and the resulting movement was a struggle against the traditional symbols of segregation as well as the operation of a paternalistic company—a paper mill owned by the Crown Zellerbach Corporation—that dominated the private economic sector. The Bogalusa movement, while based in the same racial dynamics operating in other towns, differed in two important ways. First, local worker organizations were active. Second, militant resistance, including armed self-defense, distinguished the strategy in this community from the nonviolent strategy that prevailed more generally in the movement. Bogalusa was thus atypical of the Southern movement of the times and invites our continuing attention as a special episode in the freedom struggle.

I was first involved in Bogalusa as a high school activist with the Congress for Racial Equality, working with black students as desegregation ended and new adjustments were made. We sought to link that struggle to the larger freedom struggle. My continuing study of my hometown grows out of these early experiences and the puzzles they created for me about the peculiar mixture of race and class factors in the community. As the movement has passed away, the puzzle remains: how did these struggles affect everyday life? This chapter examines the relationship between race and development in Bogalusa as that town evolved into the latest era of Southern politics.

The Setting: A Company Town

Bogalusa is located in southeastern Louisiana, in what is known as the Pearl River Valley. Its name is taken from the Choctaw Indian words *bogue lusa*, which mean "dark or smoky waters." According to 1980 census data, Bogalusa has a population of 19,520, one-third black. By 1980 estimates the average income earned by workers is $6,582 and per capita income is $3,348. The median family incomes are $15,685 for whites and $7,559 for blacks.

Bogalusa, the largest municipality in Washington Parish, was developed as a mill town in 1906. Goodyear Industries of Buffalo, New York, settled the town and established the Great Southern Lumber Company, then one of the largest paper mills in the world. Bogalusa was incorporated on July 4, 1914, under the commission form of government.[1]

In 1936, the Gaylord Container Corporation of St. Louis, Missouri, purchased the Great Southern Lumber Company, and was bought in turn by the Crown Zellerbach Corporation of San Francisco in 1955. Crown Zellerbach has turned over operation of the Bogalusa plant to its Gaylord subsidiary, which is now the largest employer and taxpayer in Bogalusa.

Race has been the primary social factor in Bogalusa since its establishment in 1906. The mill town brought a wave of unskilled black labor into the area. Black people were a common commodity around lumber camps. As laborers, they participated in a number of union-organizing efforts. In Bogalusa, they joined the carpenters' union and the timber workers' union. The membership of the timber workers' union was 75 percent black but all its officials were white. Black life was thoroughly circumscribed to the "colored quarters," where by 1920 the Great Southern Lumber Company proudly announced that "everything was done to keep Negro citizens healthy, happy and productive."[2]

Throughout the industrial development of Bogalusa, all the major corporations, including Crown Zellerbach, maintained a similar paternalism on the race question. Blacks remained in a menial position, contributing their labor but never participating in the political life of the town. As a consequence, all city and parish government decisions on taxes, school policy, or community development were carried out by all-white officials elected at large, with no ties to the black community. The town typified New South development where cooperation in economic affairs went hand in hand with separation in social and political matters.

Leadership Development

The first efforts to register blacks to vote occurred in 1950 but were not fully organized until the 1960s. The advent of the civil rights movement was a turning point in the history of black people in Bogalusa.

The initial focus of civil rights protest in Bogalusa concerned public accommodations and voter registration, led by the Bogalusa Civic and Voters League with the help of the Congress of Racial Equality (CORE).

The decisive year was 1965. After surmounting a number of maneuvers designed to frustrate the Voters League and CORE, including violence and harassment, the movement began in earnest at the beginning of 1965. The initial effort—a test of local compliance with the 1964 Civil Rights Act—created problems within the Voters League. The group's leadership at the time was split along classic lines: younger, more militant voices and older, more conservative people who generally valued change in economic areas and avoided civic protest.

In a series of striking moves, the older leaders were swept to the sidelines, where they were to remain until the late 1970s, after civil rights had been restored and economic issues had reemerged. A. Z. Young became president, Robert Hicks vice-president, and Gayle Jenkins became secretary. Young and Hicks worked at Crown Zellerbach, where they were leaders in the local Pulp, Sulphite and Papermill Workers Union; Jenkins was a cook at the local Desports Clinic.

Under their leadership, the Voters League organized a local chapter of the Deacons for Defense and Justice, widely know for their use of armed self-defense. The Deacons served as a protection force for civil rights workers who came to Bogalusa during the late 1960s. Equally important, its existence helped to erase the fear that black people, traditionally with no police protection, had long experienced.

The reinvigorated Voters League expanded beyond its initial aims to a wider goal: a comprehensive program of racial betterment, involving militant tactics. Protests were organized to achieve several basic rights: equal opportunity in employment, equal educational opportunities, desegregation of public facilities, extension of community services, inclusion of black people on decision-making boards, and removal of unconstitutional laws. Generally, demands for equal employment opportunities and the end to segregated union-ism were made to Crown Zellerbach, rather than local political institutions. An example at Crown Zellerbach—the "Big Company"—would help elimi-nate traditional racial inequities in Bogalusa.

Blacks waged a two-pronged struggle against Crown Zellerbach, attacking discriminatory practices and policies and dual unionism. Grievances were filed not only with local management, but also with corporate officers in San Francisco. At the same time, the Voters League organized a boycott and picket lines against downtown retailers. Some whites reacted to the protest with violence.

In the fall of 1965, the black community, under the leadership of the Voters League, organized against the segregated school system. Black stu-dents used picket lines and sit-ins to demonstrate against the segregated and inferior schools. The city school board responded with a "freedom of choice" plan, allowing a few black pupils to attend the "white" schools while still maintaining the basic racial pattern. Blacks continued to press for improve-ment. In 1969, with the help of the Lawyers Committee for Defense Under the Constitution, *Jenkins* v. *City of Bogalusa School Board* was filed and resulted in a federal court order requiring complete removal of segregation. Full inte-gration of the schools saw more protests, however, as black students orga-nized Students for Ultimate Liberation (SOUL) to address efforts made to re-strict their full participation in school activities.

The electoral arena was also a part of the overall strategy of the Voters League. In 1967, Robert Hicks tried to gain a seat on the school board, and A. Z. Young ran for the police jury (the parish's governing board); both lost. In 1970, Young ran for mayor, and he lost this bid as well. David Johnson, Jr., the first general vice-president of Local 189 of the International United Paper-makers at Crown Zellerbach, also ran for office in 1970—for commissioner of streets and parks—but lost. In 1971, three blacks ran unsuccessfully for the Bogalusa school board.

The primary structural obstacle preventing the election of blacks was the at-large election system. By the mid-1970s, the activities of the Voters League were focused exclusively on electoral participation, in the form of an attack against the at-large election system and the commission form of government. In 1974 the Washington Parish NAACP filed a lawsuit against the at-large election of city council members. This effort was mooted when a city charter commission proposed a reorganization of the city elections to remove the at-large feature. The school board, however, would change only with an adverse ruling in *Concerned Citizens for Good Government* v. *City of Bogalusa School Board*. After 1976, these key government bodies became accessible to black voters and candidates for the first time.

From 1965 to the mid-1970s, the Bogalusa movement was generally characterized by its protest orientation. Although its efforts to elect black political authority failed, it did produce strong, committed, and militant political leadership. The Bogalusa Civic and Voters League became a flexible force that organized and gave leadership to every phase of the movement.

By the mid-1970s, some blacks were occupying middle-level and supervisory positions at Crown Zellerbach and at other companies, such as South Central Bell Telephone. The city government employed several blacks in clerical positions and four became members of the city police force. Black employment in the retail and utilities industries increased.

In 1977, two blacks—Gayle Jenkins and Robert T. Young, brother of A. Z. Young—were elected to the Bogalusa city school board. Since September 1978, the Bogalusa city council has had two black members.[3] Both these developments resulted from the removal of the at-large election system, overturned in federal court in 1976.

These developments represent a significant and historic turn in the character of life and politics in Bogalusa. They illustrate the efforts made to overcome racial segregation, acquire basic democratic rights, obtain political authority, and win a voice in development policy.

The Rise of Economic Problems

With the election of black people to the Bogalusa city council, there has come a broadening of the political agenda to include issues that are critical to the black community. The presence of black city council members indicates a measure of access to the policymaking process, but it is marginal. Since 1979, the primary issue has been economic development. Historically, most discussions of economic development in Bogalusa have not involved the black community. However, with the political gains of the late 1970s the black community has played an increasing role in such discussions.

The problem of economic development has been primarily defined by Bogalusa's "company town" nature. Since its inception, Bogalusa has been a one-industry town. The efforts to produce an economic development strategy were precipitated by a cutback in operations at the local Crown Zellerbach plant. On August 17, 1977, the company announced that it was initiating a $100 million modernization and automation program at its Bogalusa plant; it meant closing some of the plant's operations and eliminating 1,400 of the 2,800 jobs there. By 1979, 803 employees had been laid off, most of them blacks and women.

Because Crown Zellerbach was the largest employer and taxpayer, the layoffs were viewed with considerable anguish, even though they were not entirely unexpected. The nature of the town itself was the greatest problem. Besides being dominated by a single industry, Bogalusa suffered from four basic problems that discouraged economic and industrial revitalization: (1) the enduring stigma of racism, (2) worker discontent and union activities, (3) geographical isolation from interstate highway systems, and (4) corporate paternalism and protectionism. These problems contributed to a decline in public services, a reduction of the property tax base, a decline in the retail trade, a stagnating housing market, and a decline in the employment base.

To reverse these trends and work out a comprehensive development strategy, the city established the Bogalusa Economic Development Corporation in 1979. Its primary objective was to coordinate economic development activities among local, state, and federal governmental agencies, as well as the local business community. It wanted to broaden and diversify the area's economic base and coordinate the total resources of the area toward balanced economic growth. To attract labor-intensive industries and provide jobs, the development corporation sought to establish an industrial park and to revitalize the main business district.

With the exception of the Community Development Block Grant program, these specific efforts toward economic development had no impact on the black community. Only one predominantly black area was targeted. Populas Quarters, a traditionally black residential section, received funding from the block grant program, primarily for housing renovation and rehabilitation. Although the downtown business revitalization efforts took place adjacent to a popular black entertainment area, they were not extended to this area.

The new economic development activity attracted a number of the "old line" blacks, those who had held leadership positions in the Bogalusa Civic and Voters League before 1965. Many of them were schoolteachers, insurance agents, and other professionals, and they had generally viewed themselves as being concerned with economic issues all along. Andrew Moses, president of the Voters League in the early 1960s, served as vice-president of the development corporation. J. C. Crump (now deceased), another "old line" black leader, served as chair of its minority business development committee.

The "old line" leadership remains organized around economic issues, even though economic development has been on the decline since the early 1980s. The Bogalusa Voters League no longer reflects the civic activism that characterized it from 1965 through the mid-1970s. Gayle Jenkins has been a member of the Bogalusa school board since 1977. A. Z. Young has held numerous positions in state government and with the state Democratic Party since 1972. Robert Hicks has been a supervisor at Crown Zellerbach's Gaylord Container division for more than a decade. Through such leaders, the black community is able to articulate its concerns. Built on the traditions of the Bogalusa Civic and Voters League, that kind of political authority can be welded into an effective mechanism.

Bogalusa's situation is not unique. Most small cities are faced with the

loss of their economic base to industry shutdowns and cutbacks and the inability to attract new industry. As long as it remains a one-company town,
Bogalusa will always be confronted with problems of moving forward.

Even though it continues to endure a stigma of racism, Bogalusa in recent
years has seen a breakdown of barriers to black participation. Concern for
economic development has brought about biracial cooperation on the town's
overall development efforts. Continued development of strong black leadership is needed; success in this area will benefit all of Bogalusa.

New South, Old Problem

The acquisition of black political authority in Bogalusa has meant that
black people there are faced with new realities. For one thing, because the
acquisition of black political authority is very recent, that authority is somewhat limited in traditional terms. Also, the black community has only recently become aware of the long-term possibilities of its impact on the political process. Moreover, despite the fact that federal funds have been available
since the mid-1970s, most economic development is also quite recent, and
most of it has been focused on the central business district. The development
of this district takes place at the expense of neighborhood enhancement and
development of job skills that would be of direct significance to the poor black
population. Considering all this, how are we to construct political strategies
and initiatives that can enhance black participation in ongoing economic and
industrial development?

The American South is no longer an unfettered territory of untapped resources. It never really was, as far as its labor was concerned. While racial
segregation no longer specifies the region, a complex of structural problems
does: a wider per-capita income gap, even wider for blacks, and an array of
other socioeconomic problems. Race is still the primary factor in this complex.

We must be careful not to take black participation for granted. It is really a
new phenomenon. Black politics in Bogalusa can be viewed, certainly over
the past ten years, as an awakening of the potential of the black community.
The mayor–council form of government and the district election system have
been important developments. More recently, where acquisition of black political authority has been historically and politically significant, the impact of
economic development has been crucial. We can conclude that, in large measure, the advent of black political authority in Bogalusa has created a new
political reality for the black community and the Bogalusa community as a
whole.

By linking the race problem in the American South to economic and industrial development in the region, we are able to assess the broad range of

ideological and structural factors that have shaped both phenomena. Bogalusa illustrates the evolution of black political life within the context of economic development. The recent advent of black political authority and the concomitant focus on economic development have brought the new New South to Bogalusa.[4]

NOTES

1. See Charles Waterhouse Goodyear, *The Bogalusa Story* (Buffalo N.Y.: William J. Keller, 1950), and Amy Quick, "The History of Bogalusa: The Magic City of Louisiana," *Louisiana Historical Quarterly* 20 (January 1946): 73–201.

2. Herbert Northrup, *The Negro in the Paper Industry* (Philadelphia: University of Pennsylvania Press, 1969), 96, and George B. Tindall, *The Emergence of the New South, 1913–1945* (Baton Rouge: Louisiana State University Press, 1967); Goodyear, *The Bogalusa Story*.

3. The first two blacks to hold council seats served until 1985; two others were then elected.

4. I have conducted an extensive study of the Bogalusa case since 1976. See "The Character of Black Politics in a Small Southern Town Dominated by a Multinational Corporation: Bogalusa, Louisiana, 1965–1975," M.A. thesis, Atlanta University, 1977, and "Black Political Life and the New South Development Strategy: An Analysis of Black Political Authority in Bogalusa, Louisiana, 1975–1980," Ph.D. dissertation, Atlanta University, 1982.

CHAPTER

12

Economic Slavery or Hazardous Wastes? Robeson County's Economic Menu

Richard Regan and Mac Legerton

I t is three-fourths the size of Rhode Island. It is 90 percent forests and farm-land, with a subtropical climate. Wages are low, unemployment is high. The economy is based on production of cash crops and industrial goods that are marketed and sold by outside business interests. People of color make up 63 percent of the population. Three out of four workers who are persons of color are employed in low-wage jobs. Five separate school systems were only recently merged as a result of a local referendum; there are four interspaced phone districts, and no system of public transportation exists. Punishment under the law is highly dependent on racial, economic, and social position. Violence is a common response to the widespread feelings of powerlessness.

That description fits the familiar story of a poor country in the Third World, perhaps one in Central America or southern Africa. In fact, this is a description of Robeson County, North Carolina, a rural Southern community haunted by patterns of poverty and oppression normally associated with the Third World.

Recently, eyes and ears around the world were drawn to Robeson County by a series of events that indicate the racial and economic tension in the county. On February 1, 1988, Eddie Hatcher and Timothy Jacobs armed themselves, seized the *Robesonian* newspaper office, and demanded an inves-tigation into charges of human rights violations against Native Americans and blacks and into political corruption and drug trafficking in the county. Using necessity as their defense, they testified that they feared for their lives. In Oc-tober 1988 they were acquitted by a federal jury of all charges, including hostage taking and weapons charges. Two months later they were reindicted on state charges of kidnapping.

On March 26, 1988, Julian Pierce, a Native American candidate for a newly created superior court judgeship, was murdered in his home under highly suspicious circumstances. His opponent was the highly controversial District Attorney Joe Freeman Britt, listed in the *Guinness Book of World Records* for sending more people to Death Row than any other district attorney in the world. Although official accounts deny political intent, most people believe Pierce's murder was politically motivated. Pierce won the election in spite of his murder, but Britt became the unopposed victor.

These incidents—and the questions of civil rights, drug trafficking, and abuse in the criminal justice system—have placed Robeson County in a state of shock and suspicion. The crisis stimulates memories of Alabama and Mississippi in the 1960s and has led some observers to dub Robeson County the Selma of the 1980s.

The population of Robeson County is 37 percent Native American, 26 percent black, and 37 percent white. It is the home of the Lumbee, the largest tribe of native people east of the Mississippi, and the Tuscarora tribe of North Carolina. The per capita income of blacks and native people is half that of the white population, and strong divisions remain between persons of different economic status within each race. While some political gains have been made by blacks and native people, the majority of decision makers in both public and private institutions remain white. If effective and successful organization could occur in this multiracial, divided and isolated county, it would become an example and a sign of hope for the nation.

It was out of such a need that the Center for Community Action (CCA), formerly Robeson County Clergy and Laity Concerned, was formed in 1980. Its major purpose is to make fundamental changes in the social, political, and economic environment of poor, disenfranchised people living in and around Robeson County. CCA works to unite people across racial, gender, economic, and religious lines, promote a democratic citizens' forum for problem solving, and develop leadership potential in the grassroots community.

CCA employs an empowerment model of organizing based on cluster groups of members within the county who decide, plan, and organize issue campaigns. We have found this type of organizing model more effective than the typical movement campaigns and as a result have reaped the benefits of a community-centered, locally led, and collectively owned power base.

One of the concerns CCA has addressed is economic justice and the related subject of economic blackmail. In an area desperate for decent jobs, CCA has successfully led two campaigns to stop radioactive and hazardous-waste treatment facilities from locating in our community.

Economic Background

Robeson County's economy is typical of many Southern rural counties. Most of its manufacturing concerns are the traditional Southern ones—textile, fiber, and lumber-related industries. More than half the members of its labor force are women. Almost all its jobs are low-wage. Yet while many counties throughout the region have seen the gradual loss of their traditional jobs, Robeson County has witnessed a turbulent pattern of simultaneous growth and decline, as some of the larger multinationals leave the area for Third World countries, only to be replaced by lower-wage and more hazardous industries.

One of the industries to export jobs from this rural county in recent years is Converse, Inc., the shoe manufacturer. B. F. Goodrich of Akron, Ohio (later to become Converse), first located in Lumberton, North Carolina, in 1966. Like many other industries in the South, it was attracted by the low-wage, nonunion labor force. The company soon became the county's leading employer, with a visible corporate reputation. In 1972, B. F. Goodrich leased its shoe operation to Massachusetts-based Converse and then sold the entire plant to Converse in 1978. In 1985, Converse was acquired by St. Louis, Missouri–based Interco, Inc. The plant's annual payroll has contributed as much as $18.2 million to the local economy. Production workers earn up to $6 an hour, making their jobs some of the best paid in the area.

In recent years the shoe industry has been volatile, shaped by changing consumer demands and by rising international competition. Both factors have affected Converse workers in Robeson County. In 1985, claiming that fashion was shifting away from canvas tennis shoes, Converse laid off half its 1,500 workers and transferred many jobs to Mexico. The move sent shock waves through the county's economy.[1]

Then, in 1986 the company announced it had found a new market niche, based on multicolored tennis shoes. Daily shoe production at Converse rose to 40,000 pairs; most of the 1,500 workers previously laid off were rehired.

Still, Converse daily dispatches 8,000 pairs of canvas shoes to Reynoldsa, Mexico, for labor-intensive stitching. The shoes are then shipped back to Lumberton for completion. By paying Mexican workers 65 cents an hour, Converse can avoid the high cost of sewing labor in Robeson County. By completing the shoes in Lumberton, Converse can also avoid the tariffs it would pay if the shoes were imported as a finished product. In a discernible effort to lower production costs, Converse has eliminated the possibility of hundreds more sewing jobs in the county.[2]

At the same time that Robeson County has experienced the loss of some of its best manufacturing jobs and increased vulnerability of others, trends also show new jobs being created. In a fifteen-month period in 1986 and 1987, only Charlotte, North Carolina, filled more job vacancies in the state than did rural Robeson County. Between June 1986 and April 1987, almost 4,000 persons either returned to their former jobs or received new work, making the Robeson County employment office the busiest in the state. Sounds like an economic boom? Perhaps not. Of the approximately 4,000 jobs filled within the nine-month period, only 67 paid more than $300 a week.[3]

Robeson County may be experiencing a job boom, but most of the jobs are "low pay and no say." Haleyville Drapery, for example, announced a cut-and-sew operation to make bedspreads and drapes for mobile home manufacturers. The plant would employ 50 people at just over minimum wage.[4]

An announcement that Virginia-based Rocco Enterprises would build a $15 million food-processing plant in the northeastern section of Robeson County is another piece of "let's wait and see" economic news. Rocco brings to the county a multinational reputation as the world's largest turkey processor.[5] Preliminary Rocco plans in Robeson County call for a 1988 fourth-quarter start-up, with an initial employment projection of 300 workers, expanding to 600 at full production. The forty-seven-year-old firm will eventually handle production from 100 turkey houses totaling 200,000 birds a year.[6] Rocco's advent is being called by some local observers a sign of successful economic development.

However, deeper investigation suggests reason for concern. Increasing consumer concern for healthier diets (more poultry, less beef) is creating a growing number of jobs for the rural Southern economy. There are more than 12,000 poultry workers in North Carolina alone, and they endure low wages and high rates of occupational disease and injury as they eviscerate, cut, debone, and pack chickens, turkeys, and ducklings.

Investigation shows that the moving of these jobs to Robeson County is deeply intertwined with the company's corporate performance in Dayton, Virginia. Since Rocco's takeover of the Marval Poultry Company in Dayton, life in the economically disenfranchised Shenandoah Valley has not been the same. Dayton, like many small poultry-producing towns that dot the South, resembles the picture of a classic company town. The company owns much of the property, a large realty firm, movie theaters, and a hardware store. It raises the turkeys it processes and owns the mills that make their feed.[7]

Complaints from the Dayton plant include firings of employees who develop production-induced illnesses, a 20 percent cut in the work force despite increased production, and stricter guidelines on absenteeism, sick leave, break privileges, and bathroom liberties.[8]

One former Rocco worker remarked, "They treat the workers worse than they treat the turkeys. No matter how bad a person is hurting, they won't take them off the lines."[9] Such allegations came frequently from workers victimized by carpal tunnel syndrome, a nervous disorder accompanied by numbness and swelling in the joints caused by frequent and repetitive movements. These and other inhumane conditions prompted a strike at Dayton that has lasted nearly two years.

The strike involves the aggressive United Food and Commercial Workers Union against traditionally anti-union Rocco. Since the original 500-worker walkout in June 1984, Rocco has softened its position somewhat by rehiring 300. However, hostile Rocco attempts to discredit the union have included barring union members from company property and organizing the majority of returning workers to sign a petition disowning the union. The controversy is presently lingering in the courts: the union has filed a $16 million federal suit against Rocco for bribery and racketeering.

The job growth in Robeson County, then, is a very mixed blessing. As some traditional jobs move overseas, they are replaced by lower-wage jobs in other areas, such as small cut-and-sew factories or the powerful and abusive poultry industries. But the most threatening economic news to date for Robeson County does not involve turkeys—as in many such counties, economic depression also provides the setting for hazardous wastes.

Enter Toxic-Waste Industries

In Robeson County, the scenario began in April 1984, when SCA Chemical Services announced an option to buy a forty-acre industrial site at the Laurinburg–Maxton Industrial Park in nearby Scotland County. The proposed operation was to be a chemical treatment plant for the detoxification and recovery of industrial hazardous wastes.

That proposal was followed in June 1984 by an announcement that U.S. Ecology planned to locate a low-level radioactive-waste incinerator in a black community in nearby Bladen County. To the citizens of the area, the handwriting was on the wall. Hazardous waste was beginning to migrate southward. Soon the Deep South would be known as the Dumping South. As Mac Legerton described the trend at the time, "You take a poor rural county, add a high minority population, and you have the most vulnerable community for the siting of massive waste treatment and disposal facilities. It is the same waste management equation that is being used all over the country."[10]

In fact, a number of national studies have documented the trend of locating hazardous-waste treatment facilities in rural, powerless, Southern communities, especially those where people of color live.[11] A 1983 report issued by the General Accounting Office entitled *Siting of Hazardous Waste Landfills and Their Correlation with Racial and Economic Status of Surrounding Com-*

munities noted, "Southeastern U.S. Blacks make up the majority of the population in three of four communities where hazardous waste landfills are located within EPA's eight-state Region IV. 26% of the population in all four communities have incomes below the poverty level and most of this population is Black." [12]

Recent state hazardous-waste trends and rural population compositions give residents of the coastal plain little to cheer about. As early as 1982, state officials located a polychlorinated biphenyl (PCB) landfill in Warren County, where 30 percent of the population lived in poverty and 60 percent was black. In the county of the proposed hazardous-waste facility, Scotland, 35 percent of the population is black, with 18 percent living below the poverty level. The figures grew even more significant for neighboring Robeson County, where Native Americans and blacks make up two-thirds of the population. [13]

The controversy heightened during September 1984, when British Columbia-based Genstar Corporation acquired 40 percent of SCA Chemical Services. Genstar immediately established GSX Corporation as a new waste-service subsidiary. Eventually GSX's hazardous-waste division would be transferred three times. GSX is now a subsidiary of the Canadian company Laidlaw Transportation. GSX's corporate strategy followed a national hazardous-waste industry trend. Through stock transfers and complicated corporate mergers, valuable parent assets could be insulated from lower-division liability claims.

Added concern arose when GSX acquired a hazardous-waste landfill in nearby Pinewood, South Carolina. This tiny black community has been saddled with the landfill since 1978. The controversial facility not only was polluting adjacent Lake Marion but was located directly on one of the most active underground aquifers in the Southeast. It was later confirmed that untreatable leachate from the landfill would eventually be shipped to the proposed GSX facility in Scotland County.

But of all the actors within this GSX drama, Robeson County was in the most pregnable position. If permitted at complete capacity, the GSX facility would receive wastes from ten states and other foreign countries. One of the chief concerns of Robesonians was the threat posed to the drinking water of Lumberton, the county seat. Standing only 4,000 feet from the Lumber River, and over county water wells, the GSX facility would eventually pump 500,000 gallons of treated wastewater per day into a municipal water-treatment system whose discharge was 30 miles upstream from Lumberton's intake. The potential surface-water contamination was an irreversible flaw in the GSX proposal. By the Environmental Protection Agency's own admission, GSX's discharge into a direct drinking-water source was unprecedented.

An already economically wounded Robeson County could not sustain a corporate neighbor such as GSX. As in most such cases involving siting of toxic-waste facilities, the industry used the promise of jobs and economic development to counter local citizens' concerns about the environment. However, research for the concerned citizens suggests that even such economic blackmail arguments are faulty.

The company claims that its presence will act as a magnet, drawing other industries and jobs to the area. Yet, according to the experience of Emelle, Alabama, where the world's largest chemical-waste landfill sits in a county that is 70 percent black, the only thing a toxic-waste industry attracts is more toxic waste. The only jobs the facility would create for Robeson's low-skilled labor force are low-pay, high-risk tasks in the handling and transportation phases of the treatment process. The desirable jobs will be awarded to the professional and technical specialists whose expertise most likely resides outside the confines of Robeson County. Physicists and biochemical engineers are about as rare in Robeson County as mountain ranges.

Future industry whose manufacturing depends on discharge access to surface water would be thwarted by the GSX proposal, which seeks to monopolize the remaining discharge consumption level of the Lumber River.

Real out-of-pocket costs to a public sector with an already low tax base stand to rise if GSX is permitted. Any tax revenue gained from GSX will be offset by increased expenditures for educating and training rural emergency preparedness agencies; maintenance and improvement to roads and bridges from expanded toxic waste rail and truck traffic; accident and spill cleanup, including victim and property compensation; decreased real property values adjacent to the hazardous-waste facility; and municipal waste treatment systems along the Lumber River. The city of Lumberton anticipates a capital outlay of more than $250,000 to upgrade its present waste treatment plant, and the city council has appropriated additional monies for future water wells outside the influence of the Lumber River and GSX.

Even the legal expenses connected with monitoring the impact of toxic-waste siting seriously strained the pursestrings of the local communities most threatened by the proposed hazardous-waste treatment facility. Early on in the GSX campaign, the governments of Robeson and Scotland counties and the city of Lumberton covenanted together to provide legal services against GSX, since the issue was expected to be decided in court. Bills for more than $250,000 have been incurred for lab research, consultants' testimony, attorneys' fees, and a host of other needed services. The municipal wastewater system, owned by the Laurinburg–Maxton Airport Commission, has spent thousands of dollars on research and testing in light of GSX's permit application for access to the airport's sewage treatment plant. Ultimately these costs are passed on to local taxpayers, whose meager incomes pale in significance beside the huge corporate bankrolls of GSX.

The Citizens Organize

In many poor minority communities, promises of jobs and economic development, however flawed they may be, serve to silence local concerns about the environment. In Robeson County, the Center for Community Action gave the community an organization through which to respond. In so doing, what might be considered a white, middle-class environmental issue became transformed into one of social and economic justice. Campaigns were led against both U.S. Ecology's proposal for a low-level radioactive-waste incinerator and GSX's proposal for a hazardous-waste treatment facility.

The U.S. Ecology campaign took two years but gave citizens their first experience in opposing hazardous industries. In this campaign, CCA joined forces with other citizens' groups and with the Sierra Club's radioactive-waste campaign, which provided research and scientific assistance. The two-pronged strategy—technical research united with a broad-based, triracial citizen organization—paid off. In January 1986, more than 4,000 citizens attended a public hearing in Fayetteville, North Carolina, to protest against the U.S. Ecology application. Within weeks, state officials denied two of the three permits needed by U.S. Ecology. By June 1986, the company had halted its efforts to construct the massive nuclear-waste incinerator in southeastern North Carolina.

Lessons from this campaign contributed to the battle against the GSX plan for a hazardous-waste treatment facility. Particularly confusing to state environmental decision makers was the way local Native Americans characterized GSX plans for the Lumber River as environmental racism. The river, more commonly known to most Lumbee Indians as the Lumbee River, is the very heart and soul of the largest nonreservation tribe east of the Mississippi River, most of whom live in Robeson County. To the Lumbee, the proposed location of a hazardous-waste treatment facility on their river was much more than an environmental menace; it was an attempt at cultural genocide.

Richard Regan, a Lumbee Indian, explains:

For the most part, as the Lumbee River goes, so goes the Lumbee Indians. Like the river, the Lumbees have a mystery, excitement, and violence in their history; and like the river they persevere. Despite not living on a reservation, the Lumbees have found their place along the river. We eat from, fish from, and swim in the river. We live and work on the river. We bathe in the river and farm its fertile edges. We were discovered by the Europeans on the river. Our very identity is wrapped up in the river. The river gave us isolation to develop community identity. It gave us protection from our many enemies. It gave us spiritual power to sustain our bodies and souls. While other Native American peoples cling to their sacred lands, the Lumbees claim the only river they have ever known, the Lumbee.

GSX and state officials were repeatedly warned by native Lumbees that strangers would not have the final word about their river. To the Lumbee, "Any day is a good day to die, and our river is something worth dying for."

Lumbee response to the GSX threat includes statements from such folks as Andrew Locklear, a seventy-two-year-old Indian who has fished the Lumber River for more than fifty years. "I wouldn't even think of eating a fish out of that river after they dump. They tell us the water would be safe to drink. Well, I'd like to see them process their chemicals, then fill up a glass and drink it themselves." [14]

A Lumbee second-grader read a letter to state officials during a recent GSX public hearing: "Please don't come and destroy our river. We will die without clean water. Please don't come. If you come, I'll cry until I die. Don't come, please. We wouldn't do nothing to hurt you so don't hurt our water. You wouldn't want your water polluted, and if you want to poison some water, get water from your house and poison it. We don't need your money, so keep your money." [15] Vernon V. Blackhorse of the Kau-Tu-Noh Society Singers and Dancers said shortly before performing at one GSX public hearing, "Not just the Tuscaroras, but all Indians in Robeson County are against GSX." [16]

Throughout the GSX campaign, every conceivable and practical component of Lumbee culture was used to its maximum effectiveness. Native American dance, music, and regalia were used at every major public hearing. Local Lumbee churches provided convenient meeting locations for GSX planning sessions. Leaflet distribution at these churches reached significant minority populations in every pocket of the county's nearly 1,000 square miles.

At a major barbecue fundraiser prior to the June 1987 GSX public hearing in Pembroke, Native American participation permeated the entire event. Ninety-five percent of the donated hogs came from Native American farms. A prominent Lumbee butcher and avid fisherman of the Lumber River prepared and readied the hogs for cooking. A local Lumbee vegetable farmer provided 300 pounds of cabbage for cole slaw. Three area Indian public schools processed the cole slaw. Another sister Native American tribe, the Tuscaroras, made supplies such as plates and utensils available. The largest Native American Methodist church east of the Mississippi, in the community of Prospect, brought enough pork 'n' beans for 3,000 people. The barbecue serving line was staffed by the local Indian agency, the Lumbee Regional Development Association. Practically all other needed supplies and materials were purchased from Indian businesses. Approximately 1,000 people were fed, and final proceeds from the sale were more than $1,500.

The protest against the hazardous-waste treatment facility in one of the poorest counties in the nation brought success to its citizens. On June 22, 1987, the North Carolina legislature passed legislation that would require a 1,000-to-1 dilution factor in any body of state surface water that serves a municipal drinking-water source and receives discharge from a hazardous-waste treatment facility. The new law forces GSX to either revise its proposed discharge from 500,000 gallons per day to approximately 72,000 gallons per day or abandon plans for the plant altogether. The bill passed by considerable margins in both the state house and senate, thanks to statewide concern about the GSX proposal and the implications for other state drinking-water sources.

Meanwhile, the District IV regional office of the Environmental Protection Agency (EPA) in Atlanta, which lobbied against the bill, threatened to take over North Carolina's environmental management, citing the "arbitrary and capricious" nature of the new law. Such removal of state control is unprecedented within the EPA, and appeared to be an attempt by the federal authorities to bypass local and state opposition to the treatment facility.

In response, the Center for Community Action took its grassroots campaign to Washington, where it enlisted the help of the Environmental Policy Institute, the Senate Committee on Environment and Public Works, and friendly employees at EPA to expose the agency's involvement in the siting decision. These efforts paid off when EPA agreed to meet with local citizens in Washington, and Raleigh, the state capital, to discuss state restrictions on hazardous-waste treatment.

The cumulative effect of this organizing forced four postponements of the scheduled hearings surrounding the law, a recommendation from one EPA administrator to drop the North Carolina challenge, and an indefinite postponement of the hearings until further notice. What began as a grassroots fight to save a river from pollution ended up forcing EPA to change some of its regulatory policies concerning state restrictions on hazardous-waste treatment.

At this writing, local citizens in Robeson County could cautiously declare a victory. For probably the first time, a poor, powerless community of color has protected and promoted a state environmental measure that surpasses federal standards for surface-water drinking sources. In an economically dependent county, local citizens did not succumb to economic blackmail—the promise of jobs over the environment. Theirs became a new strategy, one that balanced the promises of economic gain with an assessment of the economic, cultural, and environmental costs of toxic industries.

Conclusion

The victory over GSX was also a victory for eight years of work by the Center for Community Action to build community organization and community power in Robeson County. Rather than organizing around traditional interest groups or one-shot, issue-oriented campaigns, CCA builds its strength through local "cluster groups" in communities throughout the county. Each cluster group identifies its concerns and decides which issues to turn into campaigns. Cluster members, rather than hired staff or outside experts, participate in each step of the process, including doing research, identifying specific and realistic objectives, naming decision makers, developing effective strategies to get decision makers to the negotiating table, learning needed skills, starting, completing, and evaluating the campaign, and celebrating its victories. Realistic time frames for campaigns are established, so that the process can be evaluated and members do not become disempowered. When issues arise that call for the combined strength of the full organization, cluster groups will share and assist in united campaigns.

This method has proved to be very effective in increasing the participation of citizens and in accomplishing significant change. In the GSX campaign, the local group became the vehicle for mobilizing around what a proposed "economic development" would mean for our economy, our water, and our culture. In other campaigns, black neighborhoods have organized and obtained needed drainage from rain and flood water. Roads have been paved. In the native community of Pembroke, North Carolina, CCA members halted the construction of a major railroad line and persuaded company officials to pursue a safer, longer route through a more rural area of the county. New leadership has surfaced to provide a base for a new moral and political voice.

Victories over the policies and practices of major corporations, state and federal agencies, and local politicians are major accomplishments during these days of "doom and gloom" over the lack of citizen power and institutional accountability. Place these victories in the context of an economically dependent, predominantly low- and middle-income, black and Native American constituency, and the success is more profound.

NOTES

1. Kim R. Kenneson, "Colorful Sneakers Help Converse Rebound," (Raleigh) *News and Observer*, March 17, 1987, 10.
2. Ibid.
3. Roy Parker, Jr., "Robeson's Birthday Present: Jobs," *Fayetteville Times*, May 16, 1987.
4. Bob Horne, "Cut-and-Sew Plant Wise to Locate in Robeson County," (Lumberton) *Robesonian*, December 7, 1986.
5. Francesca Lyman, "Workers Treated Worse Than Turkeys," *Datelines*, March 18, 1987, 18.
6. Charles Jeffries, "Robeson to Get Turkey Plant," (Raleigh) *News and Observer*, May 12, 1987.

7. Lyman, "Workers Treated Worse Than Turkeys."

8. Ibid.

9. Ibid.

10. Gary Delgado, "Toxics and Minority Communities" (Oakland, Calif.: Alternative Policy Institute of the Center for Third World Organizing, July 1986), 1.

11. See, for example, Chapter 15 in this volume.

12. *Siting of Hazardous Waste Landfills and Their Correlation with Racial and Economic Status of Surrounding Communities* (Washington, D.C.: U.S. General Accounting Office, 1983), 1.

13. Ursula Baurer, "Hazardous Waste Facility Siting in North Carolina: A Case Study," part of an unpublished hazardous-waste siting study conducted by Rutgers University Center for Urban Policy Research, New Brunswick, N.J., 3.

14. Paul Roberts, "A River Too Good to Waste," *Fayetteville Observer*, June 23, 1987.

15. Crystal Quick, "More Speakers Oppose GSX at Hearing," *Laurinburg Exchange*, June 5, 1987.

16. Tom Mather, "Robeson Residents Assail Planned GSX Plant," (Raleigh) *News and Observer*, June 4, 1987.

CHAPTER

13

The Mayhaw Tree: An Informal Case Study in Homegrown Rural Economic Development

Ralph Hils

A short version of this story of grassroots economic development might go something like this: a group of concerned, courageous women decided to do something about the deteriorating economy in their rural southwestern Georgia county by starting a business to produce and export a distinctive local product for a particular market, thereby creating jobs and stimulating other local economic activity. So they did. And it worked. End of story.

Yet the story of the Mayhaw Tree, Inc., of Colquitt (Miller County), Georgia, is more than a past-tense account of one successful small business in the Southern hinterlands—even though it has attracted considerable attention from the media and the state government. The Mayhaw Tree's story is, rather, one of a continuing process, far from complete, which can tell us a great deal about people-originated economic development, including the complex of resources, determination, talent, and perceptions that generates and sustains it. This chapter attempts to describe some of that process as it has been played out over the past several years in one corner of the South's largest state. That description fittingly begins, like the enterprise described, with the mayhaw tree itself.

The Tree

A member of the *Rosaceae* family, which includes apples and nectarines as well as roses, mayhaws thrive in the wild among the swampy bays, limestone sinks, and riverine wetlands of the Gulf coastal plain. Early each May, these smallish trees (rarely taller than twenty-five feet) produce an abundance of tart applelike fruits about the size of cranberries. For as long as anyone can recall, people in the area have gathered these fruits as they ripened and fell from the trees, boiled the thin, pink pulps from the large seeds (or culls, as they're known locally), and made a remarkably tasty jelly from the resulting juice.

Like most wild trees and shrubs, the thorny mayhaws produce little or no fruit some years. In other years, including those since the founding of the Mayhaw Tree, the crop would be so plentiful that a person could easily scoop five gallons of the fruit from the shallow swamp pools in less than half an hour. Or, alternatively, individuals and entire families would make a day of harvesting mayhaws by shaking them from the trees onto sheets spread out on the ground. Traditionally, each household would put up enough jelly to last its members a year or two and still have some left for giving as gifts. And those who were unwilling or unable to get out into the swamp thickets to gather their own mayhaws would buy them from others, usually for $1 to $3 a gallon in recent times.

This cycle of gathering and preserving has gone on year after year in Miller County without interruption, even though various land reclamation projects, beginning in the Depression, decreased the mayhaw's habitat as bulldozers drained and filled wetlands to make them available for farming. Nevertheless, a sufficient area of swampy lands survives to ensure a good supply of mayhaws for anyone who cares to pick them up.

Mayhaws, therefore, in the contexts of their growth and use, are not regarded as resources or raw materials. Rural people value these trees for the gift of their fruit but also for the beauty of their blossoms and for their place in the overall ecology of the wetlands. Gathering mayhaw "berries" and turning them into food—especially a food more festive than mundane—draws people into the web of relationships that is the natural world. At the same time, it reinforces those webs of relationships that comprise the social and cultural worlds of the area. It is quite impossible, then, to appreciate a business based on processing and selling this wild food without at the same time attempting to appreciate the net of relationships, human and otherwise, from which such a business emerges and on which it depends.

Just as rural people don't take pails into the swamps to gather "raw materials," neither do they look at the jars of translucent, rose-colored jelly in their pantries and think "value-added product." A jar of mayhaw jelly, in its traditional setting, is a statement about relationships with one's surroundings, about family relationships, about the social rituals of eating together and gift giving, about the economic organization of a household that makes it possible to bring this food into its midst—from swamp to kitchen to table. It is, in fact, a bundle of cultural information that includes everything just mentioned and probably some vestigial memories of hunting and gathering activities as well. Understood in its cultural dimension, the Mayhaw Tree as a business does not lend itself readily to the usual terms and concepts of economic analysis. Its roots in the wild, in the kitchen-based nurturing activity of the family, and in the relationships among a larger rural community must first be noted and honored.

Economic development efforts that grow out of the informal economies of household and rural community differ qualitatively from development efforts driven solely by concern for the "bottom line."

Wendell Berry, the Kentucky farmer and writer, captured one such reality very succinctly in his observation that humans can add value to natural things but cannot originate that value. In other words, people can gather, process, and sell mayhaws; but they cannot create the conditions that permit the may-haw tree to flourish in the first place. Those who depend for a part of their livelihoods on mayhaws (whether in jelly or in cash derived from selling that jelly) must therefore act to ensure the continuation of that environment where the value underlying those livelihoods originates. Economic development efforts that understand the wetlands as "wasteland" and then "reclaim" that land for growing popwood or row crops threaten not only the indigenous wet-land ecology but the complex of lifeways humans have evolved to live in and with that ecology as well. Reclamation threatens to destroy part of the natural and cultural worlds in the name of economic growth; a commercial venture that derives from those worlds, on the other hand, creates economic growth precisely because it cooperates with those worlds.

Another reality underlying this kind of alternative economic development is its dependence on tradition and on the day-to-day realities of the household economy. Although household activities are not calculated as part of earning indices or the gross national product, they figure prominently in the lives of ordinary people—certainly in the lives of rural people. A jar of mayhaw jelly is the product of intense cooperation, not of intense competition. A jar of may-haw jelly is possible not because women are economically subordinate (as they are in the formal economy) but because they have the major role in carry-ing forward the traditions and practices of the household economy. Any busi-ness, therefore, that emerges from the contexts of the informal, rural economy will look and act differently from a business hatched in the conference rooms of corporate or government planners. And a large part of that difference can be explained by looking more closely at the people who create these alter-native businesses—in this instance, at the women who founded and run the Mayhaw Tree, Inc.

The Women

Like the tree for which their company is named, these women are south Georgia natives; three of them were born and raised in Miller County and the fourth moved there from Macon after her marriage. They have raised their families in Miller County and have been active in business, church, and community affairs for many years. When they decided, in the summer of 1983, to take some specific action to counteract the growing despair in the community because of the sagging agricultural economy, each was working full time in her chosen career. Joy Jinks was a social worker and nursing home consultant; Dot Wainwright covered eleven southwestern Georgia counties as a field representative of the American Cancer Society; Betty Jo Toole kept the books for several area businesses, including her family's Western Auto store; and Pat Bush worked with her husband in their business, Miller Electric.

In addition to working and raising their families, these women, with other women leaders in their town, initiated or actively supported several efforts aimed at improving the overall quality of life in their area. These projects included founding a nonprofit day-care center, which not only provides jobs for several women but also enables many poor women to work outside their homes. It was this group and their friends who came up with the idea of holding an annual Mayhaw Festival in Colquitt and sold the Merchants' Association on sponsoring it. (The festival has been held each spring since 1984.)

Joy Jinks serves as president of the chamber of commerce that they and their friends founded, Miller County's first. They also lent their active support to remodeling and renewing the Colquitt town square, to developing a city park, and to ongoing attempts to increase tourist traffic in the area. By any standard, these were successful women who had already made substantial contributions to the well-being of their community. Nevertheless, they were aware that their community and their county were in deep distress, that something more was needed.

As they tell it, they had gathered at a birthday party late that summer where the talk, as usual, reflected the community's gloom in face of increasing numbers of farm foreclosures and the precarious position of several agriculture-related businesses. Talking together, these women and some of their friends realized that if their economic situation was going to change for the better, they would have to take the initiative. As Joy Jinks put it, "We decided we were going to do something. We didn't know what, but we were going to do *something.*"

They began to meet regularly with six or eight other women who shared their readiness to act, holding what quickly became a series of informal economic analysis and planning meetings. They looked at the situation squarely and faced the reality that Miller County consistently ranked in the bottom third or quarter of all Georgia counties in the usual measures of economic growth or economic growth potential. At the same time, they recognized that their county always showed up in the top third or quarter when the state government published statistics on underemployment, educational disadvantage, illiteracy, poverty households, or health problems. They knew from their own family experiences that their county offered little to keep its young adults at home or to entice them to return after college or military service. They understood that Miller County's small population (7,000 people in 1984), lack of cultural amenities, and largely underskilled work force were most unlikely to attract the kinds of industry that state officials promoted as the key to economic prosperity in rural areas. Most of all, they came to terms with the realization that economic development was never going to come from the outside to "save" Miller County, that they were going to have to do it themselves. Furthermore, they knew that "themselves" meant the women. Many of the men, they decided, had become almost fatalistic about accepting the boom and bust cycles of agriculture, negative in their assessment of the county's potential, resistant to fundamental change in the status quo, and limited in their vision.

But they also spent time in their meetings exploring the possibilities of their situation as well. Joy Jinks describes how they went about their work:

It was very informal. We started out by looking at what had been done in the past or what had been attempted in the past. We have a small sewing plant here that employs some women, making women's undergarments. That puts some money into the economy. And there had been attempts in the past to attract some other industries, but nobody wants to come here. There's no skilled labor. There's really not enough people to employ.

We were all interested in employing women, in giving women an opportunity to earn money and to have an interesting job to do. We were also interested in using good management techniques with employees, giving them a voice in the planning and the work.

Our goal was to create some jobs, just create some jobs. We looked into several different kinds of work. Somebody told us there was a mobile home factory in Bainbridge that needed somebody to make drapes. We were interested in doing that, but it didn't work out. We talked about shipping pecans and peanuts. We gathered information and clippings from magazines about all the people who were shipping pecans, peanuts, and fruitcakes. We even tried to find people who could make pinestraw baskets. We made inquiries about people not too far from here who were making pottery and weaving. But we always would come back to the mayhaw jelly because the community was going to have its first Mayhaw Festival. That was the thing we had carved out for ourselves: the mayhaw. So we said, "What if the only place you could ever buy a peanut was the Peanut Festival in Sylvester? What if you could buy mayhaw jelly only at the Mayhaw Festival in Colquitt the second weekend each May?"

We kept coming back to the mayhaw jelly because we felt like there was a market for it, and it was something that had never been marketed. And people always say, "Why sure, it's the best jelly in the world!"

Again, it is useful to pause here and consider more closely who these women are and the significance of the story they tell about how they went about grassroots economic development. Such consideration may yield more operating principles for others interested in this approach.

In the first place, they made an effort to involve all the people concerned enough to spend their time and energy working toward an action plan. They did this informally, by "going around and talking it up" and by holding their weekly meetings over a period of months. Although the structure was informal, it proved effective in involving a broad range of community experience and insight.

Next, the people doing the analysis and the planning came from the community and were completely familiar with it. Because the women who met together shared a common history and knew the community's story, they were able to move rather quickly from analysis to planning for action. In short, they knew from their own life experiences the kinds of things it would have taken outsiders many months and many thousands of dollars to determine, as part of a state agency–run economic analysis, for instance.

Most important of all, perhaps, is the refusal of these women to accept paralyzingly negative perceptions of either their community or themselves, whether those perceptions came from within or beyond the community. Once they realized, for example, that they had been buying the notion that economic development was something that came *to* a community, they were able to free themselves to explore creative alternatives existing *within* their community. When they realized that the male leadership had bought into the fatalistic perception that the community was the victim of unmovable economic forces, they decided to take the initiative themselves rather than spend energy fruitlessly in trying to persuade the men to do something. And once they identified what they came to call "the Southern belle syndrome" (ladies don't concern themselves with things like economic development), they were able to move ahead without hesitation or apology.

And so several of the women who had been meeting decided to go into the jelly business.

The Business

As this is being written (December 1987), the Mayhaw Tree, Inc., is completing its fourth year in operation. In the fall of 1983 (well before the first Mayhaw Festival was held in Colquitt), eight women incorporated the company, selected its name, and invested $300 each to form its initial capital base. When the next crop of mayhaws became available, in the spring of 1984, they began purchasing mayhaw jelly made under contract by deli workers in a local supermarket and marketing it directly, with the Mayhaw Tree label, through gift and specialty food shows. In this way they were able to spend nearly a year realistically assessing the market for mayhaw jelly before opening their own production facility in a rented house early in the spring of 1985. And when it became evident that four of the original eight partners would be unable to devote the time demanded by this low-capital operation, the present four partners bought them out and added some additional capital funds as well. The Mayhaw Tree as a processing and a marketing entity, then, got underway on the strength of four women's investment of $1,300 each and the strength of their determination that they could demonstrate the potential of their community and their people.

After a move to another rented house with better kitchen facilities, where they began expanding their product line and refining their strategies for production and marketing, the owners finally moved the company to its present location, a small commercial building a few blocks from the town square, in the spring of 1986.

When the company began producing its own jellies independently early in 1985, it employed two full-time cooks. Today it employs five cooks in the equivalent of four full-time positions, one full-time person in charge of shipping, and upward of twenty part-time people when the mayhaws come in for processing, when large quantities of peppers and onions and cucumbers must be processed, and during the holiday giftbox packaging and shipping season. In addition to hiring part-time people, the company also relies on several dozen individuals and families who gather mayhaws and sell them to the company each spring. Because two-thirds of the company's total sales volume comes from its mayhaw products, it ensures a good supply of the fruit by offering gatherers the premium price of $5 per gallon. In 1985, the company spent $5,700 to purchase mayhaw berries; in 1987, $18,000. To demonstrate to the community the economic impact of just this one part of what some were condescendingly calling a cottage industry, the partners paid their pickers with $2 bills during the 1986 gathering season. When these $2 bills began showing up in grocery stores, gas stations, and dentists' offices, people began to get the message.

From the first, the partners realized that diversifying their product line would help to ensure the eventual success of their enterprise. They began by adding mayhaw wine jelly and, during 1985 and 1986, further expanded their offerings to include mayhaw syrup, green pepper jelly, cucumber jelly, Deep South salad dressing (which combines mayhaws and another unique Georgia product, Vidalia onions), and plantation ham sauce. In 1987 they expanded their line with the addition of low-sugar mayhaw jelly, Vidalia onion jelly, roasted and flavored pecans, and cheese–pecan pinwheel cookies, another traditional delicacy of the area. They have continued to experiment with various giftboxes as well as with various product combinations and quantities.

Like its product line, the Mayhaw Tree's gross sales have also grown rapidly during the company's first four years. In 1984 gross sales totaled more than $17,000. That figure more than doubled in 1985 to $45,000 and doubled again in 1986 to $96,000. Gross sales were up sharply in 1987. In the same period, the company's payments in wages and benefits went from $1,500 to $20,000. Although the company now shows a profit (on paper) in the neighborhood of 2 percent of gross sales, none of the partners has yet taken a salary or a return on her investment, preferring instead to reinvest the technical profit in developing new products, purchasing equipment, and expanding marketing efforts.

The conventional wisdom in the business world maintains that it takes at least five years for a new small business (if it survives that long) to show a profit. Clearly, the Mayhaw Tree has done better than that. But the growth of this business and its success as an example of grassroots economic development cannot be calculated solely in terms of increased sales or wages paid— important as these dollar values are to everyone concerned. Nor can its success be attributed solely to the partners' selective use of outside assistance of the kind provided by various state agencies (for example, the Small Business Development Centers, the Cooperative Extension Service, the Department of Industry and Trade, or Georgia Tech's Industrial Extension Service). The major element in this success story can only be found in the overall style of this company and the women who run it.

Joy Jinks works full time as manager of the operation. The other three women work part time, keeping the books, designing promotional materials, exploring new markets, servicing accounts, and working in the production and shipping areas during the busy seasons. All the partners share the work of traveling to, setting up displays for, and introducing their products at various fancy food and gift trade shows in Atlanta, New York, New Orleans, Orlando, and Dallas. They also set aside at least one full day each quarter to go off by themselves and review the total operation, develop strategies for the coming quarter, and brainstorm solutions to new or continuing problems. The results of these discussions are then presented to the regular employees for their feedback and suggestions. In this way, both partners and employees take an active role in determining the company's direction and keep the decision making thoroughly grounded in the realities of daily operation. But to get a feel for how this company works, it is necessary to visit its small plant across from a peanut warehouse at the edge of town.

The Mayhaw Tree's neat, white block building houses a small, well-lit, and attractively arranged product display area just in front of the large, clean kitchen—the heart of the operation. A small office space is tucked in between the kitchen and the large packing and shipping area. This area is linked to a walk-in freezer by a paved breezeway. The whole building is permeated by the sweet yet piquant aroma of cooking mayhaws—even when the kitchen is inactive. On a typical work day, a visitor will find women of two or three generations going about their tasks in the different areas. This activity generates an atmosphere of relaxed busyness not unlike the feel of a large kitchen where the women of an extended family have gathered to can tomatoes or prepare a fish fry. The most experienced cooks are grandmothers who tend to their work with the ease and economy of movement that comes only after many years devoted to the art of preparing food.

The way these women (men appear only as visitors, vendors, or delivery persons) relate to each other in this workplace seems to reflect the cordiality and mutual respect found among women's groupings in the larger community. No one seems hurried, and all the tasks seem to have been undertaken according to the talents and inclinations of the people involved. Employers and employees interact informally, even casually, despite differences in age and race. The overall ambience bespeaks pride in the work—and a tremendous amount of work gets done, too. The small size of the operation combined with the friendliness and mutual respect found within it would seem to promote the quality so characteristic of all the products made here. Clearly, no one here is a production unit or a faceless number.

But this company is not some small-business version of Utopia either. It competes nationally with other small producers of fancy foods, many of whom receive substantial technical and financial assistance from their state governments in marketing their products. Vermont, for instance, not only pays the shipping costs to get its producers' wares to the trade shows, it rents space for their displays as well. The state of Georgia provides no such assistance to encourage the growth of its homegrown businesses. As a result, the Mayhaw Tree has to absorb shipping and display costs (which can easily exceed $1,000 per show) and thereby compete at a comparative disadvantage. Furthermore, because the company has received no effective help from those state programs designed to enable producers to enter the international marketplace, it is forced to purchase its considerable supplies of sugar at the federally subsidized domestic price or three times the world market price available to producers who export overseas. Another structural disadvantage the company faces is the lack of commercial freezer space nearby. Because the partners cannot rent the space they need to store a year's supply of frozen mayhaws and mayhaw juice, they pay an enormous monthly electric bill to operate their own large freezer, thereby greatly increasing their overhead expenses.

Even more telling than these disadvantages is a contradiction that springs from the nature of the enterprise itself: it is almost impossible to reduce labor costs when the product is labor intensive. Other businesses can cut labor costs by automating or by creating high turnovers in production personnel, or both. But this business depends on product quality, which is possible only when most of the work is done by hand and done by experienced employees. Because the partners cannot reduce their costs in the usual ways (and in some instances would not even if they could), they are forced to spend an enormous amount of energy attending to the dozens of smaller ways they can find to lower costs and improve efficiency. Dealing with these ongoing problems and coping with the small crises that afflict any business require continual hard work and fierce commitment from all concerned.

Even though this overview of the Mayhaw Tree's growth and development as a business has been necessarily brief, it, too, contains some matters of underlying significance that ought to be stated directly. And here again, as in the other aspects of this enterprise already discussed, human and cultural factors are prominent.

The Mayhaw Tree, as a business, operates more like an extended family than a corporation. Just as in an extended family, everyone involved has input on decision making commensurate with their responsibilities. The experience of the elders in the operation is valued and the benefit of their wisdom actively solicited. The members of this business family, like multigenerational families at their best, work together to discover how each can best contribute to the good of all while at the same time helping each other to grow in responsibility. Building a business on the model of the extended family is one way to make creative use of one of the great strengths of rural communities—the persistence of family and clan ties. And it is precisely this family support system that enabled these women to launch this venture and see it through as they have.

In its products, too, this company remains faithful to its cultural roots. Some observers have attributed the Mayhaw Tree's success to the uniqueness of its main products, claiming that this enterprise is not repeatable in rural areas lacking an equivalent unmarketed resource. But what in fact is so distinctive about this enterprise is not its mayhaw jelly or mayhaw syrup but the simply reality that *all* its products come directly from the cooking traditions of the area or creative extensions of traditional recipes. It can easily be argued that the success of this business comes not from packaging mayhaw jelly but from presenting a distinctive cultural expression in a dignified and respectful way.

Also, like careful homemakers, the women of the Mayhaw Tree look for ways to create something appealing and marketable from what less observant or experienced people would consider waste. For example, cucumbers too large to meet the criteria of commercial picklers are considered culls, left to rot or sold very cheaply. But it is just these large or overripe cucumbers that make the best jelly. And ounce for ounce, the jelly sells for three or four times the price of pickles.

It seems evident that faithfulness to the traditions of the local culture, both in production and in product, means more to enterprises like this one than any actual or perceived uniqueness of the product. Novelty, at best, attracts customers just one time—fad buying, it's sometimes called. But purchasers will pay a premium price for mayhaw syrup or pepper jelly because these products allow them to participate in, literally to get a taste of, a distinctive culture very remote from their own. And these same purchasers will reorder the products not because of their novelty (which disappeared after the first purchase) but because of the quality that only small-batch preparation and careful handling can confer—a quality absent from mass-produced foods.

It is worth noting, too, that the women who began this business began it conservatively. They elected the option most likely to succeed in their circumstances and their community, the option that required no special education or training, no high start-up costs, and no indebtedness to any lending institution. Had they discovered no market interest in mayhaw products, they would have lost relatively little, at least relatively little money. So far, at least, they have shown themselves equally conservative in guiding the growth of their company. Its growth has paid for itself, in dollar terms, because the partners have relied on another conservative tactic, sweat equity investment. Anyone contemplating similar grassroots economic development efforts would do well to pay attention to these conservative maneuvers and to believe, as these women do, in the efficacy of hanging in for the long haul.

Finally, it must be said that this business is making a difference in Miller County as a business and as a sign of possibility. The number of dollars it brings into the community and the number of times those dollars change hands make a difference, particularly in a county so lightly populated. This is, as these women have often said, more than a business; it's a statement from one rural community written off as an economic disaster area to other such rural communities. It's a statement that says rural and small-town folk can still do for themselves. The governor's proclamation honoring the Mayhaw Tree and the women who founded it calls these women "an inspiring example to other entrepreneurs across the state." And he's right. But one suspects these women have worked so hard for so long not so much to prove themselves as enterpreneurs but to demonstrate their determination to do all they can to ensure the survival of their community, their land, and their traditions. And that, finally, is what economic development should be about.

Conclusion

It's probably premature at this time to try to assign any absolute significance to the Mayhaw Tree as an example of alternative, community-based economic development strategy. Nevertheless, it does have about it features that, viewed in the larger contexts of history and traditional economic development policies as practiced by Georgia and other Southern states, are compellingly suggestive.

The South has always suffered from development policies built on the economics of extraction. The region's coal, gold, copper, timber, and fiber products have always created wealth for distant processors of those materials or for absentee owners of those resources. And what has always been left behind are corrupted government officials, exhausted soils, exhausted people subject to exploitation and dislocation, and devastated local economies. The historical economic development policies of slavery for many, forcible removal for some, wealth and power for a small elite, political and economic servitude for virtually everyone else, and wholesale contempt for both the land and the values of the traditional peoples on the land provide an unpromising background for today's official development policies.

In a word, the economics of extraction are still very much with us. This can be seen quite clearly in Miller County. More peanuts are produced in Miller and its neighboring counties than anywhere else on this continent. Yet none of these counties has a facility for providing value-added processing of these peanuts. Both the peanuts and their economic potential continue to leave the state. As long as the state of Georgia continues to expend tax revenues that perpetuate the structures of extraction and exploitation, it cannot be expected to provide much support or encouragement to alternative economic development approaches.

One wonders what might happen if some significant portion of the state's economic development budget went to identifying new opportunities for rural enterpreneurs and researching the expansion potential of existing rural businesses. One wonders what might happen if the considerable resources spent on trying to get runaway industries to stop a while in Georgia on their way to Mexico or Singapore were to be spent on researching ways to decentralize the information industry and use the new electronic technologies to spread that industry into the state's rural counties. One wonders, too, what might happen if money now spent on finding ways to increase the production of grains already glutting the market were to be used instead to create a low-interest loan fund for new small businesses out in the small towns.

The Mayhaw Tree and dozens of other small businesses like it are the real hope for economic stability in rural Georgia. They demonstrate that local people can make a difference even when state government is minimally responsive to their vision and their needs. Most of all, they demonstrate that the South's traditional dependence on the economics of exploitation and extraction can be broken, that rural Georgians can recover control of their economic destinies without giving away or destroying rural Georgia.

Since this chapter was written, the Mayhaw Tree has successfully completed its critical fifth year as a small business and is well into its sixth. During this period, its owners have helped to bring about a significant shift in the attitudes and practices of various state agencies. Georgia, like Vermont, now helps to sponsor its specialty food producers at trade shows; a special foods and wine producers association has been formed under the auspices of the state agricultural department; the state is using its resources to help the Mayhaw Tree and other small companies enter international markets, notably the Japanese market.

Part II

VISIONS FOR
THE FUTURE

Development
by Corporate Design

THE IMPACT of the global economy reaches into every corner of our nation. Joblessness and the economic decline of communities bind together not only the Black Belt South and the coalfields of Appalachia, but also the farmers of the Midwest and the oil workers of Texas, the shoe workers of New England and the auto workers of Detroit. The atmosphere of scarcity—scarce jobs, scanty budgets, diminished public services—has encouraged state governments to devise extravagant and often ill-advised schemes to lure industry, and has forced some workers to accept lowered wages and more dangerous working conditions. Some call this competitive equality; others call it extortion.

The chapters in this section explore some central themes, common to all areas of our nation, in this process of "development by corporate design." Carter Garber analyzes the many hidden costs associated with General Motors's famous Saturn plant, which was attracted to tiny Spring Hill, Tennessee, by promises of tax breaks and other incentives. Chapter 14 raises numerous questions about the role of state officials in economic development and the potential role of community groups in appropriating greater control over their local economy.

Robert D. Bullard explores a form of "development" that has become common in poor communities, often rural communities of color: hazardous-waste disposal. While exposing the racist dynamics that have guided hazardous-waste siting, in Chapter 15 Bullard also points out the new and hopeful alliances between civil rights advocates and environmentalists that have arisen in opposition to this industrial practice.

Perhaps no economic trend is so pervasive or familiar as the growth of the service sector. In Chapter 16 Cindia Cameron examines the quality of work among one large group of service workers, office workers; she suggests that their low pay, lack of job security, and other problems are part of larger economic trends that are creating a "new work force." Characterized by marginal job status, a rising proportion of part-time and temporary work, and a high level of female and minority employment,

173

this new work force presents both obstacles and opportunities for those who seek to organize workers for better treatment on the job.

Ann Seidman concludes this section by situating the economic problems of Southern workers and communities in a global context (see Chapter 17). By identifying the many links between workers in the U.S. South and those in southern Africa, Seidman argues persuasively that there can be no long-term community-oriented development in the United States in the absence of greater political freedom and economic prosperity in the Third World.

CHAPTER

14

Saturn: Tomorrow's Jobs, Yesterday's Myths

Carter Garber

Saturn is providing tomorrow's jobs while preserving yesterday's values.

> —*Lamar Alexander,*
> *former governor of Tennessee*

Saturn is the pattern for the twenty-first-century industrial operation.

> —*J. L. Kewandowski, vice-president,*
> *Saturn Corporation*

We didn't have any real estate offices in Spring Hill before Saturn hit. The next day we had five. . . . Land speculators blew into town with money in hand, bought land, and flipped it.

> —*Joan W. Jackson, manager*
> *of the only bank in town*

More and more it looks like GM came to this rural area of Tennessee looking for a colony to exploit instead of a community to respect . . . . The Volunteer State better start volunteering more citizen and governmental oversight and get the free-loading GM off welfare.

> —*Ralph Nader*

On July 30, 1985, General Motors (GM) announced its decision to locate a $3.5 billion automobile plant making the new Saturn model thirty miles south of Nashville in the town of Spring Hill, Tennessee.

Governor Lamar Alexander trumpeted his state's victory in full-page newspaper ads around the country. The prize was a considerable one, for the competition for the plant had been unprecedentedly fierce. Said to be the largest one-time investment in U.S. history, Saturn has taken on almost mythical dimensions and qualities in the public mind.

But what is the real benefit of "winning Saturn," and what is the cost? Why didn't the plant go to one of the obvious high bidders like New York or Minnesota? Why did Saturn choose an agricultural community whose residents did not particularly want it while avoiding areas prepared for industry that anxiously sought it?

If the primary benefit is jobs, why aren't local people assured of being hired? If the primary benefit is tax revenues, why does the county make concessions that let the company pay only a third of what everyone else pays?

With the enticement of 6,000 manufacturing jobs and the fear of bungling their opportunity, the state, the county, and the workers were all willing to accept GM demands that they might otherwise have opposed. But once the deals had been cut, GM announced it had made a "minor" miscalculation—it would invest $1.75 billion instead of $3.5 billion. That also meant 3,000 jobs, not the 6,000 initially projected.

For decades the South has based its economic development strategy on luring industry from outside the region. This chapter looks at the region's largest industrial recruitment "success" to see if the strategy delivers on the three goals of the state government that recruited it: providing jobs for locals, improving the tax base, and increasing the quality of life for those who live nearby. It also concentrates on the decision-making role that local people played—or failed to play—in the effort to improve their community economically.

Winners Unprepared for the Prize

GM's July 1985 announcement startled citizens and elected officials in Spring Hill, Tennessee (population 1,275). Mayor George Jones said that he and county officials "learned about it the same day you did, if you were watching television. . . . It was like a star falling from the sky."

Spring Hill is an unlikely spot for one of the world's most technologically advanced manufacturing plants. Just off Interstate 65, which cuts through Tennessee's horse-raising country on its way from Nashville to Birmingham, the town lies among rolling meadows, dairies, and cornfields. Downtown Spring Hill is a strip about three quarters of a mile long of stores and businesses interspersed with houses. A branch of the First Farmers and Merchants Bank competes with the Bi-Rite grocery for status as the true center of town.

The double-wide trailer that serves as town hall is parked next to the new elementary school. Near the north end of town stand the two main social centers: the Poplar House Restaurant and the Auction Barn. The side streets are so narrow that pickup trucks have difficulty passing.

In mid-1985 Spring Hill had no full-time police officers, no fire department, no resident doctor. Of more interest to GM, it also had little experience negotiating with large companies, few other prospects for economic development, no countywide planning or zoning, no organized citizen groups to oppose the company, and no history of the labor–management antagonism that characterizes many of GM's plant sites.

Saturn, Key to Survival for GM

Spring Hill residents are minor actors, perhaps even pawns, in a grand manuever by GM and the domestic auto industry. Saturn, a subcompact, represents the company's main effort to face down Japanese car competition. GM has created the Saturn Corporation as a subsidiary with its own executives, engineers, and dealer network—and a "special" labor contract. Using computer and robot technology, the Saturn plant will eventually produce half a million cars a year with about one-third of the work force other GM facilities would need. Board chairman Roger Smith touts the Saturn operation as the key to the giant corporation's survival and competitive success as a domestic producer. Limited production is expected to begin in 1990 with 250,000 cars a year.

Communities for Sale

When GM announced on January 8,1985, that it was looking for a Saturn site, a bidding war broke out among thirty-eight states. More than 1,000 communities sought to be home for America's largest industrial investment. Twenty-six governors (including those from Alabama, Arkansas, Georgia, Kentucky, Texas, Virginia, and West Virginia) made the pilgrimage to Detroit, bearing gifts of tax breaks, land deals, new public facilities, and worker-training grants. Missouri's governor boasted of a "staggering offer" and rented three billboards in Detroit urging, "Give Us a Ring." Another billboard pleaded, "Chicago Wants You." Youngstown, Ohio, proclaimed its need for jobs through promotions by boxer Ray "Boom Boom" Mancini, a 100-car caravan to Detroit, and 200,000 letters from local residents and school children.

The states' recruitment efforts were substantial and extraordinarily expensive. Kentucky's legislature passed a $306 million educational aid package when it learned that GM considered its educational system inferior. New York's state legislature passed a bill to give Saturn 100 megawatts of free hydro-electric power for twenty years—a billion-dollar savings. Michigan offered substantial incentives to remain the center of the auto industry: $250 million in aid over ten years, $250 million in local property tax relief over twelve years, $65 million in job training, $35 million in training for suppliers' employees, a health and a day-care center, and an ombudsman to cut red tape. Michigan's governor promised to "beat any offer." Minnesota's inducements were worth at least $1.2 billion. Included were a thirty-year tax holiday, free child care for imported workers, and relocation monies and subsidized mortgages for top management.[1]

With so many suitors, GM was able to take its time. The national media provided tens of millions of dollars of free advertising for the future car. A GM-commissioned poll showed that by mid-1985 Saturn had 49 percent name recognition among the American public, even though no plant had been built, no product designed. Now, more than three years after the original announcement, GM still does not have a design. Yet it already has a success. This unparalleled public relations triumph, achieved largely because of Americans' desperation for jobs, is proudly heralded by Saturn's executives.

Was Tennessee Just Lucky?

Governor Lamar Alexander and former Senate Majority Leader Howard Baker lauded Tennessee's right-to-work law, its "pro-business climate and its hardworking labor force" to GM's Smith in early 1985. These euphemisms are characteristically used by government officials in selling the South as an exploitable region. The governor and the senator may not have actually mentioned it, but Smith's computers told him that Tennessee was in the bottom 20 percent of states in maximum benefits for disability and unemployment, in statutory protection for workers. Nor would the wage demands be great; Tennesseans are forty-second nationally in the incidence of working poor and near the bottom in terms of manufacturing wages and income distribution.[2] Since Tennessee is projected to have higher than national unemployment at least through the 1990s, this is a state that would appreciate GM—whatever its pay and benefits—for a long time to come.

Tennessee was also promoted as a state that would not be very taxing to GM. Tennessee's tax structure has been amended repeatedly for the benefit of big business: a 1 percent investment tax credit for industrial machinery, no sales tax on industrial and pollution-control machinery, a tax exemption on finished goods, a low workers' compensation insurance rate, and no personal income tax. More than 49 percent of the state's tax revenue comes from high sales taxes, which include a tax on food. Tennessee's ads announce, "Grow with a pro-business tax structure. Only four states have a lower state and local tax burden than Tennessee. Tennessee does not offer large tax concessions to attract business to the state—the tax structure is already attractive for business!" Tennessee's state government expenditures per capita and school revenues are among the lowest in the nation.[3]

With the nation watching and with his 1988 national political aspirations in mind, Tennessee's governor eagerly courted GM. Alexander, who had won one such prize—a Nissan plant—wanted another. In 1982 Nissan made the largest Japanese industrial investment in the United States at a highly automated truck and car assembly plant in Smyrna, thirty miles from Spring Hill. Ironically, his earlier success may have been the best guarantee of his second win. Since GM wanted to prove it could compete with the Japanese, why not do it on the same turf? Some of the leadership of the United Auto Workers, GM's partner in Saturn, also wanted to locate nearby in hopes that Saturn's union influence would rub off on nonunion Nissan.

Why Spring Hill and Maury County?

GM's choice of middle Tennessee joins the Southbound wave for car manufacturing facilities, including the Smyrna Nissan plant and the Toyota facility in Scott County, Kentucky. Michigan has gone to extraordinary lengths to preserve its hold on the industry, but it is clear that for both U.S. and Japanese car makers, the mid-South has become the location of choice.

In addition to its "docile" labor, Spring Hill was chosen because it lies within 500 miles of three-fourths of the U.S. domestic market. The area has a railroad and interstates and could provide 4 million gallons of water daily. In the rural setting, there were a small number of landowners from whom to acquire the 2,450-acre site.

The site GM chose lies a few miles from Maury County's border with Williamson County, Tennessee's richest and fastest-growing county, with an unemployment rate of 3.1 percent in July 1986. County Executive Robert Ring says about Saturn, "It's definitely not good for our county. I wish they had gone somewhere else." Williamson County residents are concerned about the rapid changes in their county, which is changing from an agricultural to a bedroom community feeding metropolitan Nashville's booming "office parks." The result is a controversial growth management plan that is unprecedented in the *laissez-faire* countryside of Tennessee.

Over the line in Maury County, with 9.6 percent unemployment, the planning mechanism was nonexistent. Judy Langston, a county native hired when the planning office was finally set up three months after Saturn's announcement, explains: "Maury County government did not have any land use controls, policies, or plan. We did not have any zoning or subdivision controls at all and there was not a planning commission as such." Langston and the new planning commission have worked quickly "to get the county ready to start dealing with the growth that's coming." [4]

What Did Tennessee Offer?

In an intriguing, although less than candid, statement Governor Alexander bragged, "New York offered $1.2 billion. We didn't offer a penny." [5] What did Tennessee really offer?

In addition to the usual benevolence to large corporations, the governor promised Saturn $50 million worth of roads, including a new interstate exit and a $30 million, 5-mile-long, connecting "Saturn Parkway." Spring Hill is getting a bypass, two stoplights, state-paid planners and engineers. Maury County received some $2 million from the state for increased costs of county services. The state promised $21.8 million worth of job training under Saturn control, with no requirement that Tennesseans would be trained.

Legislature Greases GM's Wheels

Tennessee's General Assembly rushed to provide housewarming gifts to the new corporate neighbor. In early 1986 Maury County legislators introduced a bill that would put a $500,000 cap on the realty transfer tax and another cap on mortgage fees. Written to benefit very large plants "such as Saturn," the bill represented a prior agreement among legislators, Saturn officials, and the governor. As a result, the state lost a one-time payment of $2.5 to $3 million; local governments lost $75,000. When he learned that General Motors badly wanted states to pass seat belt laws (to fend off federal pressure for auto manufacturers to install air bags in new cars), the governor mustered enough votes in the legislature to pass such a law. [6]

Much of the intense courting of Saturn was inspired by the lure of thousands of new jobs. But four months after Saturn's site selection, a copy of the secret labor agreement between GM and the United Auto Workers (UAW) leaked to the Spring Hill Area Concerned Citizens Group revealed that "a majority of the full initial complement of operating and skilled technicians in Saturn will come from GM–UAW units throughout the United States." [7]

Maury County officials were stunned. The disclosure came only a week after they had agreed to large tax concessions, allowing the corporate giant to pay only a third of the regular rate. They said they had done this in the expectation that the majority of jobs would be for area residents. The Citizens

Group leaders had been asking the county since early September to obtain a commitment that 80 percent of the Saturn work force would come from the county and the state. GM says it made no promises.

By July 1986 UAW Vice-President Donald Ephlin reported that union members all over the country were interested in the Saturn jobs. "We don't ..eed applications. Every day I get letters inquiring about employment." While 6,000 jobs were originally projected, Saturn now estimates 3,000 new jobs will be created—which could be filled eighteen times over by the 54,000 UAW members already laid off at other locations at the time of the site announcement.

GM Unwilling to Pay Full Property Tax

Tennessee helped Saturn choose a county with lower property tax rates than surrounding areas. Saturn then hammered Maury County officials into an unprecedented forty-year in-lieu-of-tax agreement. According to county budget director A. C. Howell, "The forty-year length was the toughest part and the part that the county disliked most about the deal. We really didn't want a forty-year deal. It was a GM idea and they took pretty much a hard line on it." GM's leverage was that its choice of this county was "tentative" until it got the deal it wanted. By withholding the UAW labor agreement from the public and county officials, GM had a further advantage.

Maury County's industrial board agreed to hold title to the site so that Saturn would not be burdened with real and personal property taxes, the county's primary revenue source. Instead, Saturn agreed to follow a separate in-lieu-of-tax schedule. The first year Saturn agreed to pay $7.5 million; in 1987 and 1988, $3.5 million each year; from 1989 to 1995, $3 million each year; and from 1996 to 2025, a rate starting at 25 percent and rising to 40 percent of the standard property tax rate. The county was pleased at being able to negotiate the larger amounts up front, since normally the property tax would not show up in significant amounts until the plant was fully built. "The plan of action is to use the front-end money to handle the initial impacts. Then we'll have to develop some mechanisms to make sure future developers have to pay their own way," says Howell.[8]

Some local residents and officials were skeptical of the deal, especially when they learned that most "high-growth" counties in other parts of the country find it impossible to make developers cover all the costs of new services. If Saturn does not pay for expanded services and if the developers who follow Saturn to Maury County do not, who will? The residents of Maury County, who currently enjoy a low 2 percent property tax rate, expect that they will have to pick up the tab.

Although the details are spelled out in an official agreement, estimates still differ on just how much the county has given away to GM. Ralph Nader has estimated that the in-lieu-of-tax deal will cost Maury County almost $57 million during the first ten years.[9] Budget director Howell figures that if the plant is built as proposed, "the full tax value [without concessions] would have been $14 million" annually, less than half the $32 million figured by the state comptroller's office and others. Even if Howell's estimate is accurate, this means that after construction during the seven-year period from 1989 to 1995, GM will pay $77 million less than the normal county tax rate.

Jim Musselman, a Nader researcher, points out that Maury County officials failed to compare what GM said it was willing to pay in property tax with what it was already paying at its facilities in Michigan and Ohio. GM wasn't about to volunteer the information: it pays almost twice as much tax on smaller-sized plants. Howell says the county did talk to a few places during the eight weeks of negotiations, but he wished there had been more time. While the company clearly benefited from the sense of time pressure, Howell says the greatest urgency came from state officials, who wanted an agreement to be reached but refrained from offering much assistance.

On February 28, 1986, Saturn ceremoniously made its first tax payment of $2 million. Its next checks were delivered in late May and September to the Maury County Industrial Development Board. Posing in front of the enlarged check, Howell wondered whether he should smile or frown. "It probably is not the best deal in the world but when you go to buy a car you don't get the deal you want. I can't tell whether it was a good deal or not. I think it was as good a deal as we could have gotten. . . . History will tell."

Will the Town Get Its Fair Share?

"Let's be honest," the mayor of Spring Hill exclaimed in late August 1985. "The plant is going to affect us the most. While the county negotiated over the property tax, we're the ones who are going to be dealing with the traffic and having our roads and our land and our homes torn apart. Nobody seems to be interested in Spring Hill."

For several weeks, state officials, Saturn, and the UAW ignored the mayor's requests for a meeting with the townspeople to explain plans and to answer citizens' questions. Only in September 1985, when Mayor George Jones warned that he might oppose zoning changes needed for initial construction, did the three groups agree to the town meeting.

Spring Hill's annual property tax revenue was around $21,000 before any GM payments. A recent property reappraisal had the effect of a major tax hike, and Mayor Jones did not want to raise taxes again to pay for new facilities. When the mayor's efforts to get a financial commitment from the county and GM failed, the city council began the procedure to annex the Saturn site, just two miles outside the city limits. This would have brought the town an estimated $8.5 million annually, instead of the $11.5 million over a forty-year period to which they eventually agreed.

When he learned about the annexation plan, Saturn's general counsel threatened that GM would leave the Spring Hill area before the company had turned one shovel of dirt. "I don't know if I'd call it blackmail," Mayor Jones told the *Flint* (Michigan) *Journal.* "I have heard accusations before that if we don't this or that, Saturn will pull out." Jones reports that during this period he received a number of death threats from developers who feared they would lose substantial profits if GM did not come.

Spring Hill's threat to annex Saturn's property, followed by Saturn's threat to leave, is credited with giving the town enough leverage with Maury County to get a larger part of the in-lieu-of-tax money. To obtain $250,000 annually, Spring Hill promised in writing not to annex the Saturn site.[10]

Speculators Descend

"We didn't have any real estate offices in Spring Hill before Saturn hit. The next day we had five," says Joan W. Jackson, the manager of the only branch bank in town. "Land speculators blew into town with money in hand, bought land, and flipped it." Two months after the announcement, land values had risen from between $1,000 and $2,000 per acre to between $5,000 and $10,000, with some land selling for as much as $35,000 per acre. Activity tripled at the county's register of deeds, which garnered more than $1 million in recording fees and transfer taxes. During the early "gold rush fever," the mayor distributed signs: "My home is not for sale. Compliments of George Jones, Mayor." He explained, "I want my neighbors to know I want to keep them."[11]

Word of the boom attracted displaced workers from around the region and the nation. As they began to come to the boom town, Mayor Jones and the board of aldermen bought them one-way tickets to Columbia or Nashville. A policeman would take the indigent newcomers to Main Street and flag down the bus (which is the only way to stop it). Legal Services personnel worry that the bus trip may await some local people as well. After Nissan was built nearby, local people with low incomes became homeless as property values rose. "The rental situation here is already deplorable," says Bill Haley, Legal Services director, based in Maury County. "We're going to see local people evicted as the landlords jack up rents to lease to outsiders. Every county in the area has a long waiting list for low-income housing now. With the tremendous real estate pressures, homelessness is going to be an overwhelming problem and the counties are doing little to address it." [12]

With the arrival of the county's largest taxpayer, local residents are afraid they will not be able to afford to stay. "It will be the people on fixed income who will suffer," says Mayor Jones. Retired schoolteacher Martha Torrence agreed. "We who are trying to continue here might have to move out of the area because of taxes."

Homeowners are not the only victims. Randy Lockridge, who farms 1,000 acres, declares that Saturn, named after the Roman god of agriculture, "will ruin farming in Spring Hill and have a negative effect on farming in all of Maury County." Dairy equipment supplier John Campbell, president of the Citizens Group, agrees that "farming's a thing of the past in Spring Hill." The closed farm implement dealership in town and the rapidly rising land prices seem to affirm his conclusion. "Many people in the community who were in favor of the project have now turned against it after seeing the way GM operates," Campbell says.

In the wake of recent elections, landowner Jim Cathey said, "We really should be voting on getting that plant here." Cathey's words echo the thoughts of thousands of Southerners suddenly faced with the rapid changes and unintended results of development decisions made secretively by a few state or local officials in pressured negotiating sessions with outside giant corporations. There are no mechanisms for public participation, much less citizen approval.

Making Modern Mythology

To all concerned, the Saturn myth is far more important than the reality. This is why the Saturn operation, which in reality is nothing more than another branch plant locating in the rural South, has captured the national imagination.

To GM, the Saturn myth represents a resurgence in thirty-eight states of the time-honored idea that "what's good for GM is good for the country." It has found that even corporate giants can be given the aid and comfort Americans usually reserve for underdogs.

The legendary dimensions of Saturn have built political careers and justified raids on public treasuries from the county to the federal level. Even in the 1986 tax reform bill, Congress showed its support by writing in a special $60 million tax break specifically for Saturn. [13]

For the union and the industry, the Saturn myth has come to symbolize the "pattern for the twenty first century industrial operation," according to Saturn's vice-president J. L. Kewandowski. The union is willing to forgo hard-fought contract elements such as seniority and grievance systems for a chance to be a partner in this undertaking.

The shiny, state-of-the-art features of the new Saturn car seem to vindicate the public's desire to believe in reindustrialization—proof that the glories of Henry Ford's revolution can come back in a high-tech form.

For Tennessee and Maury County, Saturn's myth is that the industrial recruitment lottery game can be won. There is now hope that young people will not have to leave their rural homes to find jobs. There is the illusion that our local and state officials are in charge, even as they carry out decisions made in faraway corporate boardrooms.

Despite the tremendous odds against them, communities across America have gone into a period of self-flagellation and self-blame because GM did not choose them. Most have learned nothing from the massive expenditures of time and money. They have fallen back on the losers' dictum, "Try harder next time."

In the wake of the Saturn success, the governor's State of the State speech instilled fear in the legislature that, if they didn't pass his $3 billion roads program (euphemistically called "jobs corridors"), they would lose the Saturn suppliers to one of the eleven other states within 250 miles of the new plant site. Similarly, better schools, higher sales taxes, and many other unrelated governmental items are justified to Americans on the basis of industrial recruitment.[14]

Why are Americans so vulnerable to such mythology? Because there simply are not enough jobs to go around. Saturn has proved that states, even unions, are willing to do almost anything for a few of them. A few is all Saturn will provide. While the optimistic combined number of 20,000 eventual plant and related jobs sounds impressive, Governor Alexander in more candid moments put that figure in perspective: 170,000 jobs, 10 percent of the state's total work force, were lost in 1983 to plant closings, bankruptcies, and shutdowns.[15] Saturn's *total* job impact—12 percent of what is lost annually in one state—has to be considered in the context of the overall job structure.

When industrial recruitment succeeds, few will bother to look beyond the comforting myths to the reality. Maury County now is a living example—and the real effects will not be known for years. What is known is that the usual goals of industrial recruitment—jobs for locals, a better tax base, community improvement, and an era of progress for residents—have not materialized. Many long-term residents have little hope that they ever will.

"Tomorrow's Jobs, Yesterday's Values" is the goal, according to Tennessee's public relations slogan. At 80 percent of the industry standard, Saturn will surely be paying yesterday's wages. Paying less than a third of the normal tax rate, it will foster a repeat of yesteryear's company-town scenario. Saturn is preserving those features of yesterday that corporations value—a docile, concession-prone work force located in a community already fearful that its corporate benefactor may leave or is having financial woes.

In self-appreciation festivals in each of Tennessee's ninety-five counties, citizens gathered to learn about and celebrate their past as a part of Homecoming 1986. Despite the attempted parallels between the early pioneers and those charting the frontiers of Saturn, there is a real awareness that something is being forgotten, irretrievably lost in Tennessee.

What about the values of self-reliance, of community building, of democratic local decision making, of charting one's own economic destiny? Some Tennesseans may remember that their forebears came here to escape economic dependence on the Saturns of yesteryear.

Amid the booths demonstrating barn raisings, furniture making, spinning, and even moonshine stills, Tennesseans may experience the real values needed to put all our unemployed citizens and resources back to work. While this may at first seem naive, economists across the nation confirm that most new jobs are being created by small businesses, not by large corporations. Tennessee's Economic and Community Development Department, despite its almost exclusive emphasis on industrial recruitment, documents that over a five-year period almost 70 percent of the state's new manufacturing jobs occurred in Tennessee firms that were expanding or starting up.

As the 999 loser sites ponder Maury County's situation, maybe they should be grateful. If they can wean themselves from the Saturn myth, they have a chance to develop their economy proactively rather than reactively awaiting the next announcement from a far-off corporate boardroom. Even if they are unwilling to abandon industrial recruitment as a part of their overall development strategy, they have much to learn from the mistakes made with Saturn. Government officials and citizens in Maury County and Tennessee now say they would approach the Saturn recruitment very differently.[16]

States, counties, and cities have shown that they are willing to subsidize every step of a company's business—build the roads, provide all the social and physical services, do the planning and growth management, subsidize the utilities, provide job training, waive the taxes, own the factory and land, and sometimes pay the initial wages—and also take all the risks. It is now time for governments to use these same resources to support locally generated forms of economic development. Citizens are organizing in localities across the country to demand an end to wasteful recruitment practices. They are directing their governments to invest in local corporations, both nonprofit and for profit, which will hire local people, complement the lifestyles of current residents, and build a stable local tax base and economy.

The irony is that Saturn may have done much to encourage this trend. "Loser" localities in the Saturn sweepstakes may turn to local development as their only alternative. In Maury County, where citizens for the first time have had to debate the role of government in developing the economy, the citizens are very likely to opt for an alternative the next time they are chosen the "winner." [17]

NOTES

Acknowledgments: This chapter is based on Carter Garber and Verna Fausey, "Today's Jobs at Yesterday's Wages: GM's Saturn Auto Plant Arrives in Spring Hill, Tennessee," *Southern Changes* 8, nos. 4–5 (October/November 1986): 16–24. An expanded version of the article, *Saturn: Tomorrow's Jobs, Yesterday's Wages and Myths: A Case Study of Industrial Recruitment in Rural America,* is available from the Rural Coalition (2001 S Street, NW, Suite 500, Washington, DC 20009). The authors gratefully acknowledge the assistance of Paul Elwood in interviewing and research, as well as the research funding provided by the Rural Coalition and the Economic Development Policy Project of the Southern Neighborhoods Network (SNN).

1. Additional information on other states' bids is available in Jeff Spinner, "At Any Cost: The Bidding War for GM's Saturn," *Citizens for Tax Justice Special Report* (1825 K Street, NW, Washington, DC 20006), December 15, 1985, 1–12. Also see the thirteen articles compiled by Farley Peters in *State Wars Over Saturn: A Policy Reader on Industrial Recruitment,* issued by the Conference on Alternative State and Local Policies, August 6, 1985, 1–36. This organization has now changed its name to the National Center for Policy Alternatives, 2000 Florida Avenue, NW, Washington, DC 20009.

2. "The Climate for Workers," a September 1986 study by the Southern Labor Institute, which is a special project of the Southern Regional Council, Suite 820, 161 Spring Street, NW, Atlanta, GA 30303. A summary of the study appeared in *Southern Changes* 8, nos. 4–5 (October/November 1986): 1–15. Similar low ratings for Tennessee were found among the seventy-eight measures used to judge each state's economic development policy climate in *Making the Grade: The Development Report Card for the States* (Corporation for Enterprise Development, 1725 K Street, NW, Suite 1401, Washington, DC 20006).

3. Quotation is from a 1983 promotional booklet published by the Tennessee Department of Economic and Community Development. For more on tax analysis, contact Tennesseans for Fair Taxation, c/o Tennessee Hunger Coalition, P.O. Box 120961, Nashville, TN 37212.

4. Unless otherwise cited, the quotations and facts for this article are taken from interviews with politicians, local citizens, and company and union officials conducted by SNN researchers in July–August 1986 and December 1987. Other material comes from hundreds of newspaper articles read and sorted by the SNN research team; press releases and public relations materials by the Saturn Corporation, General Motors, and

188   DEVELOPMENT BY CORPORATE DESIGN

the United Auto Workers; and the monthly minutes of the Spring Hill Area Concerned Citizens Group.

5. Also misleading the public was William Long, then Tennessee's commissioner for economic and community development. Reminding the press that, by law, Tennessee cannot offer tax abatements or gifts directly to corporations, Long said of the GM negotiations, "They didn't ask for anything; we didn't offer anything" (*Wall Street Journal*, August 2, 1985, 18).

6. The fee issue is noted in Mike Piggott, "Saturn Lobbyist's Goal Is to Guard State Tax Climate," *Nashville Banner*, June 12, 1986, and in Verna Fausey, *Public Interest Report*, June 1986, published by the Southern Neighborhoods Network, Nashville, Tenn. The seat-belt issue is discussed in Patricia Templeton, "Seat Belt Savior Swayed by Saturn," *Nashville Banner*, April 17, 1986, and in Jim O'Hara, "Buckle Up! Alexander Signs Bill," (Nashville) *Tennessean*, April 22, 1986.

7. "Memorandum of Agreement Between Saturn Corporation and UAW," June 28, 1985, i–ii, 1–30. The preamble of the memorandum traces the history of Saturn and UAW talks, which began in the spring of 1983. The document was leaked to the Spring Hill Area Concerned Citizens Group on November 13, 1985, one week after the tax agreement was finalized (Jim Musselman, "The Dark Side of Saturn: A Tennessee Community Mortgages Its Future," *Multinational Monitors*, March 31, 1986, 11).

8. This and the following information from Howell are from an interview by SNN researchers with Howell in August 1986 and from the text of the forty-year in-lieu-of-tax agreements on file at the Maury County Courthouse in Columbia, Tenn.

9. Musselman, "The Dark Side of Saturn." Nader's opinions did not find a warm reception in middle Tennessee, but his guest editorial was published as "Spring Hill, Take Lesson from Flint," (Nashville) *Tennessean*, December 15, 1985.

10. Newspapers gave wide coverage to Mayor Jones's threats to block rezoning of the site: see (Nashville) *Tennessean*, August 31, September 1, 2, 3, 4, and 5, 1986. Jones's threat to annex the Saturn site is reported in Carolyn Shoulders, "Spring Hill Untangles GM Snag," (Nashville) *Tennessean*, October 23, 1985, and Sue McClure, "Mayor's Tactics Bring Spring Hill Split," *Nashville Banner*, October 23, 1985.

11. SNN interview with Joan W. Jackson, August 1986; Tom Eblen, "Is What's Good for GM, Good for Town?" *Atlanta Journal and Constitution*, July 27, 1986, 12-A. Mayor Jones quoted in "Spring Hill Finds Solace in Labels for Its Property," (Nashville) *Tennessean*, September 7, 1985. Nine months later, the tremendous speculation had subsided and the real estate market in the area was virtually dead. However, another boom is expected when plant and town bypass construction begins in 1988–89.

12. David Graham, "Town Braces for Invasion of Drifters," (Nashville) *Tennessean*, April 21, 1986, 1-A, and "Vagrants Get One-Way Ticket Out of Spring Hill," ibid., April 11, 1986. SNN interview with Bill Haley, August 1986.

13. Alan Murray, "New Bill Gives GM Tax Break of $60 Million: Special Preferences Cleared for Facilities to Build Saturn Model," *Wall Street Journal*, August 20, 1986, and Jessica Lee, "Saturn Plant Tax Request Before Panel," (Nashville) *Tennessean*, September 2, 1986, 1-B.

14. Governor Lamar Alexander's State of the State address to the legislature, January 1986.

15. Statement at 32nd Governors' Conference on Community and Economic Development, November 1984, Nashville, Tenn.

16. For areas that seek to develop using industrial recruitment as a tool, many practical lessons for public officials and citizens can be learned from the Saturn experience. See Carter Garber, "Get Ready for Industrial Recruitment: Lessons from Saturn's Recruitment to Tennessee," *Economic Development and Law Center Report* 16, no. 5 (Spring 1987): 8–12, and *Saturn: Tomorrow's Jobs, Yesterday's Wages and Myths.*

17. Public officials and citizens who want to shift local and state governmental policy away from wasteful industrial recruitment can call on a variety of approaches that have been tried and found successful by citizens around the country. For a step-by-step approach, see Carter Garber, "You Can Change Economic Development: A How-To Guide," *Everybody's Business: A People's Guide to Economic Development,* a special edition of *Southern Exposure* 14, nos. 5–6 (September/October and November/December 1986): 115–22.

CHAPTER

15

Environmentalism, Economic Blackmail, and Civil Rights: Competing Agendas Within the Black Community

Robert D. Bullard

There is abundant evidence that blacks and low-income people are subjected to a disproportionately large amount of pollution in their neighborhoods and in their workplaces. This is especially true in the southern United States. Black communities in the South have become the dumping grounds for all types of toxins. Why has this happened? What are blacks doing to combat this threat? What is government doing to ensure that everyone has equal access to an unpolluted environment?

First of all, the black community in the South does not have extensive experience with environmental issues when compared with its white counterpart. Blacks were actively involved in the civil rights movement during the peak period of the environmental movement, roughly during the late 1960s and early 1970s. On the other hand, civil rights advocates and boosters of unrestrained economic development became closely aligned. This alliance often brought them in direct conflict with environmentalists. Pollution and health risks were the price thousands of unemployed and marginally skilled blacks had to pay for employment.

In a desperate attempt to attract new industry and jobs, and in turn broaden their tax base, many poor communities in the South relaxed their enforcement of pollution and environmental regulations or simply looked the other way when violations were discovered. Polluting industries were brought into poor black communities with little input from local leaders. When questions were raised by concerned citizens, the argument of jobs for local residents (a form of economic blackmail) was used to quell dissent. Many business firms, especially waste-disposal companies, came to view the South as a "push-over, lacking community organization, environmental consciousness, and with strong and blind pro-business politics."[1] Residents of these economically impoverished areas were often powerless against private and government polluters.

The strong pro-jobs stance, a kind of "don't bite the hand that feeds you" sentiment, permeated the black community and helped institutionalize high risks and inequities. The South's unique history, traditions, and laws institutionalized discrimination in employment, education, housing, and other areas. A plethora of federal civil rights legislation was enacted to remedy inequities that resulted from Jim Crow laws. The South during the 1950s and 1960s was the center of the civil rights movement. The 1970s catapulted the region into the national limelight again, but for different reasons. The South was now becoming a major population and economic center. Growth in the region during the 1970s was stimulated by a number of factors, including a climate pleasant enough to attract workers from other regions and the "underemployed" work force already in the region, weak labor unions and strong right-to-work laws, cheap labor and cheap land, aggressive self-promotion campaigns, and weak enforcement of environmental regulations. The South beginning in the mid-1970s was transformed from a "net exporter of people to a powerful human magnet."[2]

The South desperately attempted to rid itself of its image as a socially and economically backward region. It was vigorously promoted as the "New South." However, many of its old problems related to underdevelopment—poor education, large pool of unskilled labor, high unemployment, low wages—remained while the influx of polluting industry created new environmental problems. For example, four of the five states that led the nation in attracting polluting industry (paper, chemicals, waste disposal, and others) in the 1970s were located in the South: Texas, South Carolina, North Carolina, and Florida. Some Southern leaders continued to display a Third World approach to development: any industry is better than no industry at all. By one measure their efforts were successful: the South led all regions of the country in the number of jobs created. More than 17 million new nonagricultural jobs were added in the South between 1960 and 1985, compared with 11 million in the West and a combined total of 13 million in the Midwest and Northeast.[3]

The benefits and burdens of industrial growth were not equally shared by all Southerners. Although blacks received some of the economic benefits of the South's growth, they received more than their share of the growing industrial pollution burden.[4] For example, the South became a favorite location for hazardous-waste "superdumps," large facilities that can accept waste from other regions of the country. Not surprisingly, black communities were targeted for these facilities. Some examples of these superdumps include Chemical Waste Management's landfills in Sumter County, Alabama (the "Cadillac" of superdumps) and Lake Charles, Louisiana; Genstar's Pinewood site outside Columbia, South Carolina; the Browning-Ferris Industries site in Willow Spring, Louisiana; and the Rollins landfill in Scotlandville, Louisiana.

Local Sumter County black residents have been fighting the Chemical Waste Management facility for years. The company's 2,400-acre landfill in Emelle, however, contributes more than $2 million annually into the economies of Sumter and Greene counties, located in the western Alabama Black Belt. Local residents are paying a price for having the facility in their community. Pesticides and volatile solvents have shown up in the company's monitoring wells outside the site after less than ten years of operation.

Environmentalism as Civil Rights

Why are black communities burdened with so many of these waste facilities? Black and lower-income neighborhoods often occupy the "wrong side of the tracks" and receive different treatment when it comes to enforcement of environmental regulations. The sociospatial groupings that emerge in the South are a result of "the distribution of wealth, patterns of racial and economic discrimination, access to jobs, housing, and a host of other variables." Housing discrimination artificially restricts millions of blacks to poorer neighborhoods and areas that pose health risks from pollution and other environmental problems. Political power and economic clout are also key factors that influence the spatial distribution of nonresidential land use. Siting dilemmas involving noxious facilities, such as municipal and hazardous-waste landfills, garbage incinerators and transfer stations, and sewage treatment plants, could be resolved with a strategy based on the "politics of equity."[5]

Although there has been considerable overlap between the agendas of civil rights advocates and those of economic boosters, these agendas often conflicted with those of environmentalists. The interplay between civil rights advocacy and environmentalism has been minimal. Historically, black civil rights organizations have not been on the cutting edge of environmental issues, even those that directly affect the black community. On the other hand, many of the battles that mainstream environmentalists waged during the height of the movement had marginal effect on deteriorating conditions in inner-city areas.

The "jobs versus environment" argument has held black Southerners captive to a system that often forces them to choose between employment and a clean work environment. This either–or choice is tantamount to economic blackmail. The correlation between factors associated with disadvantage (poverty, occupations below management and professional levels, low rent, and high concentration of black residents) and poor environmental quality has been clearly documented.[6] Various forms of pollution take a heavy toll on inner-city neighborhoods as a result of the high concentration of industry and power plants, disparate enforcement of pollution laws, heavy vehicle traffic, and congested freeway systems, which often crisscross lower-income and minority neighborhoods.

Middle- and upper-class citizens have been more successful in changing the course of freeways and the siting of industrial facilities than their lower-income counterparts. Air and water pollution in central cities can be found at levels up to five times greater than in suburban areas. Exhaust fumes from automobiles are especially troublesome to neighborhoods adjacent to the heavily traveled freeways. Black children in the United States suffer from lead toxicity six times more frequently than white children.[7] Although the source of elevated lead levels in children can be difficult to pinpoint, leaded gasoline, lead-based paint, and industrial smelters are the major culprits.

Lead in the environment is caused largely by human activities. Individuals who live near lead smelters run a high risk of exposure to harmful pollutants. Residents of the mostly black and low-income West Dallas (Texas) neighborhood, for example, have for years lived with the constant bombardment of health-threatening pollutants from the nearby lead smelters.[8] As early as 1981, toxicologists in the U.S. Environmental Protection Agency (EPA) knew that air emissions from the smelters posed an immediate threat to area residents. Children who lived in nearby public housing were especially at risk.

In 1983 EPA's Office of Toxic Integration and the Center for Disease Control studied children who lived near the smelters and found high levels of lead in their blood. Contact with contaminated soil and workers who brought the toxic material home on their clothes were the major sources of lead toxicity in the children. The West Dallas Lead Pollution Task Force, a black grassroots organization, used a number of strategies to close the smelters, including litigation, lobbying for effective enforcement of the city's zoning ordinance, political pressure, and citizen protests.[9] After years of litigation, an out-of-court settlement estimated at nearly $20 million was reached in 1985 between the now-defunct RSR Corp., operator of one of the smelters, and the blacks whose children suffered irreversible brain damage from exposure to lead pollutants.

Individuals and businesses that can afford to flee do so, while the poor and less advantaged stay behind and suffer from poverty, pollution, and potential health problems. The problem for blacks is exacerbated by the factor of access to medical and health care. One in six black families had trouble getting medical care in 1982, compared with one in eleven white families. Institutional barriers (employment and housing discrimination; disparate treatment by banks, mortgage companies, and insurance firms based on geographic location—"redlining"; public policies that tend to favor the affluent over the poor; and disparate enforcement of land use and environmental regulations) relegate a large segment of the black community to less than desirable physical environments, reduce housing and residential options, limit mobility, and increase risks from exposure to potentially health-threatening toxic material.

The Dumping Grounds

The hazardous waste problem has been described as the most "serious problem facing the industrial world." The United States generates more than 250 million metric tons of hazardous waste each year, and EPA regulations cover only a fraction of this waste. Potential Love Canals are waiting to be discovered. More than 80 percent of hazardous wastes is disposed of on land; only about 10 percent is disposed of properly. Millions of tons of unregulated hazardous wastes end up at municipal landfills designed for household garbage, are released from tank trucks onto back roads, or are dumped directly into sewer systems. The practices of "moonlight dumpers" create health and environmental time bombs that may explode years later.[10]

The location of off-site hazardous-waste landfills poses an even greater threat to the minority community. Toxic-waste facilities are often located in communities with high percentages of poor, elderly, young, and black residents. An inordinate concentration of uncontrolled toxic-waste sites are found in urban areas with a high percentage of minorities; large commercial hazardous-waste landfills are more likely to be found in rural communities in the Southern Black Belt.[11] The nation's largest commercial hazardous-waste landfill is located in Emelle, Alabama (Sumter County), where blacks constitute 78.9 percent of the population. The fourth-largest is located in Scotlandville, Louisiana, where blacks make up 93 percent of the population. Together, the Emelle and Scotlandville sites account for more than one-third of the estimated landfill capacity in the United States.

The racial and economic dimension of hazardous-waste landfill siting in the southern United States was documented in a 1983 study by the U.S. General Accounting Office (GAO).[12] The study identified four off-site hazardous-waste landfills in the eight states that make up EPA's Region IV (Alabama, Florida, Georgia, Kentucky, Mississippi, North Carolina, South Carolina, and Tennessee). Blacks make up one-fifth of the population of Region IV, but three of the four hazardous-waste landfills are located in mostly black communities. Residents of these Black Belt counties are victims of a "triple whammy"—they are rural, poor, and politically powerless.

The Warren County PCB (polychlorinated biphenyl) landfill is one of the four off-site hazardous-waste landfills located in EPA's Region IV. In 1982 Warren County, North Carolina, was selected as the burial site for more than 32,000 cubic yards of soil contaminated with the highly toxic PCBs that had been illegally dumped along the roadways in fourteen North Carolina counties in 1978. The decision to select this largely black and economically poor county made more political sense than environmental sense.[13] For a while Warren County received national attention. A host of well-known black civil rights activists, political leaders, and area residents marched and protested against the construction of the disposal facility, and more than 400 protesters were arrested.

Although the 1982 protest demonstrations were unsuccessful in blocking the landfill operation, they were significant in another way: they marked the first national attempt by blacks to link environmental issues to the mainstream civil rights agenda. The demonstrations prompted Congressman Walter E. Fauntroy (Congressman from the District of Columbia), who had been active in the protest demonstrations, to initiate the 1983 GAO study of hazardous landfill siting in the South. The protest demonstrations were later instrumental in setting the stage for the Commission for Racial Justice's 1987 national study on Toxic Wastes and Race.[14] The Reverend Ben Chavis (Commission for Racial Justice) and the Reverend Joseph Lowery (Southern Christian Leadership Conference) were two of the many civil rights activists who led marches against the Warren County PCB landfill. The demonstrations translated into something more than mere protest marches; they ushered in a new era, when blacks and the poor demanded their rights to equal protection from the ravages of pollution. It is not coincidental that the National Association for the Advancement of Colored People (NAACP), the premier civil rights organization, in 1983 passed its first resolution on the hazardous-waste issue.

The Politics of Facility Siting

Finding suitable sites for municipal and hazardous-waste landfills has become a critical problem, mainly because people are anxious about living near a facility where household garbage and toxic substances are dumped. The standard public reaction to landfill site selection has been "not in my back yard," abbreviated as the "NIMBY" principle. Public officials and private industry have in many cases responded using the "PIBBY" principle— "place in blacks' back yards."[15]

Because of the illegal dumping of toxic substances at "sanitary" landfills, black and lower-income neighborhoods are especially at risk, since they are burdened with a disproportionately large share of such facilities. The waste-disposal facility siting practices of cities and private companies have contributed to black and lower-income communities becoming the dumping grounds for household garbage and illegally dumped toxic materials. From Houston to Atlanta to Tampa, black neighborhoods have been burdened with a disproportionately large share of municipal waste-disposal facilities.

The disparate landfill siting pattern is probably best illustrated in Houston, the nation's fourth-largest city, with a population of more than 1.7 million.[16] Houston has the distinction of being the only major U.S. city which has no zoning. In addition, it has the largest black population, nearly one-half million, of any city in the South; blacks make up about 28 percent of the city's population. The city's blacks remain residentially segregated. More than 81 percent of them lived in majority black areas in 1980.

From the mid-1920s through the early 1970s, Houston operated its own solid-waste disposal facilities, including five municipal landfills and eight garbage incinerators. All the city-owned landfills and six of the eight garbage incinerators were located in black neighborhoods. In other words, although blacks constituted just over one-fourth of the city's population, eleven of the thirteen city-owned solid-waste disposal facilities were located in mostly black neighborhoods.

The Houston City Council, which had remained all-white until 1972, systematically targeted black neighborhoods for the city's solid-waste disposal facilities. Black protests against these practices went unheeded until the late 1970s, when black Houstonians began a frontal assault on the siting practices of the city, the state of Texas, and private waste-disposal companies.

In 1979 residents from a predominantly black northeast Houston subdivision filed a federal lawsuit to stop the construction of a sanitary landfill in their neighborhood. This action came after they were deliberately misinformed about the clearing of land on a construction site near their subdivision. Residents were under the impression that the removal of trees on the site was in preparation for new homes, not a sanitary landfill for Houston's garbage. Residents and their attorney, Linda McKeever Bullard, charged the Texas Department of Health (the permitting agency) and Browning-Ferris Industries (the General Motors of garbage) with racial discrimination in the selection of the landfill site so close to a densely populated subdivision.

Residents were upset because the landfill site was not only near their homes but within 1,400 feet of their high school (which was not equipped with air conditioning), their athletic stadium, and their school district's administration building. The North Forest Independent School District is a small suburban district where blacks make up more than 85 percent of the student population. The district is also one of the poorest in the Houston area. Seven North Forest schools, which form a cluster, are located within a two-mile radius of the landfill. Two of the three sanitary landfills currently used to dispose of Houston's solid waste are located within this mostly black district.

After long delays and numerous attempts by the landfill proponents to disrupt and divide the community, the case finally went to trial in 1985. Although the federal judge ruled against the residents and the landfill was built, local organized resistance produced some important changes in waste-disposal siting practices and policies in Houston. First, the Houston city council, acting under intense political pressure from blacks, passed a resolution in 1980 prohibiting city-owned solid-waste trucks from dumping at the controversial landfill. Second, the Texas Department of Health updated its requirements of landfill permit applicants to include detailed land use, economic, and socioeconomic data of the area near proposed sanitary landfill sites. Third, black Houstonians sent a clear signal to the state and city government and private disposal companies that they would fight any future attempts to place garbage dumps, landfills, incinerators, and any other type of waste-disposal facility in their neighborhood.[17] From 1979 to 1987, the Texas Department of Health did not grant a single sanitary landfill permit for a disposal site in a Houston black neighborhood.

Conclusion

The 1980s have seen the emergence of a small but growing cadre of blacks who see environmental issues as civil rights issues. An alliance has been forged between organized labor, minorities, and environmental groups, as exhibited by the 1983 Urban Environment Conference workshops held in New Orleans. Environmental and civil rights issues were presented as compatible agenda items by this coalition. Environmental protection and social justice are now seen as essential parts of the same struggle. A growing number of grassroots organizations and their leaders have begun to incorporate more action-oriented strategies, such as protests, neighborhood demonstrations, picketing, political pressure, and litigation, to reduce and eliminate the toxic-waste threat. National black political leadership has also demonstrated a willingness to take a strong pro-environment stance. The League of Conservation Voters, for example, assigned the Congressional Black Caucus high marks for having one of the best pro-environment voting records.

Many black communities, however, still do not have the organization, financial resources, or personnel to mount and sustain long-term challenges to such unpopular facilities as municipal and hazardous-waste landfills, garbage

198   DEVELOPMENT BY CORPORATE DESIGN

incinerators, toxic-waste storage facilities, and industrial plants that may pose a threat to their health and safety. This problem is complicated by the fact that blacks in many cases have to go outside their communities to find the technical experts—toxicologists, hydrologists, epidemiologists, environmental engineers, land use planners, demographers, and lawyers—that may be needed to challenge the siting process. Moreover, the talent at historically black colleges and universities (most of which are located in the South and in black communities) is still untapped when it comes to providing leadership and expertise on environmental issues in the minority community. The underutilization of experts at these institutions must end if they are to remain viable partners in strengthening and improving the quality of life for people of color.

Finally, black communities in the South need to incorporate environmental safeguards into their agendas for economic development. The promise of jobs may provide short-term solutions to economically depressed black communities, but health and environmental risks can often overshadow the benefits derived from hazardous, low-paying occupations. The black community needs to use its institutions, churches, civic clubs, professional associations, civil rights and political organizations, colleges and universities to develop a network of advocates and experts who can develop and articulate long-term environmental strategies for the black community. Black Southerners, like all Americans, have a right to live and work in an unpolluted environment.

NOTES

Acknowledgment: Research for this study was supported in part by a grant from Resources for the Future.

1. Will Collette, "Somewhere Else USA: Fighting Back Against Chemical Dumpers," *Southern Neighborhoods* 9 (September 1985): 1.

2. John D. Kasarda, Michael D. Irvin, and Holly L. Hughes, "The South Is Still Rising," *American Demographics* 8 (June 1986): 34; *The President's National Urban Policy Report 1980* (Washington, D.C.: U.S. Department of Housing and Urban Development, 1980), 165–69; John D. Kasarda, "The Implications of Contemporary Trends for National Urban Policy," *Social Science Quarterly* 61 (December 1980): 373–400.

3. David R. Goldfield, *Promised Land: The South Since 1945* (Arlington Heights, Ill.: Harlan Davidson, 1987), 197. Kasarda, Irvin, and Hughes, "The South Is Still Rising," 32–40.

4. See Robert D. Bullard and Beverly H. Wright, "The Politics of Pollution: Implications for the Black Community," *Phylon* 47 (March 1985): 71–78.

5. Robert L. Lineberry, *Equality and Urban Policy: The Distribution of Municipal Public Services* (Beverly Hills, Calif.: Sage, 1977), 11. David Morell, "Siting and Politics of Equity," in *Resolving Locational Conflict,* ed. Robert W. Lake (New Brunswick, N.J.: Rutgers University Center for Urban Policy Research, 1987), 118.

6. See Robert D. Bullard and Beverly H. Wright, "Blacks and the Environment," *Humboldt Journal of Social Relations* 14 (Summer 1987): 165–84.

7. K. Mahaffey, J. L. Annest, J. Roberts, and R. S. Murphey, "National Estimates of Blood Lead Levels: United States, 1976–1980," *New England Journal of Medicine* 307 (September 1982): 573–79.

8. Jonathan Lash, Katherine Gillman, and David Sheridan, *A Season of Spoils: The Story of the Reagan Administration's Attack on the Environment* (New York: Pantheon Books, 1984), 132–39.

9. Bullard and Wright, "The Politics of Pollution," 77.

10. See Samuel S. Epstein, Lester O. Brown, and Carl Pope, *Hazardous Waste in America* (San Francisco: Sierra Club Books, 1983), 33–39; Adeline Levine, *Love Canal: Science, Politics, and People* (Lexington, Mass.: Lexington Books, 1982). Office of Technology Assessment, *Technologies and Management Strategies for Hazardous Waste Control* (Washington, D.C.: U.S. Government Printing Office, 1983), 3. Michael H. Brown, *Laying Waste: The Poisoning of America by Toxic Chemicals* (New York: Pantheon Books, 1982), 267.

11. *Siting of Hazardous Waste Landfills and Their Correlation with Racial and Economic Status in Surrounding Communities* (Washington, D.C.: U.S. General Accounting Office, 1983), 2; *Toxic Wastes and Race in the United States: A National Report on the Racial and Socioeconomic Characteristics of Communities with Hazardous Waste Sites* (New York: Commission for Racial Justice, 1987), 16; Robert D. Bullard and Beverly H. Wright, "Environmentalism and the Politics of Equity: Trends in the Black Community," *Mid-American Review of Sociology* 12 (Winter 1987): 21–38.

12. *Siting of Hazardous Waste Landfills*, 2–3.

13. Sue Pollack and JoAnn Grozuczak, *Reagan, Toxics, and Minorities* (Washington, D.C.: Urban Environment Conference, 1984), 20.

14. *Toxic Wastes and Race*, 23–27.

15. Robert D. Bullard, *Invisible Houston: The Black Experience in Boom and Bust* (College Station, Tex.: Texas A&M University Press, 1987), 70.

16. See Robert D. Bullard, "Solid Waste Sites and the Black Houston Community," *Sociological Inquiry* 53 (Spring 1983): 273–88; Robert D. Bullard, "Endangered Environs: The Price of Unplanned Growth in Boomtown Houston," *California Sociologist* 7 (Summer 1984): 85–101.

17. For a detailed account of the waste-disposal controversy in Houston see Bullard, *Invisible Houston*, chapter 6.

CHAPTER

16

New Work Force, New Organizing: The Experience of Women Office Workers and 9to5

Cindia Cameron

Atlanta newspapers offer a compelling portrait of the booming Sun Belt economy. The business sections have weekly articles detailing continued job growth and an ever-declining unemployment rate. The local-news and feature sections often include photographs of the mushrooming skyline. The classified sections include many column inches of jobs with service and clerical titles. This portrait is repeated in Nashville, Tennessee, in Charlotte, North Carolina, in Greenville, South Carolina, and in any Southern city where the skyline is bulging with new office buildings.

A quite different picture emerges when the stories of individual participants in this economic boom are put together.

Kay has a two-year business degree and ten years in her job as a tax clerk. She earns just over $10,000, and worries each year about whether the federally subsidized child-care program will have further cutbacks, eliminating her daughter's slot.

Peggye has twenty years' experience in steno and typing and can record more than 100 words per minute in both. She works full time for a new bank as a "contract" secretary, which means she receives no insurance, sick pay, or vacation, and she must pay her own employment taxes.

Juanita is a sixty-year-old accounting clerk. She entered the work force after a divorce at the age of forty five. She has been unable to find a full-time job and does not have enough income or Social Security to make any plans to retire.

Kay, Peggye, and Juanita are all members of the "new work force," which

200

is characterized by marginal working conditions, defined by the participation of women, and struggling under policies that have shifted the responsibility for health and welfare off employers and government and squarely onto the shoulders of the overburdened working family.

The new work force comprises part-time, temporary, and contract workers; older workers and youths; women and minorities. They are workers who remain in the work force for many years, although not at the same job, even returning after retirement.

The working conditions that have prevailed for women, minorities, and Southern workers for years—low pay, few benefits, and no job security—are now becoming the norm for all workers. The old work force is being remade in the image of the new.

The Service Economy as "Job Machine"

Service industries have accounted for most of the dramatic U.S. job growth over the past twenty years and virtually all new job growth in the past ten. Three service industries—retail trade, health care, and business services—accounted for more than 80 percent of the growth in private-sector service employment from 1960 to 1986. Service industries employ 75 percent of the work force and account for nearly two-thirds of total gross national product. These industries are diverse, including transportation, public schools, banking, and health care. Retail sales and government are the largest in terms of employment, followed by finance, insurance, health care, and wholesale trade.[1]

Service is also a job category. Both manufacturing and service industries contain service occupations. In fact, 13.2 percent of all workers employed by manufacturing industries work in a service or clerical occupation. Sixty percent of all service-industry workers are employed to package, finance, insure, distribute, or sell manufactured products. Service jobs encompass a wide range of salaries and conditions: from accountants, lawyers, and doctors to fast-food flippers, janitors, and file clerks.

The much-praised role of the service sector as a "job machine" must be questioned, however. When the Bureau of Labor Statistics counts new jobs, equal weight is placed on full-time and part-time positions. Part-time work has increased more rapidly in our economy than employment overall since 1970. Nearly one-quarter of all jobs created since 1980 were part time. Today 22 percent of employed people work part time, many involuntarily. One quarter of part-timers would rather work full time.

Another misleading aspect of recent job creation involves the rise of the temporary work industry. Temporary work is among the nation's fastest-growing industries, increasing more than 19 percent a year since 1970. Two-thirds of part-time and temporary workers are female, working mostly as clericals, salesclerks, and lower-paid service workers.

Moreover, some of the growth in service-industry jobs is caused by manufacturing companies replacing in-house operations with subcontractors. Janitors, for example, are replaced by a contract cleaning firm. Jobs are lost in manufacturing and gained in services, but no real change in employment has occurred—except that wages and benefits are most likely lower and job security less.

Setting New and Lower Standards

Rather than catching up to former manufacturing employment standards, service jobs have begun to generate new employment policies, lowering wage and benefit standards and decreasing the opportunity for all workers to achieve a decent standard of living. Our economy's "growth" has generated decline in place of progress. Despite increased hours of work per family, incomes and essential workplace benefits have declined or stagnated. Jobs are less secure and less likely to offer an opportunity for career advancement.

Recent studies of new job creation show that service jobs are clustered at the lower end of the pay scale, that service workers constitute the largest segment of the uninsured, and that most service workers do not have pensions. Consider these statistics:

Pay
- An estimated 44 percent of new jobs created from 1979 to 1985 yielded an annual income of $7,400 or less.

- One out of three new jobs created in this same period pays under $11,200, the poverty level for a family of four.

Health Insurance
- Two-thirds of year-round workers without health insurance work in service industries (9 million people).

- Nearly one out of four workers in retail and business services has no health insurance.

Pensions
- Only 19 percent of retail trade workers have pensions. This industry employs 17 percent of the total work force.

Women and minorities predominate in the work force of most service industries. Women today make up 44 percent of the total work force and hold 62 percent of all service-industry jobs. In six of ten service occupations with the largest growth, women are 50 percent or more of the work force: nurses, health aides, primary-school teachers, waiters, cashiers, and retail salesclerks. Race segregation by occupation is also severe: black workers make up

19 percent of the hospital work force; Hispanic workers are 23.9 percent of building service workers. By comparison, blacks are 9.9 percent of total employment and Hispanics 6.6 percent.

Despite publicity about the rapid *rate* of growth in many professional jobs, the clerical and service sectors continue to lead in absolute number of new jobs created. Today the clerical work force exceeds the number of blue-collar machine operators and laborers. One out of three employed women in the Southeast works in a clerical or administrative support position. Clerical work is the leading occupation of white women and is rapidly gaining on other service work for blacks.

A group called 9to5, National Association of Working Women, is a membership organization for women clericals and office workers. It has been taking a close look at the employment conditions in southeastern cities over the past seven years. According to the data gathered by 9to5, the descriptions of office work as the job of the future and land of opportunity merit closer, more critical inspection.

The View from Behind a Video Display Terminal

To find out how women office workers in the Southeast feel about their jobs and working conditions, 9to5 in 1986 distributed opinion surveys in three cities—Birmingham, Alabama; Nashville, Tennessee; and Greenville, South Carolina. The survey asked women about policies and conditions on the job ("Do you have paid maternity leave?" "Are men hired in or promoted to some jobs, women to others?"), asked them to rank issues in terms of importance (pay, benefits, health, safety, and so on), and left room for additional comments. The results were surprisingly uniform, despite the different character of each city and diversity of respondents.

The issues of low pay and lack of advancement opportunities ranked as number one or two in virtually every survey returned. However, in the space for additional comments, between one-third and one-half of respondents in each city remarked on the need for child care and leave time for family responsibilities.

In each of the cities, average reported pay was between $12,000 and $15,000 a year; nearly three-quarters of respondents earned $15,000 or less. Almost half reported their paycheck was the only means of support for themselves and often for other dependents.

Results from the survey were used as a means of bringing attention to problems faced by this often invisible group of workers. The survey respondents developed press releases in each city, focusing on the key survey responses. A look at the themes of these press releases gives a good picture of what activist women had to say about their conditions and aspirations.

In Birmingham the headline was "Survey Finds Ole Buddy System Prevails"; the release stressed the lack of advancement opportunities reported by respondents. A data-entry operator was quoted as saying, "While more career opportunities are available for women now, they are still paid less than men, and advancement beyond certain levels is still reserved for white men." Survey results showed that elements of an internal career ladder were notably lacking in the companies described. A majority of respondents had no accurate job description (sometimes no job description at all), no compensation for additional duties, no training opportunities, and no job posting system that would allow them to find out about other jobs in the company.

In Nashville, the unifying issue was lack of respect. The press release began this way: "Many female office workers in Nashville echo the lament 'I don't get no respect.'" One woman, who became the chapter president, commented, "Our low pay shows that our jobs are seen as insignificant, but without the clerical staff, work in this country would come to a standstill. If we were respected for the importance of our jobs and the amount of responsibility and skill required, we would be paid substantially more."

In Greenville, the overriding concern was low pay; one-third of those responding made under $12,000 a year and three-quarters made $15,000 or less. One respondent described her frustrations this way: "As a clerk, my job requires a high school degree. In fact I have an associate degree in business. I earn barely $10,000 a year after nine years with my employer. A man with a tenth-grade education can start out here as an equipment operator at over $13,000. It seems a man with physical strength gets paid for it, while a woman with typing and computer skills gets left behind in salary."

These are the issues that bring women to 9to5: the low pay that not only puts their families in financial crisis but reflects a severe undervaluing of their contributions and skills; the desire for advancement that far exceeds the opportunities; the lack of respect, which ranges from barring women from promotions to sexual harassment; and the increasingly urgent need for policies, including child care and family leave, that recognize the dual responsibilities of working parents.

Ways and Means: First Steps on the Road to Self-Organization

The 9to5 organization is a hybrid that combines elements of women's issues (child care, pay equity, sexual harassment, respect) and union issues (higher pay, job posting, increased benefits) with a community-organizing style (corporate campaigns, locally elected boards of directors, personal empowerment).

The fundamental goal that has guided 9to5 over the past fifteen years is simply to introduce office workers to the idea, the experience, and the value of organization. To reach this goal, 9to5 has employed four basic strategies: first, to raise the issues (pay, rights, and respect) to the public, in order to change the expectations of office workers; second, to create examples of change, to win concrete victories that show that change is possible and worth the risk; third, to educate the constituency on issues and legal rights, in order to build a climate of legitimacy for organizing and the knowledge of rights and how to protect them; and finally, to develop leadership among clerical workers, emphasizing both the empowerment of individuals and the training of long-term activists within the constituency.

Women office workers as an occupational group are seriously handicapped by their lack of cultural identity. Unlike farmers, coalminers, textile workers, or auto workers, they have had, until the last fifteen years, no songs, heroines, or legends; no mutual aid societies or recorded history; no experience of common struggle on their own behalf. Twenty years ago, the stenographer was likely to be isolated with her boss, often in a small establishment; today's clerical workers still share a sense of isolation from other women employees.

While the streamlining and automation of the office have brought about the collective experience of the typing pool and the "back-office operation," which employ up to hundreds of clericals in a single building, these women bring with them the isolating experience of women's role in the family. They do not stop by the bar or pool hall after work to chat with their buddies from the office; they dash off to pick up the children, the medicine, the groceries. To meet before work or to distribute leaflets, they need to make sure someone else is available to pack the lunches and get the children off to school.

More recently, even the community experience of passing out thousands of leaflets at busstops and downtown street corners in Atlanta has changed. Many large banks and insurance companies, the largest private-sector "back-office" employers, have, over the past five years, moved out to suburban office parks where the isolation of women clericals is again magnified. They work part-time shifts, commute by car, and rarely get to know people outside their own office or building in the sprawling complexes, which have no public property for leafleting or public restaurants for lunch meetings.

Overcoming this isolation, making a personal link, is what 9to5 is all about. Women who contact 9to5, through surveys, letters, or telephone calls, receive at least a personal phone call in response and, where possible, a lunchtime visit. In these conversations, the women talk about the issue that concerns them, and hear an explanation of what 9to5 is. "No, it's not a union, not a professional secretaries' group, not a social club. But yes, it is partly all those things." It is a place where women who are concerned with the conditions for clerical workers can get support and understanding and can contribute to the effort to bring about change.

The format of meetings, whether public forum, workshop, or committee meeting, is also part of the strategy and style. The agenda always includes time for women to describe their particular horror story or victory at work and some kind of inspiration or personal success. This testimony is sometimes planned but often spontaneous. Women who come and stay to be active, to take risks, to move into a new arena of visibility on their jobs and in their communities, do it in part because they have found new friends. They have found a group that is hard to find: women who are not professionals or middle-class activists, but who have in common the daily problems and dreams of making the office a better place to work.

A moving example took place in early December 1987, at a meeting in a city with a new 9to5 chapter, where women barely knew each other. Most of the planned agenda was lost to the discussion of the problem of one black woman who, after ten years on her job, had been passed over once again for promotion. After listening to her rage for half an hour, a white woman said, very quietly, "You may not like what I'm going to tell you, but here's my opinion." She gave some very straightforward suggestions: that the woman take responsibility for her own situation, not blame or expect others to handle it for her, and start on some specific actions. It was a rough dose of medicine and the room was completely silent. A few minutes later, at the end of the meeting, the black woman pulled $15 out of her pocket, money I knew was earmarked for her daughter's Christmas. "I've never been taken so seriously or given such good advice anywhere," she said. "This group is for me." It was a turning point in the level of trust and commitment among the women in that group, and some months later they established a local chapter, despite local chamber of commerce efforts to discredit the organization and generate hostile press coverage.

Once a chapter has formed, it uses survey results and discussions at meetings to develop a mandate on an issue or set of issues, such as health and safety for video display terminal (VDT) operators, career ladders, or working-family issues. With this focus, the organization moves into a public campaign using a variety of pressure tactics to force change in the targeted policy or institution. The methods of recruiting members, soliciting stories and opinions, developing a mandate, and choosing a focus have remained fairly constant over the seven years that 9to5 has been active in the South, but the targets of our pressure campaigns have been changing.

Southern Beginnings

In 1981, 9to5 made its Southern debut in Atlanta. With two full-time staff and dozens of volunteers from activist women's groups, the organization brought to public attention for the first time a view of "lovely Atlanta" as it was seen by the more than 200,000 office workers who kept the business of the city moving. Holding a public "speakout" to an overflow audience in city council chambers, office workers gave personal, moving testimony on salaries, job descriptions, advancement opportunity, working conditions, and affirmative action. The fledgling organization announced its intention to follow up on the results of its first survey by offering educational programs and seeking meetings with the local chamber of commerce and leading employers.

During the 1970s office workers' groups in the North and Midwest had developed an effective model of corporate campaigns, combining the elements of lively and imaginative public rallies (Heartless Awards on Valentine's Day, Scrooge of the Year at Christmas) with threats of investigation by federal antidiscrimination agencies and letters to boards of directors, stockholders, and customers. The organization relied on the eagerness of corporations to get out of the public eye and their willingness to make some policy compromises to keep a good public image on women's issues.

Within the first year, Atlanta 9to5, using this corporate campaign model, targeted the largest savings and loan in the state, publicizing their lack of promotions for women and minorities, low pay, and lack of benefits. The campaign brought about the first promotions of women and minorities to the level of branch manager, a job-posting procedure, and improved health benefits. Two years later a second campaign targeted a major locally based insurance company, focusing on conditions of VDT operators. As a result, the company installed glare-reduction devices, promised to consult workers in the design of new offices and equipment, and increased annual raises for the lowest-paid employees. Then it moved its entire operation out of the downtown area—out of reach of many black women who rely on public transportation and are most open to organizing ideas—to an area safely surrounded by private property, where leafleting of workers and lunchtime press conferences are impossible.

A number of trends have made the corporate campaigns of the 1970s a less favored method of organizing among 9to5 chapters. The element of surprise and the threat of antidiscrimination agencies are no longer viable. Appearing on the doorstep of a company to dramatize unfair treatment was, in the early years, all it took to get some changes made. But as word of 9to5 spread, chambers of commerce and management consultants across the country began offering training sessions on how to manage "white-collar women" and "militant feminists," like members of 9to5. Early campaigns also relied on suing banks for noncompliance with affirmative action plans required of federal contractors. After the changes in funding, enforcement, and regulations during the Reagan administration, it became much more difficult to threaten companies or to win cases. A third difficulty of this campaign style is the expense; it carries high costs in staff and member resources and time. As government and private funding sources for all kinds of advocacy became more thinly stretched in the 1980s, fewer chapters could support two or even one full-time staff person, a critical element of an intense, months-long corporate campaign. But 9to5 adjusted to the tougher financial conditions by experimenting with a new model of organization—all-volunteer chapters. The idea was to enable the movement to continue to grow by developing a model that would work in any city or town, with or without local staff. This also meant scaling back on program size and searching for new methods of winning policy change.

Responding to this new direction, the Southeast field office began operation in 1986, incorporating two existing chapters in Atlanta and Marietta, Georgia, and targeting three cities where interest in forming local chapters had been shown. In 1987 funding was obtained to open an office in Durham, North Carolina, with the mandate to develop new chapters in several cities in that state.

These new volunteer chapters have different resources, methods, and expectations. A local chapter, without staff to do the intense legwork required of a corporate campaign or a legislative effort, must define its role and goals differently. It can be discouraging to look toward the program models set in a different era by staffed chapters or by those in a different political environment. Volunteer-led chapters in Maryland, Massachusetts, Wisconsin, and California, among others, operate in a context that includes progressive labor, women's, and health coalitions, liberal legislators, and alternative community funds. All these resources make it possible for a 9to5 group to add a useful and important contribution—the voice of women office workers—to a policy campaign that might be initiated by others.

In Georgia, South Carolina, and Alabama, the political terrain is quite different. Unable to mount a large corporate campaign, smaller Southern chapters have cast about for other targets. Public policy actions, from city council resolutions on VDT protection to statewide initiatives on pay equity, are not yet promising, not likely to yield the examples of change that the organization needs to be able to point to. To give these organizations a role they can successfully play in their communities, a two-stage model has been developed. Every local organization of clerical workers, in a rural area or small town, with five members or five hundred, can set itself a goal of "exposing the problems and proposing solutions." This means surveying co-workers and workshop participants, developing press visibility and in some cases a hotline to collect examples and experience on a particular issue. These local examples, combined with national research and examples of positive corporate and public policies from other cities and states, make a powerful presentation to the local press, elected officials, planning agencies, and audiences of office workers willing to organize for improved conditions in their own offices.

The goal for every aspiring chapter is to move to stage two: directly affecting policies. This, on a moderate level, can happen where chapters have the opportunity to work in coalition with statewide organizations, or where they have a moderate or progressive elected official who is open to influence on issues such as parental leave or child care. Over the long run, the fact that problems of low pay, lack of job security, inadequate benefits, and the like are not unique to women office workers gives us hope.

The New Social Contract

As we look for a mandate, a rallying cry that might move women office workers, with their legacy of isolation and lack of collective tradition, into action, we might find a powerful tool in the framework of issues that has now taken shape in the new work force. For what truly distinguishes the new work force from the old is not the job titles, the hours of work, the sex or race of the worker, or the difference between the service and manufacturing sectors. It is the conditions of work—the dramatically changed social contract among workers, management, and government; a contract that has, in fact, lapsed.

The new work force is the result of two fundamental changes in our society: the shift to low-wage, less secure jobs; and the dramatic increase of women in the labor force, with consequent changes in family structure. The growth of the new work force has brought about a severe decline in the standard of living for U.S. families. Despite six years of economic expansion in the mid 1980s, average family income stands below its peak in 1973. And it is only the huge influx of women into the job market that has kept the rate of this decline in single, rather than double, digits.

Nearly sixty years ago, the despair and conflict of the Great Depression gave rise to similarly dramatic social and economic changes. Partly through the efforts of a massive labor movement, a new set of federally established minimum standards was passed, including the minimum wage, child labor laws, Social Security, and the forty-hour work week. Today we need a new set of standards to address the changed realities of jobs and families: policies in the areas of work and family, pay and benefits, jobs and training, and working conditions.

A September 1987 national conference cosponsored by 9to5 and the Service Employees International Union brought some of the elements of a new organizing climate into positive focus. Entitled "Solutions: Policies for the New Workforce," the conference brought together researchers, elected officials, and political analysts who discussed the economic and political significance of the shift from a manufacturing to a service-based economy. It also presented nearly fifty case studies of successful policy initiatives that address the new realities of the American work force and family—from child care to drug testing, from protections for part-time workers to pension reform.

This need for new standards may provide a new framework for organizing in the South. A new social contract would require cooperation among a broad range of community advocates. It would require the participation of public officials and elected representatives. And, for those segments of the work force and community with no tradition of self-organization, it would provide a framework to express their needs and concerns and to be involved in bringing about solutions in new ways.

For fifteen years now, 9to5's strategy has been to find the "gut" issues— whether it is who gets the coffee or how much is in the paycheck—and then play that issue on a large screen. This means telling people's stories: stories that illustrate the problem and bring it to life, and stories that provide proof that change is possible and worth taking a risk for.

The catalog of difficulties and obstacles on the road to organization is not significantly lessened by this new framework. But the effect on 9to5 members of attending the "Solutions" conference in September was encouraging. The result of the barrage of facts, statistics, and political analysis was to bring their personal situations into new focus. The frustrations of inadequate and unaffordable day care, the financial anxiety of working temporary jobs with no benefits or security, the demoralization of moving from job to job with never a promotional opportunity in sight—each personal crisis now fitted into a larger picture, a social reality rather than an individual failing.

"That's my life," said a long-time leader of Atlanta 9to5. "I am the service economy. What a relief to know that it is not just me, my problems, my failings that make me worry about having no pension and not being able to afford health insurance for my daughter."

The challenge now for 9to5 and other groups concerned with organizing among workers and communities in the new work force is to find new and exciting ways to make use of this potential rallying point. If we can do that, we can overcome some of the traditional obstacles to organizing and unleash the energy that will translate visions into solutions.

NOTE

1. These and other general statistics are from John J. Sweeney and Karen Nussbaum, *Solutions for the New Workforce: Policies for a New Social Contract* (Cabin John, Md.: Seven Locks Press, 1989).

CHAPTER

17

The Changing International
Division of Labor:
Links with Southern Africa

Ann Seidman

$\mathbf{I}$n the 1960s and 1970s, widespread publicity proclaimed an industrial boom in the Sun Belt. By the 1980s, however, plant closings and rising unemployment spelled increasing poverty for growing numbers of people living in the southeastern United States.

Why the change? This essay proposes an explanation centered on the way the post–World War II technological revolution enabled transnational corporations to shift their production in agriculture, mining, and manufacturing to take advantage of pools of even more impoverished Third World workers. In a no-win competition, they pitted wages, working conditions, and living standards in the southern United States against the near slave-labor conditions of Third World countries like South Africa. I conclude that, to end their region's poverty, the citizens of the southeastern United States—farmers, wage earners, small-business owners, and professionals—not only need to devise people-oriented economic programs to provide jobs for their population; they must also support liberation and development in Third World areas like southern Africa. In that way, they will help to lay the foundation for increased, mutually beneficial trade in a world at peace.

Background

A set of complex interacting factors causes the growing poverty in the Southeast. Some factors grow out of the region's history; some involve the region's interactions with other developing regions of the world. The South's heritage of slavery left a monoculture economy characterized by features similar to those of many Third World countries: dependence on the sale of a few crops or crude exports to uncertain national and international markets; a sharply skewed income distribution characterized by ownership of most of the region's major agricultural, mineral, and financial resources by a few wealthy families; a large reservoir of labor, especially women, desperate for additional income, willing to work at any job for below-poverty-level wages; and a resurgent racism, accompanied by violence, that turned poor whites against blacks, thwarting efforts to build the unity required to restructure the region's political economy.

Following World War II, the technological revolution in production, communications, and transportation enabled transnational corporations to maximize their global profits by shifting their investments to take advantage of pools of low-cost labor throughout the world. Collaborating with wealthy local, state, and federal groups and agencies, they initially shifted their more labor-intensive factories to exploit the resources (including low-cost labor) of the southeastern United States.

Accumulating and reinvesting capital to maximize their profits on a world scale, they expanded their operations into Third World countries where inherited political and economic structures force impoverished populations to work for even lower wages. The resulting changing international division of labor puts the working and living conditions of U.S. workers, including those in the Southeast, in direct competition with those imposed by inherited colonial structures on the increasingly marginalized peoples of Third World regions like southern Africa.

Increased military spending and extended U.S. military involvement in Africa foster this process in several ways, often under the guise of combating "communism" and exaggerated national security requirements. They provide a profitable cost-plus business for the largest transnational corporations' facilities in the United States, including those made possible by southeastern state governments willing to hold down labor, tax, and environmental costs. They finance research and development of new technologies designed to facilitate control by the largest transnational corporations over resources and labor both at home and abroad. They justify the extension of U.S. military aid to repressive African (and other Third World) governments willing to make available their national resources, including impoverished labor reserves, at even lower costs than those available in the South. Adopting an implicit (sometimes explicit) racist stance, they aid South African surrogate forces to thwart fundamental changes in the southern African regional economy.

Development and Underdevelopment in the South

Although the Civil War ended outright slavery, it left the South's basic political economic structures intact. Sharecroppers, working for wealthy plantation owners under conditions of debt peonage, cultivated cotton, tobacco, and other crops for northern industries and for export. In Appalachia, mine companies employed workers at backbreaking labor to produce coal for the railroads and expanding northern industries.

After World War I, the boll weevil decimated the South's Cotton Belt. At the same time, England developed alternative sources of cotton in Africa, especially in the Sudan and Uganda, where colonial rule forced peasants to accept lower cotton prices than those U.S. farmers demanded. Then, in the Great Depression, acreage-reduction programs paid U.S. farmers to take land out of cotton production, forcing the exodus of a third of the region's sharecroppers. As the Depression destroyed their markets, mine companies also shut down.

Pressed by small merchants and professionals, state officials sought to create a "hospitable business climate" to attract northern industry. Much like impoverished Third World governments today, they offered tax holidays and incentives; government-financed industrial areas including free public utilities and highway spur connections; and, above all, no unions and wages a third or more below the U.S. national average. To keep taxes down, governments resisted increasing funds to improve schools. Local property taxes throughout the region averaged a quarter to a third lower than national averages.[1]

Company and community leaders played on racial and sectional prejudices. The *Charleston News and Courier* in the mid-1950s warned workers against throwing in "with union officials who are brainwashed with the popular creed of mixing the races." In 1956, South Carolina's lieutenant governor alleged a conspiracy between labor unions and the National Association for the Advancement of Colored People against "the Southern way of life."[2]

In some respects, the Southeast's postwar industrialization drive succeeded. By the 1970s, all but two southeastern states could boast a higher-than-national-average rate of manufacturing employment.[3] Nevertheless, the strategy failed to eliminate the region's high poverty rates. Many new plants located in rural areas where wages remained even lower than the region's low statewide averages. By 1980, the region was home to sixty-six of the nation's seventy-five most industrialized counties—and sixty-one of its poorest.

The Shift to South Africa

As new technologies increased the mobility of transnational corporations, they shifted to even lower-wage areas in Third World countries, like South Africa. This trend emerged first in the agriculture and mining sectors. By the late 1970s, however, it had spread to labor-intensive manufacturing industries such as textiles and microelectronics.

After World War II, U.S. government policy supported the buildup of a South African military industrial complex that appeared especially attractive to U.S. corporate investors. They provided the technological and financial support that enabled a (white) minority of less than one-fifth of the population to dominate not only 30 million black South Africans but the entire southern African region.[4]

In the first three postwar decades, U.S. transnational corporations invested three times as much capital in South Africa as in the entire prewar era. By 1983, total U.S. financial involvement there, including direct investment, bank loans, and stockholdings, had soared to $14.6 billion. U.S. manufacturing firms poured more than three-fourths of the capital they invested in the entire African continent into building factories in South Africa.[5]

Until the crisis of the 1980s, U.S. investors in South Africa enjoyed high profit rates, reaching 29 percent in 1980.[6] These rates primarily reflected the fact that apartheid forced African workers to accept wages a fourth to a tenth of those earned by U.S. workers for the same kind of work. Although many U.S. transnational affiliates operated plants with advanced technologies, using mainly skilled (white) workers, they still benefited from institutionalized black poverty. First, the apartheid state provided infrastructure—water, energy, transport links, and skilled labor—for white-owned business at low cost. Second, low black wages and state subsidies enabled the parastatals to sell basic services and products to corporations at or below cost.[7] Third, by providing little social security, health care, or education for the black majority, the state held effective corporate taxes down to about 25 percent of net corporate income. Furthermore, until the mid-1980s, a double-taxation agreement between the United States and South Africa permitted U.S. firms to deduct South African taxes from their U.S. tax bills.

U.S. and other transnational manufacturers' investments in South Africa gave them access to the South African and regional markets. South Africa's 4 million high-income whites alone constituted an important market for high-priced manufactures. As the neighboring countries attained independence, the South African government deliberately spurred parastatals and private firms to invest in mechanization to reduce dependence on black labor, expanding the market for sophisticated imported machinery and equipment. Finally, South Africa's military budget, an increasingly important component of the South African market, topped $6 billion in 1987. The state-owned arms manufacturer, ARMSCOR, had contracts with 1,200 firms, of which about a third relied heavily on military sales.[8]

In addition, the transnationals gained from South Africa's domination of its neighboring countries. With a combined population of about 75 million, these constitute a land area roughly the size of the continental United States. The underdevelopment imposed by a century of colonial rule forced hundreds of thousands of their workers to migrate annually, swelling the labor pool that kept South African wages low and profits high. Furthermore, by collaborating with South African mining finance houses and parastatals, U.S. transnationals obtained the region's low-cost agricultural, forestry, and mineral raw materials. Finally, although the majority of the neighboring states' populations remained poor, their wealthy elites provided a substantial additional market.

A conscious or subconscious racist perspective may also have influenced U.S. corporate managers to invest in South Africa. The socioeconomic infrastructure of the white urban areas met all their firms' requirements. Apartheid ensured their families suburban living conditions—including cheap domestic labor—equal to if not exceeding in comfort those in the United States. These may have particularly attracted company personnel accustomed to operating in the pre–civil rights era in the American South.

By the early 1980s, U.S. transnationals began to market in Europe, and increasingly in the United States, the low-cost goods they either manufactured or purchased in South Africa, competing with higher-priced items produced by U.S. workers. At the same time, the Reagan administration adopted the policy of "constructive engagement" toward South Africa: first, to achieve a compromise between the minority South African regime and "moderate" blacks that—much like the civil rights victories in the U.S. South—would end the worst features of apartheid but leave intact the profitable economic structures; and second, to slow the pace of change in the neighboring states to allow time to cement that compromise in place. Under the guise of "combating communism," the Reagan administration expanded its direct military intervention in southern Africa. In direct collaboration with South Africa, it poured weapons into the Union for the Total Independence of Angola (UNITA), backed by South African troops and planes, which aimed to disrupt Angola's newly independent government.[9]

The Impact on Southern Jobs

Several examples will illustrate the way U.S. transnationals' shift of their business to apartheid-ruled South Africa directly affected employment and wages in the U.S. Southeast.

Stagnation of Tobacco

As new technologies shrank the world's parameters after World War II, small southeastern tobacco farmers felt the impact.[10] In 1982, tobacco still contributed almost 20 percent of total farm sales in several southeastern states and more than that in Kentucky and North Carolina. Compared to other crops, moreover, a higher proportion of the gross income generated by tobacco sales—up to 75 percent—ended up as net income to the average farm family. Nevertheless, the number of family farms in North Carolina and Kentucky had dropped to half the number that existed in 1954, and the number of flue-cured tobacco farms, where mechanization advanced more rapidly, had plummeted to 15 percent of those that existed in 1954.

Spurred by transnational tobacco companies, international competition aggravated the problems confronting small U.S. tobacco farmers. From the mid-1970s to 1983, imports of both flue-cured and burley tobacco roughly tripled. Imported burley tobacco rose from about 5 percent to 25 percent of total U.S. use, while imported flue tobacco increased from 3 percent to about 20 percent. Exports of flue-cured tobacco fell off sharply.

Seven transnational tobacco firms effectively control tobacco marketing and processing on a global scale.[11] They turned to cheaper sources of supply in Third World countries, particularly Africa.

This shift is illustrated by the case of British American Tobacco (BAT). Back in the 1920s, BAT helped white settler-farmers in Southern Rhodesia (now Zimbabwe) introduce flue-cured tobacco. By 1980, when Zimbabwe attained independence, it had become the world's second-largest exporter of flue-cured tobacco, after the United States. Tobacco made up a fourth of the country's total exports. In 1980, after the sale of tobacco to BAT and other buyers, the 1,200 white tobacco-farm owners received 58 percent of the income that remained in Zimbabwe. By contrast, 76,000 farm workers, receiving wages of (U.S.) $75 a month or less, earned only about 16 percent of the nation's tobacco income. Like the other tobacco transnationals, BAT bought tobacco leaf from other independent southern African countries, where inherited colonial structures forced African peasants to work for incomes far below those earned by small farmers in North Carolina or Kentucky.

While operating throughout southern Africa, the transnational tobacco firms located their African headquarters in South Africa. BAT, for example, owned a majority of shares in six South African companies manufacturing cigarettes and other commodities. Another major tobacco transnational, the Rothmans–Rembrandt Group, South Africa's third-largest corporation, owned more than $2 billion worth of assets in South Africa, including mining and industrial enterprises, among them one of South Africa's largest textile firms.

In short, a handful of powerful transnational tobacco corporations reaped global profits by purchasing tobacco leaf worldwide from the cheapest possible source. In consequence, the U.S. tobacco farmers in the South found their incomes in direct competition with those of southern Africa, dominated by apartheid-ruled South Africa.

The Story of Coal

After World War II, U.S. coal companies introduced increasingly capital-intensive technologies, financed in part by mergers and takeovers by transnationals, especially oil companies. In the 1970s, as the oil crisis spurred demand for an alternative fuel, U.S. transnationals multiplied their investments in coal. However, many of them invested, not in their own Appalachian coalmines, but in low-wage areas such as South Africa.[12]

The leading South African mining finance house, the Anglo American Group, operating in close collaboration with the New York–based Citicorp through its Bermuda-based Mineral Resources Corporation (MINORCA), acquired a controlling share of Newmont Mining Company, a large U.S. coal producer.[13] In turn, Newmont owned a 27.5 percent share in Peabody Holding Company, the largest coal producer in the United States. Anglo's MINORCA also joined Hudson Bay Mining and Smelting to form a joint venture, Inspiration Coal, which, in turn, owned Clintwood Mining Company and Harmon Mining Company in Virginia and Majestic Collieries Company and Sovereign Coal Corporation in Kentucky.

By the mid-1980s, U.S. coal buyers began to import coal. In 1983, as U.S. coal output plummeted by 14 percent, South African coal imports rose rapidly, providing almost a fifth of all foreign coal sold in the United States. By 1984, a third of the underground U.S. miners, mostly in the Southeast, had lost their jobs.[14]

By 1980, South Africa produced about 12 percent of the world's coal exports, a foreign-exchange earner for the apartheid regime second only to gold. South African coal competed with U.S. exports in markets in Western Europe and the Pacific Rim. It also exported coal to Israel, while the South African parastatal, ISCOR, joined the Israeli Koor Group to export South African steel, cutting into the market of the declining U.S. steel industry, once a major U.S. coal customer.

U.S. transnationals with investments in South African coal led a campaign to weaken the United Mine Workers of America (UMWA). In 1980–1981, Royal Dutch Shell and Fluor took over A. T. Massey, the fifth-largest U.S. coalmining company. Anglo-American associate, Barlow Rand, Royal Dutch Shell's affiliate Shell BP, and Fluor all own shares in the Rietspruit mine in South Africa, which annually produces 5 million tons of coal for export. Shell BP, together with a South African parastatal, also owns an oil refining and petrochemicals firm and helps South Africa evade OPEC's oil boycott. Fluor constructed South Africa's oil-from-coal facilities to help South Africa reduce its dependence on imported oil.

Under its new Shell–Fluor managers, A. T. Massey rejected the U.S. Bituminous Coal Operators Association agreement with the UMWA, insisting that the union bargain separately with each of its subsidiaries. When the union began selective strikes and peaceful picketing at Massey mines in Virginia and Kentucky, Massey brought in strike breakers and armed mercenaries as guards. The strike dragged on for more than a year, with increasing violence. An unknown assailant fired shots into the home of the local union president. A bomb blew up a local union headquarters. A delegation from the South African miners' union, who visited Appalachia, described Massey's tactics as similar to those the transnationals employed in South Africa.

Unemployment in Textiles

Other chapters in this volume have described the Southeast's loss of textile jobs in the 1980s (see Introduction and chapter 7). What is less well known is the fact that transnational firms such as Sears Roebuck, Montgomery Ward, and K-mart imported goods from firms in South Africa. Celanese, a leading U.S. textile fiber and weaving firm, manufactured synthetic cloth there. By 1986, some seventy-five factories owned by Taiwanese, and others owned by Israeli and Hong Kong businesses, operated in the *bantustans,* the land areas to which the apartheid regime has begun to remove all members of the black majority population who are not employed on white-owned farms or in white-owned mines or factories. Workers there received $7 a week, about what a North Carolina worker earned in an hour![15]

Before Congress passed a compromise sanctions law over President Reagan's veto, the administration increased South Africa's quota of textiles imports. Even if the Reagan administration had enforced the sanctions, Taiwanese firms probably would have continued to sell South African textiles to U.S. merchandisers under a made-in-Taiwan label.[16]

The Myth of a High-Tech Boom

In the 1980s atmosphere of intensified militarization, southeastern state officials accelerated their efforts to attract high-tech industries. They behaved much like the low-wage, tax-conscious industries that had for so long dominated the region. To take advantage of transport facilities and skilled labor supplies, however, they located their engineering capacity in or near the major cities. Thus, high-tech firms accelerated the "modernization" of urban areas while further impoverishing the rural population.[17]

The changing production structure and growing unemployment hit black communities the hardest. Industrialists allegedly feared that blacks' greater susceptibility to unionization and increased political strength might lead to higher wages and tax increases for more social services. Manufacturing employment grew more than twice as fast in Southern counties where blacks constituted less than 25 percent of the population as in those where they exceeded 30 percent.

Meanwhile, even high-tech firms began to shift their production plants, where two-thirds of the workers had fragmented, low-paid, unskilled jobs, to lower-wage areas outside the United States. In 1985, the electrical and electronic equipment industries lost 68,000 jobs in the United States. General Electric closed plants in Kentucky and Virginia; Burroughs, Motorola, and IBM shut down in Florida; and ITT shut down a North Carolina facility.[18] All these companies had invested in South Africa.

The story of SCI Systems, the biggest employer in Huntsville, Alabama, illustrates the conscious anti-union attitudes underlying this trend. In the mid-1980s, SCI employed 1,000 engineers and scientists, mostly from out of state, and 3,300 low-paid production workers. The plant manufactured personal computers on contract with IBM. A former SCI corporate counsel, Harvey Harkness, claimed that if SCI workers joined a union, the company would move its IBM contracts to its new factory in Graham, North Carolina, or overseas—or IBM would take its contracts away. SCI head Olin King told *Forbes* magazine, "While I expect to remain union-free in the U.S., should there be a problem, I'd be very comfortable having outside plants. You might say they are insurance."[19]

The Role of the Banks

Banks and financial institutions have also played a significant role in financing the movement of industry, first from the North to the South and then overseas to places like South Africa. The world's largest bank, Citicorp, closely linked with South Africa's Anglo American Group, led U.S. financial institutions in loans to finance South Africa's military–industrial expansion. Several of the firms represented on Citicorp's board of directors operated both in the southeastern United States and in South Africa. In 1984, its long-term loans to South Africa totaled $2.6 billion, almost as much as the combined amount lent by the next two largest U.S. lenders to that country. After Congress imposed sanctions, Citicorp sold its South African affiliate to the Anglo American Group; through its links to the MINORCA subsidiary, however, it remained in a position to help finance South African business.

The Southeast's largest regional bank, North Carolina National Bank (NCNB), directed relatively little locally generated investable surpluses to small business, minority housing, or industry in the Southeast. Instead, operating through a London affiliate, it expanded its business overseas, including South Africa.[20] One of three U.S. banks with offices in South Africa, NCNB made loans that accounted for one of every seven U.S. dollars lent directly to the South African government. As a percentage of its total assets,

NCNB had more loans outstanding in South Africa than any other U.S. bank. NCNB's chairman, a former U.S. Marine officer, explained, "I think it's [South Africa] one of the most wonderful countries in the world. . . . I've lived in a segregated society and that doesn't kill people." [21]

Increased Military Spending

As they encountered increased economic difficulties in the 1980s, all the southeastern states joined the nationwide scramble for military contracts and installations.[22] But expanded military spending failed to offset the region's mounting poverty. Instead, concentrated among a few large, typically transnational corporate contractors in a few counties, it had several negative consequences. The boom-and-bust effects of military spending cycles aggravated instability throughout the region. Even in boom years, defense contractors obtained tax-free facilities that reduced local and state revenues by millions of dollars.

The Department of Defense financed research and development of automation. This enabled transnational firms to de-skill jobs and control growing numbers of low-paid workers, moving their plants to the lowest-wage areas.

Several leading southeastern military contractors acquired holdings in South Africa, giving them a direct stake in the U.S. "constructive engagement" policy. Stringent South African military secrecy laws, backed by heavy fines, made it difficult to pinpoint the military role of these U.S. firms. Nevertheless, the latest available data provide examples.[23]

■ Union Carbide, which for decades managed the Atomic Energy Commission's Oak Ridge facilities in Tennessee, had more than $50 million in assets and employed about 1,500 workers in South Africa. There it mined and refined chromium and ferrochromium, both included by the Reagan administration in the list of so-called strategic minerals exempted from the 1986 U.S. sanctions.

■ Manufacturing airplane engines and equipment as Florida's leading military contractor, United Technologies held at least $20 million in assets and employed more than 1,220 workers in South Africa.

■ North Carolina's second-largest military contractor, the tobacco manufacturer R. J. Reynolds, held more than $12 million in direct investments and employed about 1,800 workers in South Africa.

■ Ingersoll-Rand, North Carolina's third-largest military contractor, held more than $31 million in South African assets.

■ Mississippi's fifth-largest military contractor, Sperry Corporation had $33 million worth of assets in South Africa.

By 1987, following the anti-apartheid movement's upsurge in South Africa and abroad, several U.S. military contractors sold their facilities in South

Africa. However, they contracted to provide technologies, spare parts, and even finances to the local firms that took over.[24] This group included:

- The parent of Florida's Hughes Aircraft, General Motors, which owned $140 million in assets, employed about 5,000 South African workers and admitted that its sales to South Africa's military market made its business there viable.

- General Electric, another leading Florida military contractor, had owned $140 million in assets and employed about 1,900 workers in South Africa.

- Louisiana's leading military contractor, Exxon, held more than $10 million in assets and employed 509 workers in South Africa.

- Georgia's third-largest military contractor, Goodyear Aerospace, a subsidiary of Goodyear Tire & Rubber, owned $97 million in assets and employed 2,510 workers in South Africa.

Summing Up: The Challenge

Evidence shows that transnational corporations took advantage of the post–World War II technological revolution to shift industries from the Southeast to low-wage areas, especially regional subcenters such as South Africa. Spurred by increased military spending, federal and state strategies fostered high-tech, often military-related industry that further aggravated the region's dualism, enriching the few while the many grew poorer. This reality posed a challenge to those seeking to devise more participatory, people-oriented strategies to end the South's poverty.

As long as transnational corporations can shift productive capacity to low-wage areas outside the United States, they will inevitably undermine these kinds of community efforts. To succeed, U.S. citizens need to support the struggles of Third World peoples, like those of South Africa and southern Africa, to liberate themselves, to attain parallel development of their own resources.

In southern Africa, the liberation movements have long proclaimed their aim not only to end racist rule in South Africa, but to reconstruct the intertwined South African and regional political economies to provide full employment and improved living standards for all the region's inhabitants.[25] To do this, they will need to buy the kinds of machinery and equipment that U.S. factories can build.

Thus, when they succeed, the entire vast southern African region—a land area as large as the United States—could become a far more stable, developed partner for mutually beneficial trade with the United States. On the one hand, like Angola today, they will eagerly sell their minerals to earn foreign exchange to buy the imports they will need.[26] On the other hand, as their incomes rise, they will provide a market perhaps eight to ten times the present level. Thus liberation and development in southern Africa could contribute not only to peace but full employment on both sides of the Atlantic.[27]

Attainment of these goals requires an increased awareness by U.S. citizens that U.S. political, economic, and military intervention in southern Africa strengthens South African minority rule, with a consequent negative impact on U.S. living and working conditions. The heads of state of the independent southern African nations, together with South African liberation leaders, call for an end to U.S. military intervention in Angola and implementation of more effective U.S. sanctions to hasten the end of apartheid. In their own interest, Southerners—small farmers, workers, professionals, and unemployed—should join in support for this call.

NOTES

Acknowledgment: This chapter is based on participatory research summarized in Ann Seidman, *Apartheid and the U.S. South* (Trenton, N.J.: Africa World Press, forthcoming).

1. For details on concessions, see James C. Cobb, *The Selling of the South: The Southern Crusade for Industrial Development, 1936–1980* (Baton Rouge: Louisiana State University Press, 1982), and *Industrialization and Southern Society* (Lexington: University Press of Kentucky, 1984). For property tax data, see *State and Metropolitan Area Data Book* (Washington, D.C.: U.S. Department of Commerce, 1986).

2. Quoted by James C. Cobb, "Y'all Come On Down—The Southern States' Pursuit of Industry," in *Everybody's Business: A People's Guide to Economic Development,* a special edition of *Southern Exposure* 14, nos. 5–6 (September/October and November/December 1986): 20.

3. Special circumstances explained the two major exceptions. With a large military establishment, Florida emerged as a sun trap for retired folk, tourists, and refugees from Latin American social change. Louisiana's manufacturing industry, centered around petrochemical plants located between New Orleans and Baton Rouge, paid wages higher than the national average. Nevertheless, in 1979, about a fourth of the rural inhabitants of both states struggled to survive on below-poverty-line incomes.

4. Unless otherwise cited, the analysis relating to South Africa and southern Africa in this section is from Ann Seidman, *The Roots of Crisis in Southern Africa* (Trenton, N.J.: Africa World Press, 1985).

5. The percentage of direct U.S. investments is from Anne Newman, "The U.S. Corporate Stake in South Africa," *Africa News* 24, no. 10 (May 20, 1984); Board of Governors of the Federal Reserve System, Federal Financial Institutions Examination Council, Statistical Release, E.16(26) of June 1, 1983. All other information is from *Survey of Current Business* (Washington, D.C.: U.S. Department of Commerce, annual).

6. Of U.S. foreign investments throughout the world, the rate averaged 18.4 percent (U.S. Department of Commerce, *Survey of Current Business*, August 1982).

7. Parastatals are partially state-owned corporations in basic South African industrial sectors, including electricity, railways, iron and steel industries, and the like.

8. *Quarterly Bulletin of Statistics* (Johannesburg: South African Reserve Bank, September 1979). "South Africa—The Militarism of a Society," *Solidarity News Service* (Botswana), March 1984.

9. Formulated by then U.S. Assistant Secretary of State Chester Crocker, the policy of constructive engagement and its antecedents are detailed in Seidman, *Roots of Crisis*, chapters 5 and 6. The Reagan administration's policy of military intervention stemmed from the Kissenger era (see John Stockwell, *In Search of Enemies: A CIA Story* [New York: Norton, 1978]) and continued through various secret channels until after repeal of the Clark amendment, which prohibited aid to the Angolan rebels; at that point it became public policy. See James Brooke, "U.S. Arms Airlift to Angola Rebels Is Said to Go On," *New York Times*, July 27, 1987.

10. For details on the Southeast's tobacco industry, unless otherwise cited, see William D. Toussaint, *Agriculture in the Southeast (with Particular Attention to Tobacco)*, study prepared for MDC, Inc. (Raleigh, N.C.: Economics and Business Department, North Carolina State University, 1986); also see Chapter 6.

11. Peter Taylor, *The Smoke Ring* (New York: Random House, 1984).

12. Unless otherwise cited, the information here relating to coal is from F. J. Rivers, "People and Jobs in the Southwestern Virginia Coalfields: A Report Prepared for the Commission on Religion in Appalachia and Community College Ministries (Knoxville, Tenn.: CORA, 1986). See "Unified List of U.S. Companies with Investments or Loans in South Africa or Namibia," compiled by Pacific Northwest Research Center, Inc. (New York: American Committee on Africa, 1985).

13. For detailed analysis of the Anglo American Group, see Duncan Innes, *Anglo American and the Rise of Modern South Africa* (London: Heinemann Educational Books, 1984). Newmont's partner in Peabody, the Bechtel Corporation, contributed George Shultz and Caspar Weinberger to the Reagan administration; see *Who's Who in America*, 1986.

14. See Chapter 3, this volume.

15. Alistair Sparks, "Slave Wage Paid by Profiteers with Pretoria's Backing," *The* (London) *Observer*, April 5, 1987. By the mid-1980s, South African apartheid, combined with growing unemployment, had forced 12 to 14 million people, about half the nation's black population, to live in the fragmented *bantustans*, which together constituted only 13 percent of South Africa's land area. There, without jobs or land, many died of malnutrition-related diseases, and millions of men, women, and children faced literal starvation.

16. An American Friends Service Committee (AFSC) in-house study suggests that the Reagan administration did not enforce the sanctions; cited by Jerry Hermann in an interview with the author at the AFSC office in Philadelphia, 1988.

17. Stuart Rosenfeld, "A Divided South," in *Everybody's Business;* see also Stuart A. Rosenfeld, Edward M. Bergman, and Sarah Rubin, *After the Factories:*

Changing Employment Patterns in the Rural South (Durham, N.C.: Southern Growth Policies Board, 1985).

18. Rosenfeld, "A Divided South."

19. Cited in Miller, "The Low Down on High Tech," *Everybody's Business,* 36–37.

20. Details on NCNB's role in the Southeast and South Africa may be found in "Comment on the Application of NCNB Corporation of Charlotte, North Carolina, to Acquire Centrabank, Inc. of Baltimore, Maryland and Request for a Public Hearing, Before the Board of Governors of the Federal Reserve System," by the Maryland Alliance of Responsible Investment.

21. *Charlotte Observer,* February 10, 1985.

22. See Tom Schlesinger with John Gaventa and Juliet Merrifield, *Our Own Worst Enemy: The Impact of Military Production on the Upper South* (New Market, Tenn.: Highlander Research and Education Center, 1983), for detailed information exposing the consequences of military spending. Also see supplemental maps in Paul DeLeon, ed., *Appalachia's Changing Economy* (New Market, Tenn.: Highlander Research and Education Center, 1986).

23. For these firms' role as U.S. military contractors, see Tom Schlesinger, *The Military and the South* (New Market, Tenn.: Highlander Research and Education Center, 1986); for their role in South Africa, unless otherwise cited, see "Unified List of U.S. Companies with Investments or Loans in South Africa or Namibia." Union Carbide data are from *Los Angeles Times,* January 18, 1987.

24. John D. Battersby, "U.S. Goods in South Africa," *New York Times,* July 27, 1987.

25. See the South African Freedom Charter, formulated by the African National Congress, the leading South African liberation organization, and the repeated declarations of the Southern African Coordination Conference, representing the nine independent neighboring southern African countries. Available from the office of the African National Congress of South Africa, 802 Second Ave., New York, NY 10017.

26. Despite U.S. military support of UNITA, the South African–backed contras, the United States is Angola's number-one trading partner and will probably remain so unless right-wing forces succeed in imposing sanctions to halt trade with Angola, as they now propose.

27. Seidman, *Roots of Crisis,* chapter 7.

Visions for Change

THE ARTICLES in this final section take up the challenge of articulating more general strategies and visions of change that are long-range yet rooted in the present realities of the Southern political economy. None purports to encompass all the constituencies or concerns represented in this book; indeed, the diversity that flavors the rest of the volume persists here.

The essays in this volume indicate that discontent is spread wide and deep, but there exists no common vision or strategy of change. What we find instead are pockets of resistance. Some emphasize self-help strategies for development, others advocate change in the mainstream; some are organized by race, others by gender or community. Some seek fundamental change in the economic system, others seek a larger share of the existing economic pie.

Despite the diversity, there are central themes that emerge repeatedly, and they are elaborated on in these chapters. Several contributors call into question the very definition of *economy* as commonly used in our society. Economics must be demystified, argues Wendy Luttrell, not simply by educating people about capitalism but by helping people to claim their own knowledge of and contribution to the economy. In Chapter 18 Luttrell discusses innovative educational approaches that can be used to overcome the dominant image of the economy as an external, mysterious arena that only experts can understand and no one can control.

Continuing this theme, Deborah Clifton Hils draws on the deeply spiritual traditions of her Creole culture to present a holistic view of the economy as part of a web of family and community relationships. In Chapter 19 she contrasts the materialism and environmental destruction that have accompanied industrial development with the symbiotic relationship with the earth held by many traditional peoples.

The chapters by Couto and Fisher offer proposals for economic development that is democratic and transformative. Couto (Chapter 20) argues that the provision of community-based human services should no longer be viewed as a derivative or secondary economic activity, but be developed as a key source of employment and a means to satisfy human needs. Fisher (Chapter 21) reviews recent proposals for economic renewal from both the right and the left and questions their relevance to the

225

problems of Appalachia and the South. He argues that the "real battleground is the national economy" and equips readers to evaluate the major economic policy approaches currently under debate.

The concluding essay, Chapter 22, draws on the experiences of the groups discussed in this volume to critique the mainstream perspective on economic development, including the popular affinity for educational improvement and technological innovation. While suggesting some new components for grassroots organizing, the editors draw hope and direction from the scattered but manifold efforts to redefine what constitutes the economy and to build economic democracy from the bottom up.

18

Community-Based Economics Education: A Personal, Cultural, and Political Project

Wendy Luttrell

There is a groundswell of community action across the country that may soon become a social movement. People are coming together within their communities in response to economic decline. In some instances, in direct response to plant closings, people have begun to explore collective, rather than individual, solutions to unemployment. In other instances, communities have come together to create economic alternatives such as developing new businesses, taking over existing industries, or shaping the decisions about the kinds of industry people want to bring to their region.[1] While people's collective action as *responders* to the economy is not a new phenomenon in the history of this country, there is something new in people seeing themselves as *shapers* of their own economic futures. This is particularly true in Appalachia and the South, where economic development and control have rested in the hands of people outside the region and the culture of those who must live with the consequences.

The current movement of people within Appalachia and the South to define and claim their rights as economic actors is the sociopolitical context for this study of the role of economics education. The more specific contexts framing my discussion are community-based education and development efforts that have been part of the Highlander Economics Education Project (HEEP) of the Highlander Center (see Resources). This project has a life history of its own, supporting community-based economic development groups and generating curriculum and resource materials on economics education.[2] Here I draw on and expand beyond the specific experiences and contribution of the HEEP project, in an effort to reconceptualize the role of economics education as a vehicle of social change.

I believe that economics education is a personal, cultural, and political undertaking that must nourish the development of self, knowledge, and power. The learning process must begin by discovering and validating what people already know about themselves, their lives, and community and using that as a basis for shaping their economic futures. It must also enable people to translate this self-knowledge into collective visions of and values about economic problems and possibilities. These visions and values are best formed and changed in community-based settings where participants are already embedded in ongoing social relationships or share common identities and concerns.

Ways of Knowing and Acting In the Economy

What is economic knowledge? Who has it? How do we claim economic knowledge so that we can control the development process? These are the questions that economics educators and learners face, whether or not they are aware of them. For the most part, as community residents or activists, we enter the process of economics education assuming that there are experts who know much more about the economy than we do. We think economic knowledge is something outside our experiences. In this view, the economy and its effect on people are not measured by concrete, everyday efforts to survive, but rather by government statistics, presented as facts and left to trained experts and officials to debate and resolve with public policy. This "official" knowledge of the economy, while it might relieve people of a certain responsibility, is also damaging.[3] Official economic knowledge works to minimize, underestimate, ignore, and suppress people's power to shape the economy.

Several contemporary social movements have challenged the power of "official" knowledge. For example, the black liberation movement challenged the authority of whites to define and therefore control the "problem" of blacks in America. This happened politically through voting and civil rights legislation, but also socially as blacks claimed leadership roles that had previously been denied to them.[4] Similarly, the women's movement challenged the authority of men to define and therefore control women's bodies, lives, and consciousness through the male-dominated institutions of law, religion, education, and even language, calling into question the very nature of knowledge and power.[5] The occupational and environmental health movement has challenged the authority of industry and government to define and therefore control what is dangerous to our bodies, land, and water, often exposing the political and ideological underpinnings of "scientific" facts and decisions.[6] In all these movements, people have come together to claim the knowledge of their collective experience despite overwhelming odds. Although this collective, resistant knowledge base and heritage are often dismissed or not fully recognized, they are ours to inherit in community-based economics education.

What we inherit from these social movements about people's knowledge and power is a model for putting women, minorities, the unemployed—in short, the economically disenfranchised—back into the process of defining and shaping the economy. This is the heart of economics education—understanding the participation, value, and potential power of people who are never seen as part of the economy and who have not had the opportunity to see themselves as economic actors. To tap into the collective experience and knowledge base that all these groups bring to the education process, we must first validate what they already know. Yet, to date, even "radical" approaches to economics education have tended to focus more on what people do not know about the capitalist economy than on what they do know. This has taken several forms. In one such approach, the primary focus is on establishing a common vocabulary and understanding of capitalist economic development: how profit is generated, how economic decisions are made, and who benefits.[7] Yet while this approach attempts to demystify economic terms, concepts, and language, by starting outside people's own economic experiences and knowledge it inadvertently promotes the image of the economy-as-external to people's lives and therefore outside their control.

In more traditional approaches, the economy is broken into sectors according to industry, or is divided into public versus private, service versus manufacturing, and so on, all for the purpose of understanding the role of paid workers within economic change. Unfortunately, this captures only part of the picture and limits people's ability to redefine their relationship to the economy in ways that include informal, domestic, or alternative economies. By not focusing on economies that operate alongside and intermingle with these sectors, traditional economics education makes invisible all those who contribute to the country's economic survival.

What we also inherit from these social movements about people's knowledge and power is an understanding that change is a process, not a product. If economics education is to facilitate a social movement celebrating people's knowledge and power, then it must allow for both personal and collective growth as people critically redefine their relationships to themselves and others through the educational process. There are at least four aspects to this learning process: identifying dominant images of the economy; defining people's own economic knowledge; nourishing the development of collective visions; and claiming knowledge through action.

Identifying Dominant Images of the Economy

The word *economy* conjures up many images for people. But for most of us "the economy" is seen as something external, a process almost entirely outside our personal lives and control. We think about the economy as we think about the weather. Both are subject to larger-than-life processes that can be systematically observed but never controlled. The economy, like the weather, must run its course. It is cyclical or seasonal. People deal with the "windfalls" of either profit or loss, and they must prepare themselves to cope with whatever condition the economy presents.

The economy is also something that only experts can predict. Specially trained people study external processes that operate outside the understanding of ordinary people. These professional economists are prepared to analyze the workings of the economy and to prophesy its future, but even they do not control it. In the end, it appears that no one controls the economy, and only experts can begin to comprehend it, thereby confirming people's already established sense of powerlessness.

The paradox of this contemporary cultural image of the economy-as-external is that it generates a contradictory message about people's economic role. On the one hand, because we think of the economy as a process outside ourselves and our communities, we don't see ourselves as shapers of the economy. This was made clear in the economics education class in Jellico, Tennessee, where Helen M. Lewis and John Gaventa asked students to define the words *work* and *economy* at the beginning of the course. Not surprisingly, people were quick to associate their own experiences with the word *work*, as "hard," "boring," "money," or "unemployed." On the other hand, words like *government, GNP,* and *taxes,* which were associated with the word *economy,* represented how external, distant, and institutionalized the image of the economy is. *Work* is what people do to ensure their own survival in an external and often hostile *economy.*

Yet, at the same time, when it is important to understand certain economic conditions as externally imposed, people instead take personal responsibility for financial crises. For this reason, plant closures and relocations, layoffs, wage and benefit reductions, unemployment, and all forms of social service cutbacks are viewed as the result of personal hardship or inadequacy. These external economic conditions are translated as an internal inability to compete successfully as an individual within the public economy. Through the dominant cultural image of the economy-as-external, coupled with ideologies of upward mobility, the American Dream, and equal opportunity, our society stresses that individuals are responsible for their own economic fates, yet simultaneously powerless to determine them.[8]

People's paradoxical relationship to the economy has its roots in the development of capitalist industrialization. The shift from agrarian to industrialized society fundamentally and profoundly altered personal, work, family, and community life. The nature of people's relationships to themselves, to one another, and to the marketplace was reshaped in ways that created unresolvable conflicts. And while these economic transitions defy simplistic accounts and explanations, the resultant social relationships produced popular images of the economy which must be addressed in economics education.

The advent of capitalist industrialization freed people from some of the constraints of preindustrial society while also creating new problems. On the one hand, people were no longer tied to the land, and subsistence survival was not the only option. Similarly, children could pursue other means of economic support in the form of wages, thus freeing them from the arbitrary rule of fathers or communities. Yet, at the same time, the breakdown of preindustrial family and community relations, coupled with wage labor, forced people into more separated spheres of life: work versus family, public versus private. Factories, rather than families, became the center of commercial or market production, and people's work and home lives were no longer integrated.

These two arenas of production—public and private, market and domestic—were reinforced by new gender relations and ideologies. The marketplace became associated with men, identified as a process controlled by few men but engaged in by most men. Men's activity in the public sphere was seen as productive work, and men alone became responsible for earning wages to support other family members. This primary breadwinner role and identity became equated with masculinity. On the other hand, the family became identified as a female domain. Even when women worked outside the home, women alone began to take on child rearing and homemaking as their primary roles within society. Within the family domain, women supported a domestic economy, bartering with relatives and neighbors for basic survival needs with food and clothing they produced themselves. Women's domestic work was more continuous; it was "never done" because its nature was fundamentally personal, private, and tied to the particular needs of each family member.

The lack of integration between work and family arenas of production provides one basis for the current inequality between women and men, where women's roles and activities are seen as less valuable. Also, these two separate spheres help support the economy-as-external image, an image that effectively eliminates all those who are not part of the paid work force from consideration as economic actors. Homemakers, the disabled, welfare recipients, the retired, and people who are permanently unemployed are all denied or stripped of their economic worth. In the same way, all these people, together with those who have given up hope of finding work, are discounted within government measures of the unemployment rate and become invisible as significant participants in the economy. Sexism and racism flourish in this context, which undermines people's contribution and covers up the real nature of economic discrimination.

These distinctions between work and family arenas of production have also created differences between people's strategies for coping with economic hardship. On the one hand, the distance and lack of control that most men feel is multiplied for people who are or have been denied full participation in the labor market, such as women, minorities, and the elderly. And as minority communities, to ensure survival, develop distinctive strategies that deviate from mainstream culture, they become even more marginalized in a society that rewards only those who conform. Yet, at the same time, the same groups that suffer from economic powerlessness are also more resilient in time of economic depression because they continue to have a base in the domestic, informal economy. For example, a critical role for women in the domestic economy has been to stretch resources in every way possible to meet the survival needs of families, which in times of trouble are no longer provided for by the public economy. In this way families, but especially women, absorb the costs of production for the market economy, cushioning the booms and busts.[9]

The Human-Nature-as-Self-Interest Debate

At the same time that the economy is seen as external to people's lives, the experts attempt to explain the economy in rational terms, often basing their predictions on fundamental principles about "human nature" that assume uniformity in people's responses and adaptations. The conventional wisdom about "human nature" includes the following traits: as human beings we are all efficient, calculating people who are only out for our individual gain; we base our decisions on rational criteria to maximize our own resources; and we make these rational decisions on an individual basis, without general regard for the interests or needs of others. In short, it is argued that human self-interest motivates all human behavior, but especially economic behavior. These economic experts argue that this self-interest is important for the economy—it fuels competition, competition fuels profits, profits fuel economic growth, and economic growth benefits everybody.

This notion of human nature as self-interest is also rooted in capitalist industrialization and modern sensibilities about the survival of the fittest. It is premised on applying the rules of the animal kingdom to human behavior, despite overwhelming evidence of the complex capacities of human beings to learn, adapt, change, and create.

The assumption that self-interested human nature motivates contemporary economic arrangements denies the full complexities of our humanity. First, it leaves out emotions as a factor in shaping economic decisions. But this is no surprise, given a society that casts emotions and rationality as polar opposites, perhaps even generated by different parts of the brain, and that applauds rational, objective, efficient management of the self. Yet, in daily life people know there is a fine line between emotion and rationality in their relationships, choices, and behaviors. Advertisers know that human emotions play a key role in our lives as consumers—the flood of commercials that speak to deep human desires, fears, and needs testifies to this fact. As economic actors, people find their emotions constantly impinging on decisions to consume, save, or take some jobs rather than others. In short, human self-interest as a cornerstone of capitalist economic relations simply cannot account for how people feel about themselves and others, nor can it explain how these feelings get translated into both the "rational" and "irrational" economic decisions that we make.

Second, the concept of human nature as self-interest leaves out important gender, cultural, class, racial, religious, and regional differences in self-perceptions and desires. Marketing research has explored this territory with an eye for capitalizing on the diversity of class, race, and gender self-concepts and values in selling a product. For example, while foreign cars may be popular among urban, middle-class professionals, they are scorned in working-class neighborhoods in Detroit. Similarly, personal hygiene products, such as shampoo, soap, and deodorant, that are targeted for women emphasize concerns different from those targeted for men. Advertising strategies build on the popular wisdom that "we are what we eat, wear, or drive," which simultaneously expands and limits personal options and images, solidifying people's place and identity within the social structure.[10]

Finally, the concept of human nature as self-interest obscures the real nature of the contemporary economy, which in fact fosters interdependent relationships among people. Despite an economy predicated on competition and individual maximization, collective and at times oppositional values do emerge in the struggle to make personal, community, and even national ends meet. These collective values can be traced throughout the history of our country, defying the simple self-interest model of economic growth.[11] In Appalachia and the South we see them in people's efforts to hold on to the land, protect natural resources, and establish shared traditions through community-based institutions, such as churches, unions, and schools. We also see them in people's life histories, where they balance between a quest for self-fulfillment and self-sufficiency on the one hand and, on the other, commitments to others that are part of everyday economic survival. In this quest, alternative or oppositional definitions of success and achievement arise that are not recognized or valued by the dominant society.

Economics education must deal with the complexities of these issues by standing conventional wisdom on its head. It must first make the claim that there is nothing instinctive, natural, or immutable about current economic arrangements. The task of economics education, therefore, is not only to expose the dominant images and assumptions about the economy, but to look for resistant values that are embedded in people's experience. While capitalist economic relations may indeed *shape* our ideas about human nature and motivation, they do not *determine* these ideas. Economics education must unravel the multiple and at times conflicting meanings that people attach to their own economic lives, so that we can begin the hard task of comparing, evaluating, and understanding the experiences we share with others. Viewed from this perspective, economics education is indeed a cultural project, setting out to explore how variations in people's experience, traditions, heritage, and sociopsychological development affect their economic roles, relationships, and activities.

Discovering People's Own Economic Knowledge

People's agency as economic learners and actors is best captured by their personal and family life and work histories. By sharing these economic stories people can begin to recognize and celebrate the active roles they have played within the economy. Collecting people's economic stories creates an equality; each person has a story, an idea of his or her own place in the economic process that is not based solely on wages but rather on relationships of economic survival. Getting people to reflect on all the multiple ways that family members have contributed to economic survival—through wage work, domestic work, illegal work, bartering and trading of goods and services, community work, or the emotional work of soothing wounded hearts and egos—is critical for redefining their relationship to the economy.

It is no surprise that students in community-based economics classes enjoyed doing economic oral histories with members of their family and the community. As people talked about the moonshine made by their fathers, the babies delivered by their grandmothers, the toys made by favorite aunts and uncles, or the quilts passed down from generation to generation, they recovered a piece of economic heritage that enabled them to articulate what they wanted for their own families and communities.[12] Collecting these economic stories also helped to integrate rather than separate the alternative, informal, or domestic economies into a more complete picture of what the economy is, thus challenging the economy-as-external myth.

Sharing economic stories is also an invaluable cultural activity in which variations in people's experience can be highlighted and analyzed. For example, in *Claiming What Is Ours: An Economics Experience Workbook,* the life and work histories of men and women are compared in an effort to break down false distinctions between men's and women's activities and to make visible women's contributions to economic survival. Similarly, family life and work histories are used to examine generational changes in both the nature of work and community life. Documenting community changes through people's economic stories helps to illuminate what is unique about a community. In the face of American mass culture, which emphasizes uniformity, cultural or regional differences are often seen as old-fashioned, unprogressive, or backward. People's own stories about community economic life can help to identify what is truly distinctive and worth holding on to, such as the land, religion, or natural resources, which have been driving forces in the Appalachian experience for generations, and build a sense of shared values and concerns.

Analyzing people's economic stories involves a critical examination of personal economic patterns and activities, such as consumerism. One of the most revealing assignments in the Jellico class was the import checklist. For one week, students kept track of all the groceries they bought, being sure to note where the food was produced. They were also instructed to make a checklist of all the clothes in their closets. As a result, the class discussion focused not only on the connection between local, national, and international economies, but also on people's own "needs," questioning the kinds of options we have as consumers.[13]

A critical focus on consumer and cultural values helps to counter the myth that human nature as self-interest shapes the economy and not vice versa. People intuitively know this, especially when they talk about community change, but it needs to be validated by systematically collecting and analyzing people's economic stories. For example, in the oral history materials collected by Jellico students, people emphasized how economic changes in the mountains had fostered new community relationships and values. While for many people this was expressed as nostalgia for the "good old days" when people went out of their way for one another and community life was vibrant with movie houses, stores, and church activities, there was an important parallel message: the closing of the mines, the building of the interstate, or the relocation of industry had created a new kind of individual, one isolated from collective activities and therefore less concerned about the community at large.

After collecting and analyzing these economic stories, students in two different communities—Jellico, Tennessee, and Dungannon, Virginia—came up with similar suggestions for a community-needs survey. Class discussions in Jellico had already indicated that students were concerned about mental health needs in the community. It was clear through all the community testimony that economic change had left many human needs unanswered and that economic development must address these needs. Each group identified human services—housing, restaurants, day care, and a nursing home—as their focus for economic development. This suggests an important role for economics education: one that allows people to challenge the primacy of profit motive over human needs in determining all economic planning and development.[14]

Nourishing Collective Economic Knowledge and Values

Moving from individual to collective forms of knowledge is not an easy step, but it is essential for the economic development process. It is not enough for people to gain personal insight about their own lives and place in the community; self-knowledge must also be translated into collective goals and visions for the future, especially if the agenda is economic change. While the process of collective economic visioning is often overlooked in traditional approaches to economics education, it nevertheless emerges as a galvanizing activity in the materials generated by the HEEP project. It deserves special attention.

Collective economic visioning broadens individual concerns by emphasizing people's sense of responsibility to future generations. One such visioning exercise draws on a saying among some Native Americans that "we should make every decision by considering its impact on our descendants seven generations on."[15] People are invited to consider the ten things they want to leave their descendants seven generations from now. These considerations then become part of goal-setting within the group so that discussions of what is possible are broadened rather than limited by current issues and problems. This exercise also helps to counter dominant images of individual self-interest as the single criterion of economic planning and decision making.

Collective economic visioning also gives people the opportunity to think of themselves as shapers rather than responders to public economic policy. Since most community-based groups will be forced to consider city, county, regional, or national economic initiatives, people will be better prepared to evaluate these proposals if they have had a chance to consider their own visions. One group of students in the Jellico class took this challenge seriously and drafted a community "economic bill of rights," listing the considerations they saw as important in recruiting new industry to the area, such as environmental and occupational safety and security. Their approach, which delineated the responsibility of industry to communities, provided a means by which students could articulate collective identities and interests as Jellico residents, rather than simply as individuals in need of jobs. This process also helped to clarify collective values about economic equity and justice as the class debated what kinds of tradeoffs individuals and communities should be willing to make.

One of the key dilemmas of community-based economics education is that we are all seriously limited in our imagination and knowledge of what is possible. Not only are we constrained by our own economic and cultural experiences, but we are also limited by the lack of organizational or institutional supports for ideas that oppose the status quo. As a result, economics education needs to be seen as a constant experiment in finding new ways of thinking and imagining ourselves, not only as individuals but also as groups. For this reason, much of the emphasis of the HEEP materials in both style and content deals with group processes, how people learn and work together, as a vehicle for expanding the boundaries of our economic imagination.

Claiming What Is Ours to Control

Transforming new economic knowledge into economic development practice is by no means automatic. While the popular slogan "knowledge is power" may inadvertently encourage simplistic or naive notions about human, political, or social transformation, most people know better by virtue of their own experience. Identifying what helps us to act, and what inhibits us from acting on our experience and knowledge is perhaps one of the most important goals of community-based economics education, yet it is the most underdeveloped. Although there is an extensive body of research on power relations within a community, most often referred to as "power-structure analysis," there is considerably less understanding of how people discover the source of their own power and/or powerlessness.[16]

In Jellico, Mountain Women's Exchange leader Barbara Greene has dealt directly with this issue in workshops she has developed to help people locate and redefine power for themselves and their community.[17] She begins by drawing a line on paper (calling it the "power in the community" line). She asks participants to name things or people that have power and writes their responses above the line. Then, for every person or institution that has power, she asks participants to name one that does *not* have power, and writes those responses below the line. This first step is crucial in establishing the idea that power is a relationship—for someone to have power, someone else must be without it. Power is not invisible, nor does it reside within single institutions. After the power line is complete, Barbara Greene asks people to chart themselves on it. What follows is the core of the exercise:

My going through this line and picking out where I stand in the community only helps me understand how I feel. It does not help me understand how or what people think about me. We need to work on not only how we see ourselves, but how other people see us. . . . That's the purpose of this part of the exercise, to examine our differences. We need to talk about how other people see us, and how the people on top think about the people on the bottom. What is the boss's attitude to the worker? What is the worker's attitude toward the boss?

From here participants are encouraged to discuss the difference between being a powerful individual and an individual with power. Barbara Greene invites participants to critically evaluate the meaning of power:

We have to talk about how we feel when we take control of things in our lives. It doesn't mean that we want to turn this whole power line upside down. We don't want to make all these people on the bottom be the ones who have the power and these on top be the ones who don't have the power. What we're trying to do is figure out how we can all have power together. Not that I have power over you and you have power over me, but that somehow together we're real powerful. We have power with each other, not over each other.

Economics education must challenge mystical or false concepts of power in people's everyday lives. It must examine what holds people back at each stage of the economic development process: when people process new knowledge, when they deal with officials, collect information for their community economic profile, or present economic research to their communities, and when they organize plans for economic development. For example, students in the Dungannon class were forced to deal with feelings of powerlessness when they interviewed a bank president. As they probed the official and insisted on their rights to public information, they overcame their initial discomfort and refused to be patronized. This is a good example of how the learning process itself and the claiming of new knowledge can enable students to tap into a source of power within themselves—the power not to be intimidated.

Community-Based Learning Strategies

The HEEP project, as well as community-based economic development projects around the world, is premised on an educational philosophy that views learning and knowledge as strategic. Therefore, community-based economics education must ask where is it possible to go, and how is it possible to get there. To address such strategic questions, economics education must build collective identities, interests, and concerns.

Certain learning contexts make such a cultural and political project virtually impossible, such as formal, institutionalized settings that promote individual, competitive achievement. Community-based education, however, when it takes place within already established collective settings, such as unions, churches, and community-action groups, can more readily translate knowledge into practice.

In recent years, with the proliferation of post-secondary education into off-campus sites where community colleges have sought to increase revenues through student recruitment, community-based education has taken a different form. In these contexts, students come to class bonded to each other through their common heritage and identity in a particular community. The role of economics education in these settings is to foster collective knowledge, learning, and change through these already established community relationships, confirming rather than undermining people's identification with their culture and community. The Highlander Economics Education Project has been part of this postsecondary effort to make education empowering, building bridges between the classroom and community organizations already involved in economic development. The result is a partnership that grows out of people's direct relationship to their community and its survival.

In whatever form it takes, *community-based* economics education holds the greatest potential for identifying, nourishing, and claiming economic knowledge. Its promise, however, can be fulfilled only through broader cultural and political movements and coalitions that together create a new social imagination about a fair and just economy. The seeds of these movements exist within Appalachia and the South where the voices of economically disenfranchised people are beginning to be heard. Community-based economics education must do all it can to help vocalize the effort.

NOTES

1. The Tri-State Conference on Steel is just one of many organizations that collectively address the issue of plant closures. See "Valley of Steel" as told by Jim Benn in Wendy Luttrell, *Claiming What Is Ours: An Economics Experience Workbook* (New Market, Tenn.: Highlander Research and Education Center, 1988), 135–38. *Everybody's Business: A People's Guide to Economic Development*, a special edition of *Southern Exposure* 14, nos. 5–6 (September/October and November/December 1986), is an excellent review of economic development efforts in the South.

2. These resources include *Picking Up The Pieces: Women in and out of Work in the Rural South*, 1986 (a collection of oral histories of working women); *New Direc-*

tions: Responses to the Rural Economic Crisis, 1986 (edited proceedings from a conference entitled "Community Based Economic Development: An Alternative for Southwest Virginia?"); Wendy Luttrell, *Claiming What Is Ours: An Economics Experience Workbook,* 1988; Helen Lewis and John Gaventa, *The Jellico Handbook: A Teacher's Guide to Community-Based Learning,* 1988; Sue Ella Kobak and Nina McCormack (with assistance from Nancy Robinson), *Developing Feasibility Studies for Community-Based Business Ventures,* 1988; *Claiming Our Economic History: Jellico, Tennessee,* 1988 (a compilation of oral histories collected as a class project in a community-based economics education class in Jellico); and Paul DeLeon, ed., *Appalachia's Changing Economy,* 1986 (a reader compiled by the HEEP project and the Commission on Religion in Appalachia). All are available from the Highlander Research and Education Center, Route 3, Box 370, New Market, TN 37820.

3. See John Gaventa, "The Powerful, The Powerless and The Experts," working paper (New Market, Tenn.: Highlander Center, 1984).

4. Challenging the knowledge and authority of whites is perhaps most clearly seen in the writings of black nationalists such as Malcolm X, H. Rap Brown, Huey Newton, Bobby Seale, Imamu Baraka, the Soledad Brothers, and Angela Davis. See also the book by Black Power advocates Charles Hamilton and Stokely Carmichael, *Black Power: The Politics of Liberation in America* (New York: Random House, 1967).

5. This is perhaps clearest in the women's health movement. See Boston Women's Health Collective, *The New Our Bodies, Ourselves: A Book by and for Women,* (New York: Simon & Schuster, 1984); Linda Gordon, *Women's Body, Women's Right: A Social History of Birth Control in America* (New York: Grossman, 1976); Sheryl Burt Ruzek, *The Women's Health Movement: Feminist Alternatives to Medical Control* (New York: Praeger, 1978). See Dale Spender, *Men's Studies Modified: The Impact of Feminism on the Academic Disciplines* (Elmsford, N.Y.: Pergamon Press, 1981), for a discussion of how the women's movement challenges traditional academic disciplines.

6. For example, Juliet Merrifield, "Putting the Scientists in Their Place: Participatory Research in Environmental and Occupational Health," working paper (New Market, Tenn.: Highlander Center, 1988); Nicholas Freudenberg, *Not in Our Backyards! Community Action for Health and the Environment* (New York: Monthly Review Press, 1984); and Barbara Ellen Smith, *Digging Our Own Graves: Coal Miners and the Struggle over Black Lung Disease* (Philadelphia, Pa.: Temple University Press, 1987).

7. I am referring here to the Center for Popular Economics developed by economists at the University of Massachusetts, Amherst. *Capitalism for Beginners* by Robert Lekachman and Borin Van Loon (New York: Pantheon Books, 1981) is another example of attempts by radical economists to demystify the economy.

8. William Ryan defines this process as "blaming the victim" and describes the ways in which various social institutions contribute to people's self-blame, thereby obscuring the structural forces behind poverty (*Blaming the Victim* [New York: Vintage Books, 1976]). Richard Sennett and Jonathan Cobb in their book *The Hidden Injuries of Class* (New York: Vintage Books, 1973) and Lillian Rubin in *Worlds of Pain: Life in the Working-Class Family* (New York: Basic Books, 1976) also discuss how working-class people blame themselves rather than structural constraints for not being

upwardly mobile, which, the authors argue, is one of many built-in methods of social control.

9. Ruth Milkman, "Women's Work and Economic Crisis: Some Lessons of the Great Depression," *Review of Radical Political Economics* 8, no. 1 (Spring 1976): 73–98; Lois Rita Helmbold, *Making Choices, Making Do: Survival Strategies of Black and White Working-Class Women During the Great Depression* (Urbana: University of Illinois Press, forthcoming).

10. See Stuart Ewen, *Captains of Consciousness* (New York: McGraw-Hill, 1976) for a history of the advertising industry and its ability to create new personal and psychological needs.

11. For example, Herbert Gutman traces the conflict of values over work in American history in *Work, Culture and Society in Industrializing America: Essays in American Working-Class and Social History* (New York: Knopf, 1976).

12. See *Claiming Our Economic History: Jellico, Tennessee.*

13. See Lewis and Gaventa, *The Jellico Handbook,* for a description of the import-checklist exercise.

14. See Chapter 20, for a discussion of economic development that addresses human services.

15. See Luttrell, *Claiming What Is Ours,* 103–5, for collective economic visioning exercises.

16. Most power-structure research was modeled on G. William Domhoff's work, including *Who Rules America?* (Englewood Cliffs, N.J.: Prentice-Hall, 1967); *Who Rules America Now? A View for the 80's* (Englewood Cliffs, N.J.: Prentice-Hall, 1983); *Who Really Rules: New Haven and Community Power Re-examined* (New Brunswick, N.J.: Transaction Books, 1978); *Power Structure Research* (Beverly Hills, Calif.: Sage, 1980); *Power Elite and Organizations,* (Beverly Hills, Calif.: Sage, 1987).

17. See Luttrell, *Claiming What Is Ours,* 63–69, for Barbara Greene's exercise.

19

Interactions of Economics and Spirituality: Some Perspectives from Creole Culture

Deborah Clifton Hils

W e were born of Black Water at the beginning of time. This is the water of life that flows from the womb of the Mother Earth—whom we refer to as the Water Mother. The Water Mother gave birth to many nations in the Black Water. All the peoples, all the animals, all the plants, and all entities like fog are born of the Black Water. We come to be through it. We return to our ancestors through it. Wherever the Black Water flowed, it left living beings. So it left us in four places on the land: the marsh, the bayou, the big woods, the prairie. Everything in the land is imaged in the circle of life. This circle is called *le moyeu*. All our festivals are a turning of *le moyeu*.

When all these things were understood by our ancestors, they came together and formed a spiritual bond. This bond is called *la sympathie*. The prophet Chahta was the first one to set down the laws of the bond. These laws were spelled out not by writing but by the talking stick, the *poteau-mitain*. The *poteau-mitain* is also called *istruma* or *baton rouge*. Other prophets and teachers followed Chahta. Among them were Black Hawk, Toussaint, and Lafitte. Those who are joined together in the bond of *sympathie* are called a *cru*, or a *krewe* in the American language. So we are a people of the krewes. If a person is in the bond, he's in our blood. We don't make war with those who are in our blood.

Long before the white man ever came into our lives or into the land, there was a great civilization that developed among those who were in the bond.

Our homes were near the bayous, and we traveled freely through the marshes, bayous, prairies, big woods, and onto the sea when we wished. Then the white man came and invented himself and said we were savages that had to be civilized. White men didn't understand about the bond. Not content with civilizing us and not understanding how the world was made, they went to other countries and forced the people there to come to the land of Black Water. This made a big confusion. But some of these people—all except the *américains,* in fact—were able to understand the bond, so they came with us and are still in *sympathie* with us in spite of everything. So we hold to the Black Water, our prophets' memories, the bond, the circle of life, the four clans, and the talking stick because we've found that these are things that endure. And we call ourselves, and are called, *Créole* because we are the people joined in the bond, the people of the krewes, and native people of this Black Water land.

After the time of the original bond, other peoples came to the land. If they tasted the Black Water with us and came into the *sympathie* with us, they are like blood to us. But if they didn't come into the bond, they are still foreigners. The *américains*—they have never wanted to come in.

For me, and for most of the people I'm acquainted with, economic realities are all tied up with cultural and spiritual realities. As a Creole person, I've been taught by my culture to see things in terms of a way of living, family, community, and relationships. And all these go back a long way. They go so far back in time, in fact, that no one has ever been able to reliably pinpoint exactly *when* they began.

We come from Louisiana. We're native to Louisiana. We're irreplaceably identified with Louisiana. It's as simple as that. With the type of cyclical understanding of history we have, anything that has the potential for disrupting our complex and deeply rooted web of lifestyle, family, community, and relationships is seen as either insane or oppressive and is either ignored, avoided, or resisted—but never invited home and into our intimate circle. So these four considerations are the starting points, the focus, of any analysis of reality I do.

I speak in personal terms because a lot of Creole people tend to look at things in terms of how they affect them personally. Let's look first at the consideration of *family.* My lifestyle revolves around my family. I have a big family, although not so big as some. My family is actually spread over several states and ethnic groups in the Mississippi Valley and Great Lakes as well as in California. There's three or four languages spoken: Creole, English, French, and Spanish. My family has lived in the same basic geographic area since forever. We've lived in the same five- or six-parish area of southern Louisiana alone for over 300 years.

Connected with family is the consideration of *community.* My family is a community, and that community is part of a bigger community that relates to other communities. That bigger community is our nation—the Creole nation—and that nation connects to a whole web of other nations that we're related to.

This brings me to the consideration of *relationships*. That includes both the family and community ties already mentioned plus our relationships to our land and all the plants and animals that are part of it. So I also have to consider my relationship to the prairies and marshes of Southwest Louisiana and Southeast Texas, which are the spiritual homeland of our family; and through that my relationship to the other ecological areas created by the Mississippi River; and my relationships to other life forms like rice, corn, cane, cypresses, alligators, crawfish, egrets, and Canada geese, to name just a few. *Lifestyle* is the celebration of all these considerations. The way of living of our people is to be conscious of and thankful for all these values, to recognize that we are part of nature.

So all these basic considerations are interconnected. Each one has a bearing on all the others. What sustains this web of living, family, community, and relationships? The answer that comes to me most immediately is the River.

Every person and every thing mentioned so far is connected directly or indirectly to the life cycle of the Mississippi River and its interaction with the land and sea. So we're dependent on the River. If something were to happen to the River to radically alter its life cycle, it could threaten our lives and identity, too. And that is happening at the present time. But what's happening right now, today, is the fruition of a long cycle of destruction. It's happened in three stages: first it was decided to "tame" the Mississippi by damming it up and confining it to one channel. Then it was decided to turn the Mississippi into the sewer of America. Then it was decided to dam up and alter the major tributaries of the River—most notably the Tennessee—still further reducing the water flow and thus the capacity of the River to renew itself and dependent life forms. The combination of these factors has thrown the life cycle of the whole interior drainage system of this continent out of whack. On the way to achieving this "miracle" of industrial development, countless people were driven off the land, entire nations and other species have been destroyed, cultures obliterated, graves disturbed, and all manner of other damage done. So today, from the mouth of the St. Lawrence, through the cold wetlands of Minnesota and Manitoba, to the delta of the Mississippi, we have one vast stagnant garbage sluice. Our trash washes up on the shores of the Yucatan Peninsula and numerous Caribbean islands   for all we know it floats all the way to Africa.

The level of contaminants along the Mississippi drainage area is so high that it's now irretrievably worked its way into the food chain. We hunt, fish, trap, grow vegetables, eat, and drink at our own peril. Now the land itself is eroding, and the entire region is plagued by unseasonal droughts and violent storms. This is threatening, to say the least. You could call it an economic problem if you want. You could also call it cultural or spiritual or both. Where does one draw the line?

Obviously someone has made big money from building all those dams and locks, filling the waters with all that waste, and pumping all those minerals out of the ground. Somebody has also made big money treating people for all the artificially induced diseases, burying the victims, and speculating on the land and property ripped off from the survivors. And that's all economic—no doubt about it.

Culturally speaking, the current state of affairs has permitted the establishment of industrialism in a vast area of the interior of this continent and conveniently eradicated or put on the defensive the indigenous cultures of the area. But the cultural and economic clash between the indigenous peoples and others who live as part of nature on the one hand, and the devotees of industrialism (whether in its capitalist or socialist disguise) on the other, is also a philosophical and spiritual clash. Where do we draw the line? Where can we?

To get some understanding of what's happening to the Creole people, one has to understand something of the life cycle of the Mississippi River and its relationship to Creole culture. And that's a spiritual relationship. To get some understanding of that, one has to look at the Mississippi at its source. This requires a different way of looking at things from what one is perhaps used to.

To indigenous peoples, North America is not something on a contrived map, separated by artificially drawn lines representing Canada, the United States, Mexico, and a whole host of Central American and Caribbean countries, all dissected into equally artificial states, provinces, and time zones. To indigenous peoples, North America is a huge island. This island is shaped something like a turtle riding on an alligator's back, as the alligator picks its way among a host of smaller islands. In fact, most refer to the continent by its indigenous name of Great Turtle Island. This Turtle Island is cut by many rivers and lakes. Mountains run around the outer edges, and in between are forests, plateaus, and deserts. Around the coasts and down through the center are marshes, grasslands, wetlands, swamps, and rain forests. These natural features and the alternation of seasonal wind and water currents surrounding Turtle Island form the *natural* geographic and social divisions that have always been adhered to. A map of North America drawn to reflect indigenous social realities would look very different from the currently accepted one.[1]

Running through the heart of Turtle Island—from around Great Slave Lake in the north, through the Great Lakes and into the central parts of (what's been artificially designated as) Minnesota and Wisconsin—is a vast wetland area. It could be described as the turtle's heart. This wetland drains off in four directions. To the west it becomes the McKenzie River system, whose delta empties into the Arctic Ocean. To the north it becomes the Lake Winnipeg system, whose waters drain off into the Nelson and Churchill rivers and into Hudson's Bay. To the east it drains through the Great Lakes into the St. Lawrence River and ultimately into the Atlantic Ocean. To the south it drains into the Mississippi River, which, with its tributaries, ultimately empties its delta into the Gulf of Mexico. So these four river systems are like a circulatory system pumping life through a living body. The environmental balance maintained by this vast drainage system is very delicate. The balance between salt and fresh waters, freeze and thaw, flood and siltification, wet seasons and dry that is regulated by North America's internal drainage system is vital to every form of life on this continent. It's from the geological point of view a very active system, changing from year to year.

The Mississippi has its origins deep in the heart of Turtle Island. In a low-lying, wet, foggy, mosquito-breeding land, subjected to seasonal extremes of temperature ranging from subarctic cold to tropical heat. Yet it's a land teeming with life and ideas, a land that has always produced a rich variety of human cultures. There are many peoples besides Creoles whose legends trace their origins to the Mississippi River and its life cycle.

All speak of emerging into the world in a wet, foggy, swampy land where finding a small bit of high, dry ground was an event of epic proportions. All speak of a mother figure whose divine gift was to discover a way to live happily and securely in such an environment. All speak of powerful water creatures—fish, birds, reptiles, and amphibians, most especially the turtle—who become teachers, helpers, and guardians. All speak of the wonder of the sun breaking through the fog. All speak of the people's prosperity and ultimate overpopulation, decadence, and illness in the wetlands (usually brought on by giving in to the urge to material power and domination, symbolized by bad medicine which disrupts the delicate life balance). All speak of interminable migrations through pea-soup fog in search of healing, renewal, enlightenment, led usually by a prophetic figure. All speak of the many peoples encountered along this journey; of comparing medicines with them and of struggling to reach understanding with them rather than fighting. All speak of settling down again somewhere in this vast watery world to start the cycle all over again. Each speaks in its own way, in its own language, out of its own social experience, yet all speak about the same things.

Four rivers flow in four directions out of the womb of a turtle. Each has a life cycle of flood and ebb tide that leaves four lands: prairie, forest, black-water swamps or bogs, and open marsh. Each of those lands is a clan. Each has high ground and low ground. If every clan shares its high ground with the shifting of the tides, there's more than enough of everything for everybody. If the clans talk together, if they seek spiritual renewal and understanding together, if each clan respects the role of the other clans, if they wait for the sun to break through the fog and follow the real light of the sun instead of running off after the false light of the *feu follet,* things go well. This way of sharing, waiting, understanding, will lead to prosperity and happiness—even while living in a land of fog, trembling earth, and shifting rivers. The false light, the *feu follet,* can be power, money, material things, jealousy, bad medicine, or rejection of the natural law—that is, the unwillingness to live with the fog and move with the tide. Its attraction is hypnotically powerful. It's also fatal. The *feu follet* will get you lost. Those who fall for its twinkling light wander off into the mist and are never heard from again; or if by some chance they do return, it's only as a *zombi.* Victims of the *feu follet* are never master of themselves again. This is some of what we've learned from the River.

Creole people don't fear the power of the River, the floating land, the rain forest, or the hurricane winds. Where others see something to fear, we see only forces of power and beauty—dangerous, yes, if played with—but also guardians of the doorway to understanding and a renewed life. They give us more than they could ever take away. The Creole says, "Better a good understanding than a fine house." The *américain* seems to want his house to be fine and thinks the forces that give understanding are a threat to that finery. The *américain* wants to tame the River and seed the hurricane, because these seem to stand in the way of his desire to live in the flood channel. The Creole says, "You can't play with God," and builds his house with loose joints on high ground. We have a hard time understanding just what makes the *américain* tick. He doesn't seem to enjoy anything other than making money; and even when he has more of that than you can shake a stick at, he still doesn't seem to enjoy life any more than the poor man.

Why do you people want to poison the River? Because it won't stay within the limits dictated by your flood-control system? Or because of your own inability to live happily in this land? And if you can't be happy at home, where can you be happy in this life? Or maybe you don't really feel at home in this country. Why else would you be destroying it? How can you feel at home, when you don't even know the proper name of your own country, or understand the significance of the turtles you run over on the interstate?

It's said that everyone knows their own mother. So who would give poison to the woman who gave them birth? That's what you do when you inject toxic chemicals into the earth. Or maybe you weren't born in this country, too, and that's why you don't seem to recognize your own mother. Or maybe it's just because you have yet to learn your mother's name.

It takes a really deep self-hatred for someone to try and kill his or her own mother. Your mother is the reason you have a body. She's the one who brings you to a material level of existence, by giving up her body, her life if need be, for you. Essentially, to try and kill your mother is tantamount to saying you hate the body you're in, that you're a human being. And that's self-hate. It's a hatred of *flesh,* of sexuality, since that's what makes it possible for flesh to reproduce itself. So to destroy your mother is the same as destroying yourself. And from our point of view, one's human mother is the manifestation of the earth, the mother of us all, because flesh is earth, and the earth is the expression of the female aspect of the Creator's life force. So we tend to put poisoning a river on the same level as rape, abortion, matricide, child abuse, and questioning God. All those acts are symptoms of the same disease—self-hate. There is a terrific contradiction in a country that craves love from all the world, but doesn't love itself; in a country that wants to police and democratize the world, but can't even say the name of its own land.

And this brings us down to a basic problem. Every nation of people has its own understanding of social reality, its vision, its life experience. As a nation, we Creoles have an experience too. But the defining points of our experience are very different from those of the dominant American society. Even our borders and frontiers are drawn in different places and in different ways. Take, for example, these neat geographic divisions between North and South, America–Canada–Latin America. These are not really relevant for me.

Creole people, for example, traditionally consider Mexico to be everything south and west of San Antonio and Galveston, because to us there's a natural cultural, linguistic, and ecological border there. At the same time, Mexico, though a distinct culture from our own, is very closely related to us—so closely in fact, that one can't really talk about Creoles and Louisiana without also talking about Mexico. How does Mexico fit into the dominant culture's categories? Who decides?

To a Creole person, there are neighborhoods in Chicago, Los Angeles, and San Francisco that are as much a part of our reality as Lafayette, Louisiana. In fact, you can't fully understand what goes on in a place like Lafayette on the day-to-day level without understanding something about all the Creoles from Lafayette who live all or part of their lives in California. And what about the Chicanos in Houston who speak a Spanish laced with Cajun French and get off on *boudin* and jazz? Or the Creoles in Port Arthur, Texas, and Lake Charles, Louisiana, who ride in rodeos and devour unbelievable quantities of home-cooked Mexican food? Where do all these people fit into the *américain's* neat little analyses of who we are and where we come from?

Our way of life as Creoles is very tied into Canada, Latin America, and the West Coast. To the dominant society, the Canadian border is an international reality and sign of peace between two friendly nations. To Creoles, Cajuns, Acadians, Native Americans, and *Québecois*—all of whom have living, not fictional, relatives on both sides of it, all of whom belong to nations arbitrarily divided by it—the Canadian border is basically a nuisance and a constant reminder that our homeland is under a foreign occupation. So if I attempt to talk about our lives in terms familiar to and accepted in the dominant society, I have to leave out important factors that are directly involved and put in others that have no connection to us.

Unlike the dominant industrial society, however, we keep to ourselves. We live in our own way within our own borders and work out our agreements with our neighbors as need and opportunity arise. We're not out imposing our ways and our understanding on the whole world. We don't have a manifest-destiny policy or a Monroe Doctrine. We haven't defined the whole Western Hemisphere as "our backyard." We aren't out drawing imaginary borders and ramming them down other peoples' throats at gunpoint. Our "national security interests" are tied up in there being enough ducks and geese in the marshes for us to feed ourselves, in being able to eat without fear the crabs we catch out of the Mississippi backwaters, and in wondering who'll become the next King of Zydeco—a decision which, contrary to popular belief, is made neither in New Orleans nor by the Burger King Corporation (see Burger King's "Cajun Whaler" commercial).

To the extent that the *américains* are drawing borders, filling pigeonholes, establishing categories, and pushing them down our throats; to the extent that their manifest-destiny policies hurt us, our relatives, friends, and allies; to the extent that their passion for "taming" the spirits of nature reduces the duck and geese population and contributes to the erosion of our land base; to the extent that the pollutants created by their "industrial miracle" poison both us and our crabs; to the extent that the dominant American society poses a threat to our way of life, to our families, our community, our relationships—to that extent we and other indigenous peoples will continue to perceive the *américain* as a threatening and unwelcome foreigner in our country.

A Native American poet, John Trudell, a man I have a lot of respect for, describes the spiritual clash between the indigenous and industrial societies as being due to the action of an evil force he calls "Warmaker." Warmaker's doings, according to Trudell, are not always in the spectacular forms of open violence. Warmaker's main stock in trade is self-hate, which causes us to make war on ourselves, to get caught up in a self-destructive pattern of behavior. We're all potential victims of Warmaker, because we all have inside of us that small seed of insecurity that Warmaker preys on.

The Creole way is not to give Warmaker a chance. So our whole culture is set up to try and remove or neutralize as much as possible the causes of self-hate by learning to be comfortable with our bodies, with the life force within and around us, with the force that makes us human. Our way is not to take things too seriously, to take ourselves and all of life with a big grain of salt. Otherwise, we leave the way open for John Trudell's Warmaker. When we can be happy in our home and in our own country, we don't need to be at war with ourselves, our environment, or other people. Laughter, music, symbolism, celebration, love, the sounds of life—these will throw Warmaker right off your bumper.

NOTE

1. It would look a lot closer to a series of maps published a few years ago by the University of California at Davis—maps that were in fact prepared by indigenous scholars. See Jack D. Forbes, *Atlas of Native History* (Davis: University of California, 1981).

CHAPTER

20

Toward a Human Service Economy

Richard A. Couto

A human service economy centers on community organizations providing basic human services as a strategy of economic development. This chapter interprets past community organizing efforts, especially in health care, as forerunners of a human service economy. The central argument of this chapter is that we must part with economic development strategies that envision human services as a consequence of another form of economic activity, such as job creation, and instead articulate strategies in which the provision of human services, in and of itself, is an important form of economic activity for low-income communities.

Historical Background

Historically, Appalachia and the rural South have had a social service infrastructure directly related to a few dominant industries. The coal towns, steel towns, mill towns, and plantations that still dot the region make this apparent. The infrastructure usually included wage employment, education, housing, and health care, and sometimes the company or the plantation owner provided them all. Access to these services hinged on employment at the steel plant, the textile mill, the coal mine, or on the plantation. The less skilled and organized a work force was, as in the case of sharecroppers, the poorer the social services were. At their worst, social services were grossly inadequate, serving as mechanisms of debt-bondage and control of the labor force. Workers owed their souls—and their social services—to the company store.

In many communities in the South, the social service infrastructure was developed by these industries, as a spinoff of economic development. With the decline of these traditional industries, as we have seen throughout the case studies in this volume, the social services infrastructure has also dissipated, decayed, and sometimes disappeared.

Another way to understand the current crisis in human services for rural communities is to think of them as "social capital." When industries such as mining, textile manufacturing, and agriculture invested in the development of the region, they also invested social capital; that is, they provided the services necessary to maintain their work force at least at a minimal level of survival. As capital disinvests in the region, through mine and plant closings, or as automation replaces the need for labor, there is also a decline in the social capital through which human services historically have been provided.

Nevertheless, dominant strategies of economic development still link the provision of social capital for human services to the recruitment of private capital. These strategies generally prescribe industrial recruitment as the antidote to the dire need for improved social services. They assume that finding a company to locate in a community will mean jobs, and that jobs will mean more money in the community to improve housing, health care, or education. As discussed in Chapter 14, this strategy has reached mythical proportions, especially in the poorest communities. Essentially it means looking backward to a day when more social services were available because of employment in one or a few dominant industries.

In experience, of course, the linkage of social capital to private capital has several shortcomings. First, the poor areas of the South provide ample witness that economic development is no guarantee of adequate or equitable housing, health care, or education. Second, some industries locate in poor communities specifically *because* they find the lack of social services attractive. Poor communities can provide an abundant supply of low-cost, unskilled labor that requires little social capital investment to maintain or reproduce. Public officials in such communities are more likely to support high-risk economic activity, such as toxic dumping or strip mining, because of the desperate need for economic alternatives.

Finally, even when a community receives a "plum," such as a Saturn plant, it may find that some social capital is negotiated away (see Chapter 14). In a competitive environment, corporate investment may no longer bring with it social investment, but may in fact require social subsidies to house, educate, and provide health care for the new work force. Most often, workers themselves provide this social capital, although now the mechanisms are the property tax, sales tax, and the like, rather than the company scrip and checkoffs of former company towns.

We need to replace the myths of industrial plums with an economic development strategy that meets human needs as a form of economic activity in and of itself, not merely as a consequence of other economic activity. The provision of social services to meet human needs could offer employment opportunities for residents in low-income communities, in such areas as transportation, home health care, adult education classes, preschool programs, day care for the frail elderly and children, and restoration of the environment. Such investment would focus on the development of community rather than simply on the maintenance of a work force. Community development is at the heart of a human service economy.

This vision of a human service economy is not utopian. It is expressed in the literature that Steve Fisher reviews and describes as the progressive economic model (see Chapter 21). This model understands that stimulating the economy, perhaps even to full employment, is by itself not adequate unless we also deal explicitly with the distribution of benefits and costs of economic activity and target areas and groups with greater needs for human services.

The human service economy even has a conservative aspect. It urges education, training, and employment opportunities for residents in low-income areas and not merely increases in welfare payments. The human service economy could even be redemptive of the present service sector of the economy, with its part-time, low-wage, and no-benefits employment.

Community Health Clinics

Community-led efforts to improve health care in Appalachia and in the rural South are examples of new social capital investment. They bring health care to areas where it might have dwindled as part of the general decline of the social service infrastructure. Throughout the region, community-controlled clinics have become one form of community organization.

The impetus for these local efforts often came from funding opportunities at the federal level, such as the Office of Health Affairs in the Office of Economic Opportunity or the Appalachian Regional Commission. Less often, foundations or church groups provided funds for local efforts. Many different initiatives catalyzed local leadership to initiate clinic services. The Vanderbilt Student Health Coalition helped local residents in southwestern Virginia, eastern and western Tennessee, and eastern Kentucky form twenty-five health councils and twenty-one primary-care clinics. The United Mine Workers of America hired staff that had comparable results in West Virginia. Local civil rights groups incorporated health into their agendas. The combination of public resources and limited assistance to local leaders proved successful in generating local leadership in clinic development in scores of communities in the rural South.

These community health efforts follow on the previous health care provision of an economic base that has changed. It is not unusual, for example, in coalmining communities, for new clinics to locate in buildings formerly used by company doctors and infirmaries. In essence, these local efforts raise social capital where it has declined and invest it in social services that have disappeared. These health efforts have been sustained only by the most strenuous commitments of local residents and assisting professionals. Local administrators and residents, organized into health councils, recruit professionals and raise funds for clinics, even in the face of huge deficits related to patients' inability to pay for health care.

This perspective permits us to view the administrators, boards, and staff of these community health centers as entrepreneurs of social capital. They gather scarce resources and invest them as risk capital to meet human needs in areas where private capital and public programs have not and perhaps would not otherwise invest social capital. They provide their services as a right, and separate themselves completely from the assumption made by private capital that one has no right to services that one cannot pay for. Their work also mitigates the worst consequences of unsatisfactory economic performance in low-income communities.

The work of community-controlled health centers to mitigate the lack of services often means that their efforts spill over into other concerns such as housing, water and sewage, and education. In black communities in the rural South especially, community clinics became powerful actors in the economy and politics of their counties. The clinic serving Beaufort–Jasper, South Carolina, for example, provided an array of services, including organizing food-buying cooperatives to deal with hunger. On nearby Johns Island, another community health program developed moderate-cost housing, a sewage-treatment facility, a nursing home for old people, and a pharmacy. In Lee County, Arkansas, voter-registration drives and the first effort to elect blacks to public office since the nineteenth century followed from the development of a health clinic sponsored by the Office of Economic Opportunity.

As these groups become effective, and exceed the minimal delivery of services that have historically been provided, they may face opposition from those who have traditionally controlled service expenditures and delivery. For instance, when the Office of Health Affairs (OHA) of the Office of Economic Opportunity provided the all-white board of health in Lowndes County, Alabama, with funds to construct a clinic building, there was no protest. Efforts to bring that clinic building and the program under the control of the primarily black community it served, however, brought about one of the most severe conflicts in OHA. Similarly, attempts to provide the black community organization of Lee County, Arkansas, with funds to construct a clinic building set off another controversy in OHA. The Sea Islands Comprehensive Health Care Corporation in South Carolina also became embroiled in conflict when it bought land and proposed permanent buildings for the clinics. Ophie Franklin, former administrator of the health program on Johns Island recalled, "As long as we were in those trailers, we had no problems." But the problems of this group and many others began when local social capital entrepreneurs sought new forms of social capital investment, such as land and permanent buildings for services to address human needs. Such "excess" brings opposition and a demand to return to a lower level of social capital investment or a change in the control of the capital resources.

In addition, there is opposition to these social capital entrepreneurs because of the political returns of their work. Several leaders in each of the clinics just named are deeply involved in electoral politics. In the communities, the health centers were an integral part of the effort to elect black people to local public office. These efforts were the first in the county's history, or the first since Reconstruction. The candidates, especially those involved in the health centers' organization, stressed the need for more jobs, improved housing, health care, and other human needs. Political change follows from effective social capital investment, which is another reason effective social capital entrepreneurs engender political opposition.

The history of community health centers provides an example of the role of community organizations in struggling for a human services economy. This history also suggests the role of the politics of portion, protest, and preference in the process of community development.

The politics of *portion* is the struggle of communities to obtain their fair share of the social capital that is available for communities in need of human services. Sometimes this role is conducted by nonprofit voluntary agencies such as the health councils. Other times, groups work to achieve political office so they can use government to acquire public funds for education, roads, water systems, sewers, and so forth. Burke County, Georgia, offers an example of the acquisition of social capital through change in local government (see Chapter 10).

This volume is also replete with examples of the politics of *protest* about some aspect of the local economy. Southerners for Economic Justice and the Workers' Rights Project protest the terms and conditions of labor for some groups in South Carolina. Community organizations of minorities in Robeson County, North Carolina, and elsewhere protest the environmental degradation that accompanies economic activity, proposed or underway, in their areas (see Chapters 12 and 15). Protest against economic activity that pollutes or contaminates is also an effort to maintain the environment as social capital, which meets human needs in the community and provides a basis for alternative economic activity in the future. Likewise, the protest against existing tax policies by Kentuckians For The Commonwealth is also an effort to increase public revenues, which could go to social service delivery.

Protest against one form of development involves, at least by inference, the politics of *preference* for another form of development. Community leaders active in this work often articulate a vision of the economics they prefer. They understand their struggle for a portion of social capital for needed services, or their protests over inappropriate development, as a small, first step to a preferred economy. The preferences most often include, as a first priority, the opportunity for all people to work at jobs that pay enough to support families in comfort, or at least security. These preferences then extend to housing, improved education, recreation for young people, and additional services for old people, including home services, transportation, and social activities. One looks in vain in these pages for a county or community that has achieved more than a glimmer of possibility of this preferred economy. The struggles of protest and portion are necessary to achieve some amount of social capital, but they are not sufficient by themselves to institute the preferred human service economy. Rather, they must become building blocks for the broader systemic change, in which the provision of human services is understood as a fundamental human right and an integral part of development.

Family, Church, and Union as Mediating Structures

In addition to the importance of community organization in building a human service economy, we must also look at the role of other mediating structures in the community in mitigating the worst consequences of negative economic development—specifically, the family, the church, and the labor unions.[1] Their roles will remain important in the human service economy.

The Family

The family is the basic unit of the production and reproduction of the labor force, and so it is not surprising that it reflects changes in the labor force. The male wage earner has declined in labor force participation and has fewer high-wage employment opportunities. Women are entering the work force in greater proportion at a time when middle-wage-sector employment is declining. In two-parent households, women's wages often maintain basic needs—health, housing, education, transportation—at a time of decline in the real and social wage, and a corresponding erosion in social capital investment.

Although attention to the increased role of women, and especially married women, in providing basic family needs is important, it should not obfuscate the continuing inadequacy of employment opportunities for female heads of families in providing basic needs (see Chapters 5 and 16). The feminization of poverty is actually a measure of the inadequate public support of women, through transfer payments or employment opportunities, in their roles of re-production and parenting.

Men and women have adopted new roles as wage earners to accommodate to the changes of the economy. A human services economy will recognize those changes. First, it must establish a minimum wage that gives individual wage earners and their dependents sufficient income to provide for basic needs. At the present time, two full-time wage earners working at minimum wage cannot keep a family of four out of poverty. Second, the human service economy will extend wages or income for work that is not now paid. The care of dependents, both the frail elderly and the very young, is important work with social value often done within the family by an unpaid caregiver. It is an example of work that the human service economy will reward with wages.

Services such as day care will be expanded in a human service economy, for several reasons. First, there is a need for the care of young children and other dependents whose caregivers work, as is increasingly the case in two-parent households. Second, programs of day care are training and employ-ment opportunities for local people. Thus, day care illustrates the important new forms of social capital of a human service economy.

The Church

The church has shown unusual initiatives as an economic actor in the re-cent crisis. In Appalachia the church has addressed some of the underlying causes of the human hardships for which it provides relief. The Catholic Bishops' pastoral letter on Appalachia, *This Land Is Home to Me,* preceded similar statements on the economy at the national level; it is a critique of the rundown of social capital investment within the region.[2] The Commission on Religion in Appalachia (CORA) is an example of ecumenical cooperation around economic issues that is more than twenty years old.

As public sources of social capital have declined, the church has become more important as a source of social capital in modest amounts. The Cam-paign for Human Development of the Catholic Church has provided support for Kentuckians For The Commonwealth and several other efforts recounted in this volume. CORA, as a funnel of funds from national Protestant denomina-tions, has provided "risk" social capital to entrepreneurs such as Southerners for Economic Justice, Mountain Women's Exchange, the Dungannon Develop-ment Corporation, and other local efforts. Clergy and laypeople with substan-tial religious commitments have played an important role of providing stable staffs to community organizations despite low and sometimes irregular wages.

Although this is important, it is necessary for the church and others to complement the provision of services with the development of leadership at the local level. The most basic form of social capital is local leadership, and the church is one of the few institutions with the resources and the freedom to develop it. The experiences of social capital entrepreneurs recounted in this volume reinforce the idea that efforts at one time provide a foundation for efforts at a later time. The Coal Employment Project, for example, built on earlier efforts of Save Our Cumberland Mountains and the East Tennessee Research Corporation (see Chapter 4). Likewise, health councils often built on the union organizing experience of some residents or similar experience acquired in the civil rights movement. The point is that the church is uniquely suited to the task of investing in the initial development of local leadership as well as supporting it in its later expressions.

Another important social capital entrepreneurial role of the church is gathering and disseminating information. The decline of information on human needs is part of the overall decline in social capital investment and one which the church can uniquely counteract. The church is national and international, and thus represents the only organization in the region with national and global contacts that parallel the corporations active in the region. The church is thus in a unique position to relate economic changes within the region to national and international trends. CORA has recently stimulated discussion on the economic crisis in the region through publications and a series of hearings.[3] This provides essential support for the work of other local groups which are protesting the current economy and articulating a vision of a preferred economy.

The Unions

Organized labor is also an important mediating organization within Appalachia and other rural parts of the South. The net effect of unions has been to mitigate some of the worst consequences of economic conditions and policies. Organized groups of former workers have also been active in gaining compensation, another form of social capital, for victims of occupational respiratory illnesses—for example, black lung and brown lung. In addition to compensation, there have been efforts to control and reduce the factors that bring on these illnesses. These positive consequences accrue not only to the members of the unions but to community residents and workers in companies without unions as well.

The current economic crisis is calling for a new role for organized labor, one that is only slowly evolving. Union membership is declining and major new producers are setting up plants without union labor. During this time of crisis, management is demanding and acquiring greater control over the working conditions and wages that labor had once controlled. At a time of increases in the pool of surplus labor and a decline in the real and social wage of labor, unions are very important in slowing the decline in the conditions of labor.

But the future role of unions extends beyond the traditional workplace relations. Unions have traditionally gained higher wages and benefits with which workers could acquire forms of social capital such as health care, housing, and education. Not only are higher wages more difficult to negotiate and benefits harder to maintain, but in many cases decent housing, health care, and education are not available at any price to workers where government and private corporations disinvest in social services. Unions need to examine the public policies by which corporations evade the provision of revenues for social capital. To be most effective in social capital investment, unions need to ally with other mediating structures, including the church and community organizations, and address along with them the needs of their workers' communities as well as the terms of their labor.

New Forms of Social Capital Investment

While community organizations, the family, church, and unions help to mitigate the worst effects of the economic crisis, more fundamental changes are also needed. The primary element of a human needs economy is a public program of social capital—that is to say, a public program that provides an adequate level of education, housing, health, and environmental quality where they are lacking. Such a program will require new forms of capital investment for human needs.

One key factor is the question of whether social capital should come from the private or the public sector. Historically, social capital follows in varying degrees upon the needs of private capital. Some maintain that private capital provides adequately for social purposes and that public sources of social capital are not needed. The market is entrusted to determine the supply of and demand for social capital. Others maintain that private capital is insufficient, and that the public sector must supplement it.

Generally, these differences are debated within a narrow section of a continuum of what *could be* possible. There are times in our history, such as the New Deal and the War on Poverty, when public policy shifts toward the public provision of social capital. Then those policies are amended, and public policy moves toward the private provision of social capital. With the Reagan administration, we saw a dramatic swing to the private end of the social-capital spectrum. This not only meant a reduction in public funds for social services, but also that public services looked more and more like those in the private sector. In practice this meant, for example, that some community health clinics closed. Administrators and boards of those that remain in operation have been brought into conformity with political and economic elites of the area. Further, the clinics are required by new federal policies to resemble the practice of physicians, hospitals, and other medical care providers and not to conflict with them in any way. Also, the private approach to social investment in health means that National Health Service Corps participants are given "private practice assignments" with federal dollars.

The first step in the human service economy is establishing public sources of social capital. Without it, there is simply no economic base for services to those in need. This in turn requires new revenues from new taxes or from changed spending patterns. To be consistent with a human service economy, taxation must be progressive, must fall on forms of wealth rather than income, and must redistribute wealth among Americans so that those with less of it acquire more.

New revenues would also come from radically new patterns of government spending. We can have more public revenues to spend on human services if we spend less on other items. In practice, the human service economy is in large measure a peace economy and requires reduced expenditures on weapons and armed forces. There is room for defense in a human service economy, but the emphasis is on waging peace. Waging peace entails ending the needless death and pain in places like the Appalachian and Southern communities described in this volume, communities where we have come to accept death and pain as an all-too-familiar consequence of a poor economy.

Should we enter serious debate about such systemic changes, we have acquired enough experience in community development in rural communities, particularly in community health centers, to suggest the elements a national program would need. First, a human service economy in low-income communities should entail services that local people can provide themselves or can be trained to provide, and that can employ them. Examples are ancillary and paraprofessional roles in health care, early childhood development, housing repair and construction, environmental monitoring and restoration, and the like.

Second, the services should be controlled by a community corporation administered by a local person, and, whenever possible, with a board of community residents who are clients of the services. Third, work in these services should include supervision and in-service training and advancement in human service careers. Fourth, an economic base for local services and for the provision of professional staff that is not available locally must be provided through funds from state and national government.

Fifth, the human service economy entails the development of local leadership, with the expectation that it will, in turn, initiate new services. It is important to recall how many new community organizing efforts came from earlier efforts, as leaders recognized and responded to needs. Many different institutions, including colleges and unions, can assist local leaders. Finally, local organizations that do provide human services must also spend some time organizing political support among the people they serve and at the state and national level through policy advocacy groups.

There is substantial importance in a human service economy. It focuses directly on meeting the human needs of individuals in a community, not indirectly as a consequence of the workings of private capital. It provides employment through service delivery. It provides the opportunity for both work and social service in communities where industry is unlikely to locate and for populations whom private investment is not likely to serve. This means that the human service economy can reach the worst cases and in fact can be targeted for them successfully, unlike current economic development strategies. Likewise, the human service economy can provide for decentralized administration that is sensitive to cultural differences among those served.[4]

There are, of course, limits to this economy. For instance, the number of jobs that can be provided in some areas may well not meet the total need. Yet creating jobs through meeting human needs is a radically important first step toward the broader agenda. And the limits and difficulties should not limit the importance of recognizing the models for change that we already have in our own region. In the wake of a declining, deindustrializing economy, community organizations, families, churches, unions, and other groups have emerged as the providers of basic human needs. In their struggles to help pick up the pieces of the current crisis, they are also the harbingers of a new human service economy.

NOTES

1. See Peter L. Berger and Richard John Neuhaus, *To Empower People: The Role of Mediating Structures in Public Policy* (Washington, D.C.: American Enterprise Institute for Public Policy Research, 1977). These three institutions and organizations are called mediating structures because they stand between individuals in their private lives and the large institutions of public life. Liberals and conservatives alike, albeit for different reasons perhaps, recognize and extol the noneconomic role of mediating structures. The American Enterprise Institute and the Heritage Foundation support mediating structures as part of an effort to privatize the response to public problems and to reduce government expenditures on social needs. Those with less conservative views endorse mediating structures because they decentralize government functions and permit greater local control of and participation in public programs. Part of the new emphasis on mediating structures, even among conservatives, includes empowering them to do for groups of poor and powerless people what the affluent and powerful can do for themselves. For less conservative discussions of mediating structures and em-

powerment, see David E. Price, "Community, Mediating Structures, and Public Policy," *Soundings* 62, no. 4 (Winter 1980): 369–94, and Richard A. Couto, "Redemptive Organizations and the Politics of Hope," *Clinical Sociology Review* 7 (1989): 64–79.

2. Catholic Bishops of Appalachia, *This Land Is Home to Me: A Pastoral Letter on Powerlessness in Appalachia.* Reprinted in Joseph Hacala, S.J., *Dream of the Mountains' Struggle: Appalachian Pastoral Five Years Later* (Prestonsburg, Ky.: Catholic Committee on Appalachia, 1982).

3. See Richard A. Couto, *Appalachia—An American Tomorrow* (1984) and *Economic Transformation: The Appalachia Case* (1986), both produced by CORA, Knoxville, Tenn.

4. These last two characteristics are important to any progressive economic reform, as Steve Fisher points out in Chapter 21.

CHAPTER

21

National Economic Renewal Programs and Their Implications for Appalachia and the South

Steve Fisher

Study economics to avoid being deceived by economists.

—Joan Robinson

To plead the possibility of the merely possible, losing in the process all right to insist on the desirability of what would be better, is finally to lose even the possible.

—Wendell Berry

Most analysts of Appalachian and Southern rural economies have described regional economic problems as a consequence either of a conflict between tradition and agents of modernism (corporations or professionals) or of rural people's inability to comprehend the rationality of modern society and hence to benefit from it. Such descriptions have helped to perpetuate the notion that Appalachians and Southerners are unlike everybody else, that they have unique kinds of economic problems that can somehow be solved from within, alone.

The idea that Appalachia and the South are different from, at odds with, or exploited by the rest of the country obscures important internal struggles within both regions as well as many similarities between them and the rest of the capitalist world. The problems of Appalachia and the South may be more

263

severe than those in some other sections of the country or may have a regional flavor, but they do not originate from fundamentally different causes. Nor are they fundamentally different from those of rural people throughout the world. Appalachia and the South are part of the mainstream world economy.

Responses to the economic crisis in Appalachia and the South must begin with the realization that the root causes are national in scope. As several essays in this volume make clear, current regional economic problems are, in large part, the result of the profound transformation of the American economy as a whole. It is now conventional wisdom that the United States faces a severe economic crisis, and that simple restoration of things as they once were is neither practical nor plausible. Cries for economic renewal are heard far and wide, with economists of all ideological stripes offering alternative economic renewal programs. Given the connection between regional economic problems and national economic policy, it is essential that those working for a more just and democratic economic order in Appalachia and the South understand and participate in the public dialogue over these alternative economic programs.

Reaganomics

The popular media have lumped together conservative proposals for economic renewal under the rubric of "Reaganomics." President Ronald Reagan entered office in 1981 with an economic agenda based on five goals espoused by virtually all conservatives. He sought (1) a substantial redistribution of income, wealth, and economic power toward the corporate sector and upper-income individuals; (2) a smaller role for the public sector and major reductions in taxes and public expenditures, especially in social welfare spending; (3) a decline in wages and working conditions to reduce labor costs; (4) a military buildup and a foreign policy that would increase U.S. power internationally and strengthen the profit-making capacity of U.S. corporations abroad; and (5) a reduction and reorientation of government regulatory activity that previously aided consumers, workers, minorities, women, and the environment.[1]

Reaganomics has had some successes. Since the economy hit bottom in the deep 1981–1982 recession, it has been marked by continuous, though modest, growth. Inflation is under control, and there have been gains in disposable personal income. Reaganomics' greatest accomplishment has been a dramatic increase in corporate profits and income for the wealthy. Since 1980, real after-tax corporate profits have increased an average 12.2 percent a year, compared with pre-1973 average growth of 3.1 percent. Supporters claimed that this upward income redistribution would lead to increased productivity and investment that would "trickle down" to workers in terms of higher employment and growing real wages. But the predicted "trickle-down" has not occurred. Despite a slight increase in productivity, real average annual earnings for workers declined $102 between 1980 and 1985. If wage growth had matched the rise in productivity, average annual wages would be approximately $1,000 higher.[2]

In addition to a massive increase in the federal deficit, low wages, and a growing inequality in the distribution of income and wealth, there have been other costs to the economic recovery under Reaganomics. These include increases in poverty, reduced social welfare spending, a widening of the income gap among races, high real interest rates, and an unprecedented growth in the trade deficit. Further, the Reagan administration weakened or often failed to enforce civil rights, environmental pollution, occupational health and safety, and consumer protection laws. In addition, it undertook the largest military buildup since World War II.

In sum, Reaganomics has supplied what the Republican Party and business conservatives have long sought—a theory that can justify inequality. Its real excitement is not the prospect of economic growth but the lure of personal and corporate aggrandizement. Despite its "free-market" rhetoric, Reaganomics is not an anti-big-government package. Budget cuts in social welfare programs are more than matched by increases in military spending. Moreover, many corporations either sell only to the government or depend on government to get cheap resources, exclusive franchises, or inside information.[3] Given its ability to reduce real wage levels, taxes, business regulations, and the power of unions, it is not surprising that Reaganomics has enjoyed some economic success. But the economy remains mired in industrial decline, and an enormous budgetary deficit has been engendered. The social and economic costs have been appallingly high and unequally shared. For the wealthy and the corporate sector, Reaganomics has brought a higher standard of living and more profits, but for many working and poor people throughout Appalachia and the South, it has been and remains a losing proposition.

Industrial Policy

Acknowledging that New Deal liberalism has reached a dead end, many liberals have been searching for an economic alternative to Reaganomics. One widely discussed plan generating support among liberal Democratic politicians has been popularly labeled "industrial policy." In essence it calls for the establishment of a more intimate relationship among government, business, and labor in an effort to restructure important segments of the economy.

Industrial policy advocates believe that the U.S. economy is undergoing a

fundamental transformation in response to changes in the international economic environment. The United States no longer dominates the world economy, and many of its basic industries, such as automobiles and steel, are faring
poorly in competition with European, Japanese, and Third World companies.
This has contributed to the "deindustrialization" of the U.S. economy—the
decline in investment in basic production industries and the resulting loss of
jobs and disruption of communities. The major reason for U.S. failure in
international competition, claim industrial-policy supporters, is the success of
industrial policies in other nations and the absence of a coherent policy in the
United States.[4]

For industrial-policy proponents, free-market notions are hopelessly inadequate to meet today's changing economic conditions. The problem is not,
as supporters of Reaganomics insist, that government is too big, but that it is
too weak and incompetent. An active government is necessary to ensure
greater profitability and growth for the nation's major industries. The idea of
unlimited competition is potentially destructive and must be replaced by a
concept of cooperation between the government and the nation's leading economic actors. This cooperation requires new consultative mechanisms that
have historically been called "corporatist," a term intended to indicate the
extent to which a unified system, subject to central control, has been created
out of formerly distinct and competing interests.[5] In place of the regulatory
state, liberal industrial-policy supporters are proposing a general framework
for managed capitalism.

While the various industrial-policy plans do not always agree on specifics,
some major policy goals, in large part drawn from Japanese and West German
models, can be identified: (1) policies, such as worker retraining, to ease adjustment to industrial decline; (2) government financial assistance for research
and development; (3) improvement in financial mechanisms, particularly the
establishment of a government-supported financial institution capable of providing large sums to industries; (4) direct government support, both for key
new industries and such established industries as steel, automobiles, and energy that have a large impact on the entire economy (this would involve
"picking the winners"—identifying those industries most likely to be successful in the future); and (5) coordination of existing policies. Such coordination could be mainly advisory, in the form of disseminating information or
trying to build economywide consensus on policy issues. Or it could involve
creation of a planning agency, with authority to influence the way firms allo-
cate their resources.[6]

While there are differences, all the industrial-policy proposals seek to base
economic recovery on a strengthened private sector. They share the basic goal
of making national economic policy more rational in the sense of harnessing it

to the needs of contemporary corporate capitalism. But an industrial policy based on capitalist rationality will inevitably be at odds with equity and democracy.

Industrial policy will promote inequity because its basic theme is increased corporate subsidization, redistributing scarce resources and rewards upward instead of generally. While most of the proposals call for a new social contract—a system of cooperation among business, government, and organized labor—even the most liberal schemes define the corporate role as central. Government is to perform a useful function in socializing the risk of capital formation, but government power is intended to complement rather than challenge corporate decisions and to help insulate those decisions from popular influence. Organized labor is offered a voice in economic decision making in exchange for adopting the problems and goals of the corporate sector as its own. Industrial policy would lower rather than raise wages and benefits, would reduce rather than preserve blue-collar jobs, and would marginalize rather than strengthen industrial unionism. As labor analyst Kim Moody points out, industrial policy is not a means for labor and government to gain some control over corporate behavior, but a way for business to further coordinate its investment and trade plans while reducing its labor costs.[7]

Industrial policy will undermine democracy because it is elitist at its core. Most plans involve some degree of centralized planning and control. Since planning is a delicate and controversial process, vulnerable to disruption by political pressure, many of the proposals seek ways to limit popular input in the planning process. They establish a central but politically insulated planning body that would, using profitability as its chief criterion, set the nation's economic priorities. It is true that organized labor would have a voice in picking economic winners and losers, but unions represent less than 20 percent of the work force. A few proposals include consumer representatives on the planning body, but none includes farmers, environmentalists, the unemployed, the poor, women, or persons of color. Political scientist William Connolly insists that if an industrial-policy program (which he refers to as "reindustrialization") were converted into practice, it would mean the de-democratization of the United States. It would, he says,

place the most crucial economic decisions beyond the reach of public accountability and would shunt constituencies and public needs that do not fit into the reindustrialization syndrome toward the margins of economic life and social legitimacy. If reindustrialization gains hegemony, public elections will persist. But the range of options debated will be narrow, and the state's capacity to discipline those who do not exercise self-discipline will be extended.[8]

Industrial-policy advocates argue that we all share a harmony of interests in which the needs of the whole should take precedence over the claims of any sector, class, race, or group. But their proposals leave the current distribution of political and economic power in place. Thus, as Kenneth Dolbeare makes clear, denying or repressing conflicts will work to the advantage of those who presently reap the rewards from the established order of things. In this sense, industrial policy rationalizes the allocation of pain; it is an appeal that seeks to divert people from recognizing that the system does not work for them—or at least not so well as it does for others.[9]

Industrial policy would probably help the economy function better than it now does. Long-term planning, investment, and research should improve our competitive position abroad. However, as Robert Lekachman reminds us, industrial policy should "not be confused with full employment, democratic planning, or a fair redistribution of the nation's income and wealth. Progress on these fronts demands strategies more radical than subsidies to business that are better targeted." Industrial policy's plausibility arises primarily from the prestige of its proponents, from the fact that its costs would be both lower and less vindictive than those imposed by Reaganomics, and from the reality that no other serious alternatives are being widely discussed.[10]

Progressive Proposals

Generally speaking, the left in the United States has had little success in challenging mainstream assumptions and proposals about the nation's economy. Progressive explanations and models too often have been drawn from European and Third World experiences rather than from a clear-headed knowledge of our nation's history, of the institutions and interests that have shaped our national development, and of popular struggles for social control of land, work, and resources. These works frequently have been presented in Marxist jargon, making them inaccessible to non-Marxist academics, much less to the general populace. Their most fundamental failure has been an inability to articulate an appealing vision of the future that is grounded in a concrete program of reform. Most Americans are unwilling to risk what they have for vague and unclear alternatives, and progressive schemes have usually done little more than call for a people-centered economy or some version of democratic socialism, concepts left so vague as to be virtually meaningless.

Recently, however, a number of books and articles by progressive social scientists and activists have appeared that set forth comprehensive programs for the reconstruction of the U.S. economy.[11] These works make a conscious effort to avoid mind-numbing jargon. They are also deliberately nonutopian, focusing on short-range, concrete proposals their authors believe can be implemented in the near future.

Although they disagree on specifics, all agree that the central problem with the economy involves the corporate sector's having too much power and control, not, as mainstream economists insist, too little.

Contemporary U.S. left economists share with mainstream economists a preoccupation with economic growth and productivity. They agree with industrial-policy advocates that such growth requires increased public-sector involvement and strategic planning. But progressives have an entirely different process in mind, one that places the burden on the rich, not the poor, and that divides the national product more equitably. Instead of mainstream economists' pro-business, trickle-down approach to economic recovery, progressives propose a trickle-up strategy, one designed to move away from concentrated economic power toward greater democratic participation and an improved, rather than lower, standard of living for the majority of the population.

Most of the progressive schemes emphasize wage-led growth through a combination of real full-employment policies and a higher minimum wage. The rebuilding of the nation's deteriorating infrastructure, especially the transportation system, and the development of new and decentralized energy-producing capabilities would be at the core of the full-employment program. Along with the full-employment efforts, progressives would institute a shorter standard work week and flexible work hours, public subsidy of home child care as well as child-care facilities, and a vast national health insurance program.

Although many of these works suggest a greater reliance on publicly owned firms, especially where they are necessary to free public decision making from excessive private influence or to serve as a yardstick by which to measure performance and pricing in key economic sectors, few call for a substantial nationalization of industries. Their alternative to private ownership or state socialism is some form of worker control. This could include fully worker-owned companies, co-participation in management, or the establishment of democratic production incentives and job-security guarantees. Progressives favor economic democracy for both social justice and efficiency reasons, arguing that workers who identify with the goals of a company through a sense of ownership or involvement in key decisions will work more productively.

The progressives' espousal of economic democracy extends to democratic participation and control over the economy through the use of governmental power. In their programs, government, freed from the control of the corporate planning system, would take the lead in establishing mechanisms for social control over investment, money, and institutions for democratic planning. The former would be achieved through regulating banks and insurance companies, liberalizing labor laws to give workers more effective control of pension funds, establishing a national development bank, democratizing the Federal Reserve Board, or developing a public holding company. Government planning would take its cues from the results of a national "needs inventory"—a vast survey to determine what people believe they need most. A more just economic order would also involve economic conversion planning, a process through which outdated or unnecessary military production facilities could be converted to civilian production.

The common theme underlying all the progressive proposals is the expansion of democratic rights as part of the solution to our economic troubles. Most of the authors believe this can best be achieved through decentralization and community control. Some of the plans call for the establishment of community enterprises, businesses in which decision-making power is held by boards elected by production workers, members of the surrounding community, or some combination of both. They also call for the creation of municipal and state banks and planning agencies to facilitate local development. The rule, say Gar Alperovitz and Jeff Faux, coordinators of the National Center for Economic Alternatives, is that if a public function can be performed at a more local level, it should be.[12]

Economic democrats offer a variety of proposals to finance all this new activity: reductions in the military budget, a radically improved progressive income tax system, and a corporate income tax with tighter controls over foreign profits and deductions.[13] The largest new source of income would be generated from the tax revenue derived from full employment. Finally, while progressives do not believe their programs will necessarily lead to inflation, most, in an effort to reassure the populace, describe a series of standby inflation controls.

Although ignored by mainstream economists and policymakers, these economic democracy proposals have sparked a vigorous debate on the left. Much of the controversy concerns these programs' emphases on more rapid economic growth and full employment. Challengers to this latter priority raise two points: first, deindustrialization and technological change are making full employment less and less likely and are exposing workers to lower-paying jobs; second, demands for full employment ignore the sharp inequalities in job access between white males and women and people of color, as well as the extra burdens women bear of housework and child support. These critics propose instead a program centering on the defense and expansion of the welfare state. Such a strategy would highlight the importance of basic income support, not linked to employment, for the most disadvantaged in our society.[14]

Environmentalists complain that a growth oriented economic policy ignores ecological issues. They worry that such a policy will continue to deplete nonrenewable resources and assault the earth's biosystemic balance; they call on progressives to replace their traditional concern with quantitative indices of economic life with a focus on the quality of our lives.[15] They propose a non-growth or "steady-state" economic policy, an emphasis on alternative technology, or some form of bioregionalism (the organization of society into small, autonomous units delineated by ecological parameters and informed by a sense of place).

Those who stress the importance of economic revival and full employment agree with the orientation and objectives of their critics but argue that their concerns are misplaced. For example, technological change need not produce unemployment if, through rapid automation, hours worked are continually reduced in order to share employment among those who need it. And economic growth need not deplete nonrenewable resources if accompanied by energy policies promoting conservation and the development of renewable energy sources. Moreover, neglect of a full-employment program and calls for a no-growth economy threaten to widen the gulf between those who already enjoy secure employment and a satisfactory standard of living and those who require support from others.[16] While this debate is often described as a conflict between competing camps, there is an increasing realization that the various positions are complementary rather than competing, that no inherent contradiction exists between programs for economic renewal and concerns for income levels or ecological balance.[17]

Some on the left criticize the economic democracy programs for not being "radical" enough. True economic democracy, they insist, is possible only under socialism, whereas these recent programs are designed to be technically feasible in a market economy with substantial private ownership. As such, they are little more than a new New Deal that could once again strengthen rather than undermine the legitimacy of corporate capitalism. It is not the left's job, say these critics, to tell corporations how to solve problems created by their system. The goal must be long-term transformation, not short-term reforms, and such an effort requires an avowedly socialist program.[18] But most of these critics admit that such a program has no chance of attracting immediate political support since, for most Americans, socialism still seems remote at best, repugnant at worst. Given this, the architects of the economic democracy proposals argue that the challenge for progressives today is to identify reforms that, though they may fall short of socialism, place concrete limits on corporate power and, in so doing, provide an opportunity for workers and consumers to question the sanctity of corporate privilege and to realize that a more democratic economic structure is possible.

There are others on the left who charge that the problem with these proposals is not that they do not go far enough but that they are overly optimistic, that they minimize the difficulties of achieving economic democracy and understate the extent of the changes required. The sheer size of the United States, its complexity, the power of the corporate sector, and the weakness of organized labor combine to make the attempt enormously difficult. Serious efforts at economic democracy would provoke a long period of turmoil because corporate leaders would see such reforms as a frontal attack on their economic power and would likely begin a capital strike—a refusal by big corporations and the wealthy to invest or even produce.[19]

What is needed, then, is not only an economic democracy program but also a realistic strategy for ways to achieve it in the face of fierce opposition. Most of the progressive writers have failed to address adequately this question of strategy. They seem to assume their programmatic objectives will be attained through populist spontaneous combustion.[20] They seldom do more than assert that through "popular mobilization" a broad-based democratic coalition will arise to educate the populace and lead it to a more democratic political and economic order. Such assertions fail to address a number of very difficult questions. Who would be in this coalition? How can the various single-issue movements of the day—labor, environmental, feminist, minority, and peace groups—overcome their differences and realize that their goals are bound together with the problems of economic renewal? How should such a coalition respond to the use of racism, sexism, and anticommunism by mainstream politicians to divide and conquer? Should the coalition focus its attention on the national or local level? Should it become involved in electoral politics? Failure to address these and related strategic questions on ways to bring about fundamental economic change seriously undermines the credibility of the progressive agenda.

Finally, the progressive plans tend to equate democracy with decentralization, but to decentralize authority is not necessarily to democratize it. For instance, in *Beyond the Wasteland,* the authors offer local school boards as effective examples of local democracy that should be emulated. School board elections, however, often are marked by low turnout, school board members do not always represent their districts, and the boards are often controlled by professionals. Progressives must devote more attention to the question of how to increase the average citizen's ability to participate.[21]

Conclusion

I refuse to express myself with [political people's] words, their labels, their slogans. . . . I express myself with my words: good, bad, and worse. And I say: If it serves the people, it is good. If it doesn't serve the people, it is bad.

—*Lech Walesa*

If grass-roots movements have arisen to challenge successfully the most deeply felt personal attitudes about race and sex, is it too much to imagine that a politics can be fashioned to remove an obsolete and demonstrably unworkable economic ideology that is squandering our material well-being and destroying our experience of real community?

—Gar Alperovitz and Jeff Faux,
Rebuilding America

The search for solutions to the economic crisis in Appalachia and the South must begin with the understanding that the real battleground is the national economy, and that the central economic decision of the late 1980s and 1990s will be whether to direct government's economic role toward regressive or progressive ends. The issue is not whether government will play a role, but rather who will control it and who will benefit.

The persistent and widespread poverty in Appalachia and the South is a direct consequence of the pro-business, top-down strategy of economic development. The underlying thread of past economic strategies in these regions has been the systematic arrangement of their resources for the benefit of corporate concerns. Such an arrangement has left many Appalachians and Southerners economically and politically powerless. Yet recent economic reform proposals by regional governors and policy boards are designed to strengthen the corporate role.

The progressive economic model poses a direct challenge to the mainstream assumptions that anything good for people is bad for the economy and that efficient planning can be controlled only by a rational few. By asserting that the solution to the current economic crisis lies in using government power to challenge rather than strengthen the corporate sector and by making concrete suggestions for democratic economic reforms, the progressive model places institutional and structural change on the national agenda and provides the framework for an alternative economic vision.

The progressive model in no sense provides pat solutions to the economic problems of Appalachia and the South. Its value lies in establishing the economy as contested terrain. By undermining the notion that the economy is unchangeable and by treating humans as something other than instruments for calculation, the progressive model helps us understand that we have choices— in particular, the choice to define what we want, rather than simply reacting to the latest economic outrage. By providing an opportunity for local and regional groups to make connections between their concrete situations and larger economic and political forces and to think creatively about the kind of economic system they want, the progressive model can serve as an important tool for economic education and change in Appalachia and the South.

The progressive model has serious shortcomings; it must be worked on, debated, improved. Those struggling for economic justice in Appalachia and the South can contribute to this effort in several ways. First, they can work to ensure that their particular problems and needs are treated seriously. Progressive economists, like their mainstream counterparts, largely ignore rural issues and concerns. Some of the studies fail even to mention the agricultural sector, and those that do are mainly concerned with "ensuring nutritious food at a reasonable price."[22] There is little recognition of the problems faced by citizens of resource-based economies or areas with highly concentrated land ownership. Several works make vague pleas for land reform, but none offers concrete steps to protect family farmers, to regain control of the land and resources, or to enhance the viability of rural communities.

Second, Appalachians and Southerners know from firsthand experience that capitalist economic development too often has destroyed the cultural integrity of the people who are its supposed beneficiaries. As several articles in this volume illustrate, local and regional groups are working to find new and imaginative ways to integrate cultural values into their economic and political activities. They have learned that economic alternatives, no matter how humane, will not rouse people to action; economic policy must speak directly to people's consciousness, culture, and daily practices of life. Thus Appalachian and Southern activitists should insist that the right to preservation of cultural integrity play a more central role in the progressive agenda.

Third, the fact that the roots of economic problems in Appalachia and the South are national in scope does not diminish the importance of efforts to establish alternative economic institutions and programs on the local level. On the contrary, people's direct relationship to their community and its survival should be the starting point from which regional, national, and international economic issues are examined. In this way, people are encouraged to view their daily experiences as the key component in the process of understanding and changing how the economy works.[23] Many of the economic reforms that have occurred in U.S. history have been presaged by state and local experiments. Community economic reform efforts in Appalachia and the South (some of which are discussed in this volume) can become progressive "incubators" for change—schools for the development of grassroots leaders, the testing of new economic ideas, and the promotion of democratic attitudes and skills.

Finally, activists in Appalachia and the South can play an important role in developing a realistic strategy for achieving fundamental economic change. The first step is to look critically at the recent history of resistance in Appalachia and the South. This resistance has involved two different approaches.[24] One approach consists of a number of activities frequently grouped together under the rubric of "grassroots economic development." The primary concern of these activities is to improve the financial well-being of low-income people by fostering economic independence and self-reliance. Goals vary among advocates and practitioners and include efforts to attract new industry, generate locally controlled jobs within a community, establish and promote arts and crafts cooperatives, and supply technical advice and skills.

These grassroots efforts at economic development respond to people's immediate needs and can provide models for the future. However, these efforts have usually had little impact on the overall economic underdevelopment of Appalachia or the South. Their contribution to economic development has been limited by several factors. First, they have largely remained small enterprises, whose direct economic benefit extends only to a limited number of people. Second, though many of these enterprises are organized cooperatively, there has been little effort to extend this model of ownership and control to other segments of the economy. Third, there has been a tendency among some of these groups to fall victim to the same market mentality that pervades the mainstream economy. Participants, occupied with the protection of their own economic concerns, have been reluctant to join social justice efforts that challenge local economic and political power structures.

The second approach involves direct challenges to corporate and government development. The primary concern is to stop a particular type of development by organizing people who are directly affected by it. Groups and communities have been organized against strip mining, toxic-waste dumping, dam projects, synthetic fuel plants, oil and gas leasing, and occupational health and safety hazards. These efforts have stopped some development schemes and forced changes in others; they have frequently taught people in a community how to work together and have made them more aware of the political and economic forces that affect their lives. Yet, overall, opposition of this sort has been sporadic at best and has failed more than it has succeeded. Such groups are inevitably short of funds and resources. They frequently find themselves having to choose between meeting the immediate needs of their constituents and building a power base and a program for broader social change. They spend their time reacting to the development schemes of others and seldom have the time or resources to formulate and pose creative alternatives.

Both types of resistance efforts face a number of obstacles: the power of status quo political and economic forces, feelings of powerlessness and cynicism among their constituency, the lack of capital, and more. The ability of these change-oriented groups to respond effectively to these and other obstacles is undermined by the divisions between the two approaches. These divisions result from problems over turf, specialization of function, and the lack of a common vision. To be successful, economic development strategies must find ways to eliminate the tensions between groups doing advocacy work and those engaged in trying to create locally owned and controlled businesses. The progressive model provides an opportunity to break new ground by suggesting that the idea of economic development should be broadened to include the notion that citizens in Appalachia, the South, and elsewhere have a right to expect certain things from any economy. Among these are:

- The right to meaningful work that is not life-threatening in either the short or long term. This implies both a safe workplace and a safe environment.
- The right to economic security, in terms of both job security and equitable remuneration for work done.
- The right to participate as fully as possible in any decision making affecting their livelihoods.
- The right to the preservation of cultural integrity.

This definition implies that most citizen groups in Appalachia and the South are engaged in activities somehow related to economic development. This is true whether the battle is over strip mining in eastern Tennessee or providing construction jobs for low-income women in Mississippi. Such a definition does away with the dichotomy between economic development organizations and political organizations. Grassroots economic development cooperatives are as political in nature as struggles over taxation and land reform are economic. If, on the one hand, citizen groups limit themselves to strictly economic aims, they may end up being co-opted and buying into their own economic oppression. If, on the other hand, organizations limit themselves to strictly political opposition, they may end up always on the defensive, unable to offer creative alternatives that effectively respond to people's immediate needs.

A comprehensive strategy that integrates both approaches would lead to the sharing of ideas, resources, and capital. Such a strategy would pave the way for coalitions that would simultaneously be (1) coalitions of opposition that would oppose development as usual and expose it for the economic exploitation that it has been; (2) coalitions of advocacy that would serve as advocates for those victimized by corporate and governmental development efforts; and (3) coalitions for the creation of alternatives in which organizations currently involved in grassroots economic developmpent could serve as a building block for new and creative economic change efforts in Appalachia and the South.

NOTES

Acknowledgment: Funding for this research was provided by the Emory and Henry College Faculty Development Fund and a James Still Fellowship for Advanced Study in the Humanities and Social Science (Appalachian College Program, University of Kentucky).

1. James Campen and Arthur MacEwan, "Crisis, Contradictions and Conservative Controversies in Contemporary U.S. Capitalism," *Review of Radical Political Economics* 14 (Fall 1982): 7. A more complete annotated bibliography on varying economic strategies is available from Steve Fisher, Emory and Henry College, Box BBB, Emory, VA 24327.

2. "Reaganomics Report Card," *Dollars & Sense* (May 1987): 7, 8.

3. Samuel Bowles, David Gordon, and Thomas Weisskopf, *Beyond the Wasteland* (Garden City, N.Y.: Anchor Press–Doubleday, 1983), 196. Martin Carnoy, Derek Shearer, and Russell Rumberger, *A New Social Contract* (New York: Harper & Row, 1983), 21; and John Judis, "The Way the World Doesn't Work," *Working Papers for a New Society* 8 (May–June 1981): 48; Gar Alperovitz and Jeff Faux, *Rebuilding America* (New York: Pantheon, 1984), 13–16; and Kenneth Dolbeare, *Democracy at Risk: The Politics of Economic Renewal*, rev. ed. (Chatham, N.J.: Chatham House, 1986), 101–2.

4. Barry Bluestone and Bennett Harrison, *The Deindustrialization of America: Plant Closings, Community Abandonment, and the Dismantling of Basic Industry* (New York: Basic Books, 1982). William Hudson, "The Feasibility of a Comprehensive U.S. Industrial Policy," *Political Science Quarterly* 10 (Fall 1985): 463–64.

5. Dolbeare, *Democracy at Risk*, 7; and Frank Hearn, "The Corporatist Mood in the United States," *Telos*, no. 56 (Summer 1983): 41–57.

6. Hudson, "Feasibility," 464–65.

7. Kim Moody, "Labor's Misplaced Hopes," *Progressive* 48, no. 11 (November 1984): 32.

8. William Connolly, "The Politics of Reindustrialization," *Democracy* 1 (July 1981): 17. See also Robert C. Grady, "Reindustrialization, Liberal Democracy, and Corporatist Representation," *Political Science Quarterly* 101, no. 3 (1986): 415–32.

9. Dolbeare, *Democracy at Risk*, 119–20.

10. Robert Lekachman, "Paying for Progress," in *Proposals for America from the Democratic Left*, ed. Irving Howe (New York: Pantheon, 1984), 107. Sumner Rosen, "Economics for People," in *Beyond Reagan*, ed. Alan Gartner, Colin Greer, and Frank Riesman (New York: Harper & Row, 1984), 27.

11. For a list of the progressive works consulted for this discussion, see the bibliography by the author cited in n. 1.

12. Alperovitz and Faux, *Rebuilding America*, 262.

13. Dolbeare, *Democracy at Risk*, 150–51.

14. For a good summary of the full-employment debate, see *Progressive Agenda: A Monthly Newsletter from the Center for Democratic Alternatives*, no. 1 (February 1986).

15. For a good summary of the environmental debate, see *Progressive Agenda: A Monthly Newsletter from the Center for Democratic Alternatives*, no. 2 (May 1986).

16. Ibid.

17. David Gordon and Susan Brown, "Vox Pop," *Nation*, October 4, 1986, 301.

18. The Editors, "The Responsibility of the Left," *Monthly Review* 34 (December 1982): 1–9; Martin Hart-Landsberg and Jerry Lembcke, "Economic Democracy: Re-

forming or Transforming Capitalism," *Insurgent Sociologist* 10 (Winter 1981): 104–9; and Stanley Aronowitz, "Socialism and Beyond: Remaking the American Left," *Socialist Review* 13:3, no. 69 (May–June 1983): 31–32.

19. For a discussion of the possibility of a capital strike, see Dolbeare, *Democracy at Risk,* 154; Frank Ackerman, *Hazardous to Our Wealth: Economic Policies in the 1980s* (Boston: South End Press, 1986), 166; and Robert Collier, "Democratizing the Private Sector: Populism, Capitalism, and Capital Strike," *Socialist Review* 14:6, no. 80 (March–April 1985): 42.

20. Charles Andrian, "Capitalism and Democracy Reappraised," *Western Political Quarterly* 37 (December 1984): 659.

21. Alan Draper, "The Left and Economic Policy: A Review," *Insurgent Sociologist* 13 (Summer–Fall 1985): 120; and Charles Knight, "Progressive Economic Policy: An Overview," *Social Policy* 17 (Fall 1986): 8; Bowles, Gordon, and Weisskopf, *Beyond the Wasteland.*

22. Carnoy, Shearer, Rumberger, *A New Social Contract,* 231.

23. See Chapter 18, this volume.

24. On May 14–16, 1982, more than forty people met at the Highlander Research and Education Center in New Market, Tenn., to discuss economic development strategies in the 1980s. Background papers for the meeting were written by Bill Duncan, Doug Gamble, Bill Horton, Sally Maggard, and Tom Miller. My discussion of economic development strategies and the need for coalition building in Appalachia and the South is a synthesis of some of the ideas expressed at the workshop and in the background papers. In particular, I have relied heavily upon the analyses by Horton and Maggard. The Mott Foundation provided funding for the workshop and the background papers.

CHAPTER

22

Toward a New Debate:
Development, Democracy,
and Dignity

John Gaventa, Barbara Ellen Smith,
and Alex Willingham

T he essays in this book have revealed the impact of economic restructuring on community life and community struggle in Appalachia and the South. These voices and stories have rarely been heard, especially outside their region. In the national media and literature, the images of economic decline one finds are of the closing steel mills of Pittsburgh, the laid-off auto worker in Detroit, the drought-stricken farmer in the Midwest, and the emergence of an "underclass" in the inner cities. Far less visible have been the stories of closings of mines in Appalachia and textile mills in the rural South, the debt-ridden farmer in the Kentucky Tobacco Belt, and marginalized communities in the Georgia Black Belt. Equally unknown are the rich and impressive experiences of grassroots communities responding to economic change and decline in ways that can be instructive and inspiring to those concerned with economic organizing and empowerment across the nation.

Part of the invisibility of economic decline in the South grows from the dominant image of the Sun Belt that emerged in the 1970s. The growth of the "Sun Belt South" was presented as the bright spot on the national landscape, whose economic boom served to offset the declining "Frost Best" or "Rust Belt" of the industrialized North. Even in the 1988 political conventions in Atlanta, this image was retained as the media pointed to the glitter of Atlanta, New Orleans, or Charlotte as evidence of a new and booming South, which was supplanting the story of poverty and hardship of a Southern past.

But these chapters have revealed a different picture. As the national economy shifts from manufacturing to services and finances, as plants close and relocate overseas, as the economic gap grows between rural and urban areas, Appalachia and the South are faced with greater poverty than ever before, and with new dimensions of economic injustice for its workers, farmers, women, people of color, and rural communities.

The South plays a special role in the unfolding of this economic crisis in the United States. Long seen as a region outside the mainstream, a region attempting to catch up to the national standard, in the last several decades the region has in fact attracted capital and undergone a process of integration into the national economy. But meanwhile, that national economy itself was changing. The relatively low wages of new service jobs, the difficult working conditions and nonunion status of workers, the economic uncertainty created by capital mobility that the region has experienced are becoming the standard for workers across the country.[1]

Because the crisis is not unique, the struggles reflected in this volume— efforts to gain dignity and respect, to challenge economic injustice and build equitable alternatives—also have a special national relevance today. In this concluding chapter, we examine some of the questions about strategies for change that the current situation poses. We argue that the nature of the crisis poses new limitations for mainstream economic development models as well as for historical social movements. Finally, we suggest that underlying the diversity of these essays are themes that help to forge a new definition and vision of the economy, one that links development and growth to democracy and dignity.

Beyond Development by Corporate Design

In recent decades, the dominant economic development model for the region has involved creating a favorable business climate that would lure industry into the region.[2] In the name of maintaining the business climate, workers received low wages, communities provided tax and other concessions to industry, dissent was sometimes silenced. Based on the traditional notion of trickle-down economics, the assumption was that what was good for business was good for workers and communities.

To some extent, within its own definitions of success, the business-climate model of development worked. Thousands of plants came to the region. The overall standard of living rose.

Today, however, this "success" is waning. Industries that once sought what the South had to offer are moving elsewhere. New plants are not locating in the region as rapidly as they once did; those that do are clustering in certain "hot spots," deepening the internal patterns of uneven development. In the mid-1980s, a series of policy reports began to warn of a new poverty in the region, especially in rural areas. The 1986 Commission on the Future of the South, for instance, described the region as being "half way home and a long way to go." In its 1986 report, *Shadows in the Sunbelt*, MDC, a research firm in North Carolina, warned that the smokestack-chasing strategy of industrial recruitment was outdated.

> The situation is analogous to the great buffalo hunts of the last century. The stampede of plants to the South is definitely over—especially in the rural areas that lack a skilled workforce, transportation, infrastructure and cultural amenities. Yet the hunters continue in their pursuit, hoping to bag one of the remaining hides.[3]

As the industrial recruitment strategy began to fail, the business-climate measure of development came under intense questioning. The Southern Regional Council has argued that while the South historically may have provided a favorable climate for business, the climate has been "chilly" for workers and communities. In studies in 1986 and 1988, the council found that although the Southeast ranked high in job growth, its states were at the bottom when ranked according to a dozen different indicators of labor climate. Indeed, working people were much more likely to be poor, have hazardous jobs, and lack workplace protection and compensation in the South than elsewhere in the nation.[4]

While these and other reports were important for calling attention to the resurgent poverty and for questioning the industrial recruitment model of development, their analyses often failed to examine the full extent to which national economic restructuring was affecting the region. For instance, the assumption was usually made that the crisis was only a rural one. Analysts referred to the "two Souths": contrasting those few urban areas that are booming and the rural areas where plants are closing, jobs are being lost, farms being foreclosed.[5]

But the crisis is not only in small towns and rural communities. Even *within* the cities of the region there are two Souths. Atlanta is the third fastest-growing metropolitan area nationally, but the poverty in its core city is second only to Newark's.[6] Every morning, pools of the unemployed stand on the corners, hoping to be picked up for day labor. Economic refugees arrive daily from the rural areas looking for work that is not to be found there either. Homelessness is increasing.

Even where development has occurred, many of the essays in this volume ask us to delve beneath the Sun Belt glitter to question the quality of growth. The new service jobs in Atlanta often bring minimum wages and workplace indignities to the primarily female workers they employ, just as the high-tech pharmaceutical industry has brought workplace harassment and dangerous chemical hazards to low-wage workers in North Carolina. Beneath GM's new Saturn plant outside Nashville is also the old Southern development story of corporate paternalism and community dependency. Beneath the Cajun craze in New Orleans is also the co-optation of indigenous culture.

By focusing only on rural areas and treating the crisis as somewhat separated from an otherwise "healthy" economy, the calls for reform also are limited. For instance, some suggest that rural communities may no longer be viable, and urge that the solution to the problem lies in migration to the cities elsewhere in the country. Such recommendations ignore the fact that there are few places for rural people to go, and that displacement in the countryside only contributes to problems such as homelessness in the city. Others have urged tourism as a path to rural revitalization, without pausing to consider that where tourism has emerged, in places such as Gatlinburg, Tennessee, or the Sea Islands, South Carolina, it has often contributed to loss of traditional forms of survival and the creation of seasonal low-wage service jobs.[7]

Other more progressive strategists urge that the region should become more "internationally competitive" through better education for its people, more efficient technology, greater cultural opportunities, and improved infrastructure. Although such steps may be useful, they remain within the traditional model of changing the South to suit the needs of business, improving the business climate without necessarily improving the climate for workers and communities.

An example of the difficult nature of the problem may be seen in the proposals to rely on technology to revitalize the industrial base of the region. Here the argument is often made that, to encourage the region to compete more effectively internationally, productivity must be improved through modernization. Yet although technology may increase output, it often does so by displacing workers with machines. As we saw in the case of the West Virginia coalfields, the end result may be greater profits and productivity for business, but also increased displacement for workers and further decline of rural communities. In this sense, the technology strategy calls into question the fundamental premise of the trickle-down approach to regional development—industrial development by itself may no longer translate into the creation of jobs and the development of communities.

Another example of the limits of business-climate reformism is found in the argument about education and economic development. Historically, the South has lagged behind the rest of the nation in areas of educational attainment; its rates of adult illiteracy and high school dropouts are significantly higher than those for the rest of the nation. For many years, Southern elites saw a low-skill, low-wage work force as a way to attract basic industries; but policymakers are now seeing lack of education as a barrier to economic development. A recent report from the Southern Growth Policies Board stated, "An educated, skilled, flexible workforce will be the key to southern economic development. . . . *The lack of these skills* [emphasis added] prevents the region from achieving the productivity gains that it could otherwise accomplish. . . . The new southern economy will have to build on the *mental* strengths of its labor force." [8]

Such arguments are difficult to oppose, for most will agree that educational quality and opportunity should be improved. And it is very likely that increased education will lead to increased productivity and job creation in some areas or for some people. But to argue that the lack of economic development lies in the lack of an educated work force rapidly borders on a new version of blaming the victims of economic crisis, rather than its root causes. First, as we have seen in essays from Burke County, Georgia, or from the coalfields of Kentucky, the region's educational difficulties are in fact tied to historical policies such as segregated schools or a low tax base for corporate property holders.

Second, one cannot assume that, even *with* a more educated work force, the new high-skill jobs will come to the communities that need them the most. Under current arrangements, there is little way an underfunded school system in a rural, poor area can compete with a well-funded one in an urban growth area, or that even with educational improvements these communities will be able to compete for the same scarce high-tech jobs. Instead, many of the new jobs that do come to the poorer communities may in fact require a *less* educated, not a more educated, work force. In hearings in West Virginia on the economic crisis, one local activist told the story of a school superintendent who argued that reading was no longer a necessary skill upon which to be spending scarce resources; the only jobs available were at the fast-food restaurants, where cash registers were picture-coded anyway! [9] Educating the victims of crisis, without getting at the roots of the crisis (such as equal financing for schools and the scarcity of quality jobs in the first place), may allow some individuals to move up the economic ladder, but may also simply become a new way of blaming those who do not succeed for failures over which they have little control.

In sum, economic restructuring calls into question the old adage that "what's good for business is good for the community." The demands of the global economy for greater and greater competition, and the ability of capital to move to the communities that offer the least costs, mean that a favorable business climate may become less and less compatible with a favorable climate for workers and communities. More far-reaching solutions are needed, ones that reverse historical priorities and demand that capital be accountable to the needs of community.

Such a change in priorities is not likely, of course, to come through reforms from the top. Historically, more fundamental change arises from social movements at the grassroots. Here, however, lies the further problem. While the current economic crisis poses difficulties for mainstream models of reform, so, too, does it present obstacles for traditional modes of social protest.

The Limits of Traditional Movements

Historically, the hardships of Appalachia and the South have in turn been crucibles for change. Class, racial, gender, and community inequalities have led to a rich history of grassroots struggles for justice. But the changing economy also presents new obstacles to traditional modes of popular struggle.

Perhaps most obvious is the impact of the current crisis on the labor movement. Historically, the region has given us many examples of heroic labor struggles. The conditions of the miners in the 1920s and 1930s led to the emergence of John L. Lewis and the United Mine Workers of America, and contributed to the formation of the Congress of Industrial Organizations. In the 1960s and 1970s, the struggles of miners to organize against Duke Power in Harlan County, Kentucky, or of textile workers to win against J. P. Stevens gained national attention. Now layoffs and mine and mill closings threaten to undermine the gains of previous years. The ability of capital to relocate has created a climate of economic fear and blackmail that chills workplace protest. Plant closings and deindustrialization have weakened the power of traditional labor organizations to bargain for a fairer share of the economic pie. Indeed, the nature of the economic pie itself is changing, as service jobs replace factory jobs and as a new international division of labor forces U.S. workers to compete globally.

Similarly, the South historically has spawned movements for greater racial equity. The 1950s and 1960s saw new demands for long-denied civil, political, and economic participation among blacks. However, we have seen time and again in this volume that the gains in racial equity made in the South, while not to be overlooked, are deeply circumscribed by persistent and deepening economic inequities. Although blacks have made political gains in many areas, and although *some* blacks, especially in urban areas, have made economic progress, for most people the 1980s have brought a widening of the economic gap. Per capita income for blacks in the rural South in 1980 was $3,300, less than one-third of the national average. Research in the 1980s shows a negative correlation between levels of black population and economic growth—the greater the proportion of blacks in a county, the fewer new job opportunities were created.[10] Where jobs do come, they often are in hazardous industries, such as in Robeson County, North Carolina, or Emelle, Alabama.

Similarly, while some strides have been made for women in the region, there are still wide economic disparities. In the Appalachian coalfields in the 1970s, women received national and international attention for gaining well-paid jobs in the male-dominated mining industry, only to find an equal place on the unemployment line when the closings of the 1980s came. Often, women have entered the work force in large numbers only to find their jobs part of a low-wage, insecure service industry. Meanwhile, in many rural communities, such as in West Virginia, lack of virtually *any* jobs means that the participation of women in the labor force is still among the lowest in the country. For women who also are black and rural, the situation is particularly hard: almost 60 percent lived in poverty in 1983.[11]

Similar limitations may be found in the strategies of empowerment based on community issues such as welfare rights, the environment, health care, and schools. Though perhaps less known than that in other parts of the country, Appalachia and the South have developed a rich tradition of community organizing, much of it growing from the War on Poverty and civil rights efforts of the 1960s. Frustrated with change at the national level, community organizing emphasized action on pragmatic, winnable issues at the local level. But changing economic circumstances pose new difficulties. National cuts in social services have revived the need for national action, while at the same time making the local struggles to survive all the more difficult. Desperate to make ends meet, some local governments are all too willing to make concessions, on the environment, perhaps, in the hope of luring industry or retaining jobs. Meanwhile, the ability of industry to hop, skip, and jump globally, playing communities against one another, demands an international perspective that often has been absent from local work.

On the one hand, then, changing economic circumstances call into question strategies of change "from the bottom" that were thought to have promise only a decade ago. Moreover, the different traditions of struggle along racial, class, gender, or community lines can lead to divisiveness, especially in periods of political defeat and economic decline. On the other hand, as many of the essays in this volume have reminded us, the current restructuring may also provide an opportunity for developing new strategies and for building new coalitions. And the rich history of grassroots struggle which past hardship has formed may be used as a base of strength and resilience for approaching the new situation.

Toward New Strategies

This book itself represents one such attempt to provide a new unity out of diverse historical experiences. As part of the process that developed the book, the contributors and others came together for a series of workshops that discussed not only the impact of economic change but also new strategies for achieving economic justice. Although the task is by no means complete, these discussions can contribute to some tentative statements about the ways in which economic crisis and restructuring are also shaping new agendas for social change.

If nothing else, the essays in this volume indicate to us a new level of participation by grassroots citizens on matters of the economy. The new participation transcends class, racial, gender, and community lines. It is characterized not only by demands for a fair share of the economic pie but also by demands for redefining the very basis of economic priorities and economic decision making. Indeed, the failure of the dominant economic policies to provide for fair and equitable economic change presents the economy as "contestable terrain," a legitimate arena for grassroots action and dissent.

The new participation on the economy is particularly important given the region's history. Perhaps more than elsewhere in the country, economic dependency accompanied by direct disenfranchisement of the black population has provided little opportunity for popular participation on public affairs. Even where popular demands did arise, the control of a small, conservative elite meant that mass opinion could easily be manipulated and steered away from questions of the fundamental economic order. Race, religion, and patriotism (in the form of race-baiting or red-baiting) were symbols that could be invoked against social change.

The climate of nonparticipation also provided little room for linking the concerns of economic development with those of democratic action. Development was done *to* and *for* local communities, not *by* the people themselves. Over time, the separation between the economic and the political, at least at the local level, meant that ordinary people saw the economy as something to be dependent upon, not act upon. Even as local economies failed, workers and communities often tended to accept and adapt, explaining their hard luck in terms of the natural "booms and busts" of the economy, or "the business prerogative," or their own lack of skills and education.

The traditional separation at the grassroots level between economic development and democratic participation makes the stories of struggle and change in this volume all the more significant. In numerous ways, over and over, we have seen grassroots people acting for themselves on an economy that traditionally has not been considered theirs. Yet the strategies for the new participation are also highly diverse. They vary in part according to the economic context in which grassroots groups find themselves, and range from alternative development, to fighting to save traditional jobs and communities, to organizing and empowering the new.

With the failure of the traditional model of development from without, many local groups have turned to creating their own alternative development from within. The strategy of creating alternative development builds on local skills and resources, such as we have seen in the women's economic development efforts in West Virginia (Chapter 5) or with the Mayhaw Tree project in south Georgia (Chapter 13). Though not limited to them, this strategy seems strongest among communities and groups who traditionally have been excluded from the formal economy. In the process of creating alternatives to traditional development, they create new models of local control, self-reliance, and participation.[12]

Other groups described in this volume work to develop strategies that challenge the control and responsibility of those who have defined the traditional development policies in the region. Struggles to fight plant closings and protect workers' rights in existing industries are important, for they challenge the accountability of capital to community and insist that the rights of workers and communities are more important than a blind belief in maintaining a favorable climate for business. These battles against deindustrialization by default are often taking place in communities whose history has been shaped by earlier processes of industrialization by a formal economy, and they involve coalminers, textile workers, other workers, and their unions.

Other groups represented in the volume are questioning the benefits of the new development that the formal economy is creating. This has been seen in the organizing of women office workers in Atlanta (Chapter 16) or in the critique of the new industrial recruitment policies that focus on attracting mega-manufacturing plants (Chapter 15). The strategies and constituencies involved in organizing around new jobs may be quite different from those involved in workplace organizing in the past. They are often led by new entrants to the work force, especially women and people of color, and they link community and workplace issues.

The struggles for alternative development, for protecting old jobs and communities, and for organizing the new are at one level diverse and separate. But at another level, the efforts are interconnected: they all speak to the common concern of creating spaces in which grassroots communities act and participate in defining their own economic futures. The questions, they suggest, are not only about substituting one set of policies for another. Rather, they are about who shall participate in shaping the policies in the first place, and how success will be defined. They ask not only "development for whose interests?" but also "development by whom? toward what end?" They reflect demands not only for economic development but also for economic democracy, not only for growth but also for quality and dignity.

The process of broadening the definition of who participates in the development debate leads, of course, to different definitions of what constitutes success. As strategies to take charge rebuild the link between "community" and "economy," it becomes artificial to separate the economy as a single issue from other concerns. At the local level, "the economy" is part of a broad web of relationships which includes the relationship not only to a job or employer but also to the land and environment, as we saw in the struggle by citizens in Robeson County to protect the Lumbee River (Chapter 12) or in the efforts in Kentucky against strip mining the mountains (Chapter 2). Economic concerns become more holistic, more than just a paycheck. They also involve personal relationships to family, community, and culture.

Within that web, just as demands for development cannot be separated from demands for participation, neither can they be separated from concerns of dignity and equity, be they based on class, race, or gender. The mutual struggles for development and for dignity mean crossing barriers that traditionally have divided social groups in the South and elsewhere. Throughout these studies we have seen hopeful ways in which diverse movements are interacting and supporting one another. The movement for women's employment in the mines worked patiently, and in the end, successfully to link up with the traditional, predominantly male union (Chapter 4). The building of cooperatives in Alabama and Georgia (see Chapters 7 and 13) grew from and strengthened the demands for black political participation. The creative new organization of workers in South Carolina, the Workers' Rights Project, prides itself on the leadership that women and blacks are giving to it (see Chapter 9).

Similarly, other newly formed efforts are bringing together unions, civil rights organizations, and community groups to link their common concerns. In November 1987, more than 5,000 people marched in Nashville as part of the Jobs with Justice campaign, one of the largest demonstrations in the region since the civil rights movement. Later coalminers and other union members joined the leaders of the Southern Christian Leadership Conference for a symbolic march across the South, representing a new unity across race and region that was not present twenty years ago.

At the same time, there is much to be done if these local efforts are to translate themselves into a movement. More steps and strategies are needed to link and expand the emerging community-based activity.

First, the new participation on the economy implies the need for economic education. Education, in this sense, is not for the purpose of adapting to new jobs in an economic model over which people have no control, but is for helping people recognize the validity of their own knowledge of their economy and begin to create new definitions of development that would be successful in their terms (see Chapter 18). It is a process of gaining the economic literacy needed to act and participate in economic decision making and economic change.

Second, the movement for economic justice must begin to translate its increased awareness and activism about economic matters into new, more democratic economic policy. In many ways the failure of the traditional state and local economic policies based on the industrial recruitment model has created a policy vacuum which is ripe for new ideas that could be supported by diverse and broad constituencies. Federal legislative and policy interventions were crucial to the growth of the civil rights movement in the South. In the same way, the movement around economic issues must involve governmental participation if local action is to be sustained. And, given trends in the federal government that favor devolving many policies for economic well-being back to the states, the local level takes on new significance as a building block for policy change.

Indeed, there are examples of the political process's being effectively used to address economic concerns. In Kentucky, the successful public referendum against the broad-form deed represented a citizens' victory against the historic economic power of the coal industry. In South Carolina, the Workers' Rights Project has also been successful in gaining new policies on worker compensation. In West Virginia, Pennsylvania, and Ohio, the Tri-State Conference on Steel has proposed a public Steel Valley Authority, which would involve local governments, unions, and community groups in economic planning for the area. In West Virginia, a conservative governor, Arch Moore, challenged traditional business prerogatives by suing Newell Company for $615 million after it decided to close its Anchor Hocking Glass plant, which had previously been subsidized by low-interest state loans.[13] In Arkansas, a state-supported Rural Development Bank is exploring ways of using state pension funds for local development. All these are only examples of ways the state and local arena is becoming an arena for new policies for a more democratic economy—a process that must continue.

While emphasizing local grassroots action, we have argued at the same time here that the regional economic crisis is part and parcel of a national and international crisis as well. Just as constituencies and issues must be linked within the region, so, too, must locally based movements make links with those concerned about change in the larger arena. To do so involves building horizontal links with other regions and groups in the country whose own futures are being played off against our own. We must recognize that while important gains have been made in our region, they have often been achieved with the help of broader structures—progressive churches, unions, foundations, some government agencies—which now often battle for their own survival at the national level. We must also tie local efforts to national ones, remembering that the linkage needs to be a two-way process, one that mandates national groups to hear and include the voice of the grassroots and the grassroots to join movements for a more progressive agenda nationally (see Chapter 21).

Finally, the nature of the current crisis challenges us to link local and international concerns. Often, in our movements for social change, domestic concerns have been seen as separate from international issues. The movement of capital and industries from home to abroad and the playing off of workers and communities across national boundaries link local and international concerns in a new way. In recent years, many groups in the region have begun to respond to the new conditions by developing their own grassroots interchanges with groups affected by similar issues elsewhere. The Africa Peace Tour sponsored in 1987 by church and community groups linked economic and political concerns in southern Africa to those in the Deep South (see Chapter 17). A tour of health and safety activists from India following the Bhopal disaster linked groups questioning the location of hazardous industries, which occurs in poor communities here as well as abroad.[14] Similar exchanges have brought together leaders of cooperatives in Nicaragua and Alabama and of rank-and-file democratic unions in Mexico and Tennessee.

While national and international restructuring serves on the one hand to deepen inequities in the South and to challenge traditional models of economic development and social change, so, too, has it spawned the seeds of a new movement. At the moment, the movement is at the grassroots, relatively invisible to the national eye. To grow, it will need broader economic education, coalition building, policy development, and national and international linkages. But as the new participation builds, it has the possibility of transforming contemporary economic restructuring into a new model of development, one that links matters of the economy to matters of democracy and dignity—at the local level as well as in the broader arena.

NOTES

1. See, for example, Bennett Harrison and Barry Bluestone, *Corporate Restructuring and the Polarizing of America* (New York: Basic Books, 1988).

2. See, for instance, the analysis of James C. Cobb, *The Selling of the South: The Southern Crusade for Industrial Development, 1936–1980* (Baton Rouge: Louisiana State University Press, 1982).

3. *Shadows in the Sunbelt* (Chapel Hill, N.C.: MDC, 1986), 10. Report of the 1986 Commission on the Future of the South, *Halfway Home and a Long Way to Go* (Durham, N.C.: Southern Growth Policies Board, 1986), 5. See further discussion in the introduction to this volume.

4. Southern Regional Council, "The Climate for Work ern Changes 8, nos. 4–5 (October–November 1986), 2– gional Council Press Release, September 3, 1988.

5. General arguments along this line may be found *Rural South in Crisis: Challenges for the Future* (Boulc 1988), 51–61.

6. "Atlanta's Two Worlds: Wealth and Poverty, Mag *Street Journal,* February 28, 1989, 1.

7. See, for example, Barbara Ellen Smith, "Question body's Business: A People's Guide to Economic Develc *Southern Exposure* 14, nos. 5–6 (September/Octobe 1986): 40–41.

8. "Adult Functional Literacy in the South: Program a Regional Approach," *Southern Growth Policies Boc* 1988): 1.

9. See *Economic Transformation: The Appalach* Commission on Religion in Appalachia, 1986), 11.

10. Beaulieu, *Rural South in Crisis,* 57. Stuart Ros *Everybody's Business,* 14. See also Stuart Rosenfeld, Beaulieu, *Rural South in Crisis,* 51–61.

11. Beaulieu, *Rural South in Crisis,* 4.

12. For other accounts of grassroots developm *Business.*

13. "Corporate Shutdowns Draw Fire," *Knoxvill*

14. See, for example, Anil Agarwal, Juliet Mer *Place to Run: Local Realities and Global Issues of the* Tenn.: Highlander Research and Education Center, 1!

About the Contributors

Resources

ABOUT THE CONTRIBUTORS

J O H N B O O K S E R - F E I S T E R is communications director of Southerners for Economic Justice and was editor of *Everybody's Business: A People's Guide to Economic Development*, a special edition of *Southern Exposure* 14, nos. 5–6 (September/October and November/December 1986). *Southern Exposure* is published by the Institute for Southern Studies, Durham, N.C.

R O B E R T D. B U L L A R D is an associate professor of sociology with the Energy and Resources Group at the University of California at Berkeley and author of numerous articles on toxic wastes and racial issues. He also is author of *Invisible Houston: The Black Experience in Boom and Bust* and *In Search of the New South* and co-author of *Houston: Growth and Decline in a Sunbelt Boomtown*.

C I N D I A C A M E R O N has worked for 9to5 since 1983, first as staff director for the Atlanta chapter and, since 1986, as field organizer for the Southeast region. She has also worked in a variety of office and clerical jobs and taught in labor education and adult education programs in New York, New Jersey, and West Virginia.

R I C H A R D A. C O U T O is a professor and coordinator of research at the Institute of Government at Tennessee State University, and senior research associate at the Vanderbilt Institute of Public Policy Studies. He was formerly director of the Center for Health Services at Vanderbilt University.

P A U L D E L E O N is resource center coordinator at the Highlander Research and Education Center.

S T E V E F I S H E R is a professor of political science at Emory and Henry College in Emory, Virginia, and has written extensively on various aspects of the political economy of Appalachia.

C A R T E R G A R B E R is an economic development consultant and writer, currently working for CEPAD, an ecumenical development agency in Central America. Previously, he worked extensively with community-based organizations in the South. He is the founder of Southern Neighborhoods Network in Nashville and has written extensively on issues of Southern economic development.

J O H N G A V E N T A is an assistant professor of sociology at the University of Tennessee and research director at the Highlander Research and Education Center. He has written widely about development issues in the Appalachian region, including the

295

award-winning *Power and Powerlessness: Quiescence and Rebellion in an Appalachian Valley* (Urbana: University of Illinois Press, 1980).

BETTY JEAN HALL, an attorney from Kentucky, was the founder of the Coal Employment Project. She currently is director of women's programs at the Occupational Safety and Health Law Center in Washington, D.C.

HAL HAMILTON is director of the Community Farm Alliance and a farmer in Henry County, Kentucky, where he won a Master Conservationist Award in 1986. He was a founding director of the North American Farm Alliance, the National Save the Family Farm Coalition, the Kentucky Resources Council, the Kentucky Farmlands Committee, and the Kentucky New Farm Coalition. He served on Governor Martha Layne Collins's alfalfa marketing task force in 1987 and currently serves on the Lieutenant Governor's agricultural advisory panel.

RICKEY HILL is associate professor of political science and chair of the department of political science and history at South Carolina State College in Orangeburg, S.C. He has published review articles in the *Journal of Politics,* the *Journal of Negro History,* and the *Hampton Review,* as well as a recent essay, "The Contemporary Black Predicament: Crisis and Political Obligations," in Franklin D. Jones et al., *Readings in American Political Issues* (Dubuque, Iowa: Kendall/Hunt, 1987). He has been a frequent political commentator and analyst on state and national political issues.

DEBORAH CLIFTON HILS is a Creole poet, linguist, and cultural conservationist who works with Franco-American, Native American, and minority communities on a variety of concerns, ranging from language planning, to religious freedom in prisons, to leadership development. Her special area of interest is in working with the most traditional members of these communities. Language planning is a branch of applied linguistics that deals with literacy, language standardization, preservation of oral traditions, and the like in indigenous, Third World, or minority communities.

RALPH HILS farms some small acreage in the mountains of northern Georgia. He is a freelance writer, editor, and researcher. His most recent book is *Market What You Grow: A Guide for Small Farmers,* available from the Chicot Press, Box 53198, Atlanta, GA 30355.

MAC LEGERTON is a writer, speaker, trainer, and consultant for peace and justice organizations. He is executive director of the Center for Community Action in Lumberton, North Carolina, and an ordained minister in the United Church of Christ.

HELEN M. LEWIS is a sociologist and a staff member of the Highlander Research and Education Center. She has written widely on Appalachian issues, and is one of the editors of *Colonialism in Modern American: The Appalachian Case* (Boone, N.C.: Appalachian Consortium Press, 1978). She also contributed the introduction to the recent book of photographs by Builder Levy, *Images of Appalachian Coalfields* (Philadelphia: Temple University Press, 1989).

WENDY LUTTRELL is a sociologist and educator who currently teaches at Duke University and is conducting research on black and white working-class women learners. She has served as a writer and consultant on the Highlander Economics Education Project.

CLARE MCBRIEN works with the education programs of the Ivanhoe Civic League, Ivanhoe, Virginia.

RICHARD REGAN is a Lumbee Native American from Pembroke, North Carolina. He is a Baptist minister and serves as staff member of the Robeson County Center for Community Action.

ANN SEIDMAN is a professor in the International Development and Social Change Program at Clark University in Worcester, Massachusetts. She has written a dozen books on international economic issues as well as many articles on related topics. In 1987 she served as a consultant to the Africa Peace Tour, sponsored by religious and nongovernmental voluntary agencies, in the U.S. South.

BARBARA ELLEN SMITH is former research and education director of the Southeast Women's Employment Coalition. She is the author of numerous articles on labor and women's issues in the South, and of *Digging Our Own Graves: Coal Miners and the Struggle Over Black Lung Disease* (Philadelphia: Temple University Press, 1987) and *Women of the Rural South: Economic Status and Prospects* (Lexington, Ky.: Southeast Women's Employment Coalition, 1986).

KRISTIN LAYNG SZAKOS is a freelance writer and editor of the *Appalachian Reader*, a quarterly publication covering citizens' organizations in Appalachia. She lives in the eastern Kentucky community of Banner.

CHARLES D. M. TAYLOR has been the state coordinator of the Carolina Alliance for Fair Employment of WRP, Inc. (formerly Workers' Rights Project) since 1982.

MAXINE WALLER is president of the Ivanhoe (Virginia) Civic League and was a Southern Appalachian Leadership Fellow.

CHRIS WEISS is a founder of Women and Employment in Charleston, West Virginia, and served as its director until 1988. She currently works for Women's World Banking and the Ms. Foundation, and serves as a consultant on women's economic development issues.

CARROLL L. WESSINGER is a Lutheran minister who has been involved in community development in Appalachia for many years.

ALEX WILLINGHAM is a professor of political science at Williams College, Williams, Massachusetts. He was formerly research director at the Southern Regional Council and a consultant on voting rights issues in the South. He is editor of the *Voting Rights Review* and has written on voting rights and black political participation for a number of journals, including *Southern Changes, Social Science Quarterly,* and *Urban League Review.*

LEAH WISE is executive director of Southerners for Economic Justice in Durham, North Carolina, and an active member of a number of social justice organizations, including the North Carolina Committee Against Religious and Racial Violence in Durham, and the Interreligious Economic Crisis Organizing Network in New York.

MIKE YARROW is an associate professor of sociology at Ithaca College in Ithaca, New York. He has written about coalminers for a number of years, based on interviews conducted in the coalfields since 1978. He and his wife Ruth spent 1986–87 interviewing unemployed miners and their wives in southern West Virginia and Virginia.

RESOURCES

Compiled by Paul DeLeon

BELOW is a list of some of the key community-based organizations that are discussed in this volume, with addresses, contact people, and major activities. Readers seeking further information should follow up with these groups directly.

Amalgamated Clothing and Textile Workers Union, GTA Area Joint Board, 1124 Broadway, Knoxville, TN 37917; 615/525–2139. Doug Gamble, Mark Pitt. Workplace organizing; leadership development.

American Civil Liberties Union (ACLU), Southeast Regional Office, 44 Forsyth Street NW, Atlanta, GA 30303; 404/523–2721. Laughlin McDonald. Legal assistance to citizen suits for the enforcement of the federal Voting Rights Act.

Bogalusa Civic and Voters League, 1600 North Avenue (corner of Martin Luther King Drive), Bogalusa, LA 70427; 504/732–3194. Gayle Jenkins. Organizing and voter education in support of chosen candidates.

Burke County Improvement Association, 917 Martin Luther King Drive, Waynesboro, GA 30830; 404/554–3805. Herman Lodge. Community awareness; neighborhood organizing on school and civil rights issues.

Carolina Alliance for Fair Employment of the Workers' Rights Project, 110D Chick Springs Roads, Greenville, SC 29609; 803/235–2926. Charles Taylor. Workplace organizing, community education, and litigation.

Center for Community Action, P.O. Box 723, Lumberton, NC 28359; 919/739–7851. Mac Legerton. Research, organizing, and leadership development on civil rights, employee rights, and toxic-waste issues.

Center for Health Services, Station 17, Vanderbilt University, Nashville, TN 37232; 615/322–4773. Barbara Clinton. Sponsors student and professional research on environment and health issues, visiting medical teams, and on-site community health workers in southern Appalachia.

Coal Employment Project, 17 Emory Place, Knoxville, TN 37917; 615/637–7905. Madeline Rogero. National network helps women get and keep jobs in mining industries, provides legal support to end sexual harassment and discrimination, and develops programs to address issues of leadership development, parental leave, and workplace safety and health.

Community Farm Alliance, Nerinx, KY 40049; 502/865–2037. Hal Hamilton. This membership group works on farm credit, pricing, marketing, foreclosures, and other issues through organizing, advocacy, and training.

Commission on Religion in Appalachia (CORA), P.O. Box 10867, Knoxville, TN 37919; 615/584–6133. Jim Sessions. Issues occasional reports on the regional economy, sponsors small-scale development and grassroots advocacy projects, and publishes *CORAspondent.*

Federation of Southern Cooperatives, P.O. Box 95, Epes, AL 35460; 205/652–9676. John Zippert. Coordinates training, housing, and agricultural development projects among 130 black-majority cooperatives.

Highlander Research and Education Center, Route 3, Box 370, New Market, TN 37820; 615/933–3443. John Gaventa. Adult education and research on economic, environmental, social, and cultural issues; resource center and publications.

Institute for Southern Studies, 604 West Chapel Street, Durham, NC 27701; 919/688–8167. Meredith Emmett. Research, education, organizing. Publishes *Southern Exposure;* sponsors the southern finance banking research project.

Ivanhoe Civic League, P.O. Box 201, Ivanhoe, VA 24350; 703/699–1383. Maxine Waller. Community development, including small enterprise, housing renovation, education, historical research.

Kentuckians For The Commonwealth, P.O. Box 864, Prestonsburg, KY 41653; 606/886–0043. Joe Szakos. Citizens' work on taxation, environment, and coalfields issues.

The Mayhaw Tree, Inc., Colquitt, GA 31737; 912/758–3227. Joy Jinks. Locally owned gift-food business uses local talent and resources as an intentional way of strengthening the community.

Mountain Women's Exchange, 205 Fifth Street, Jellico, TN 37762; 615/784–8780. Wanda Perkins, Phyllis Miller. Adult education, job skills training, small enterprise, school issues.

National Association for the Advancement of Colored People (NAACP), Regional Office, 970 Martin Luther King Jr. Drive SW, Suite 203, Atlanta, GA 30314; 404/688–6506. Earl T. Shinhoster. This national membership organization offers legal assistance and organizational support to constituents dealing with questions of civil rights in employment, housing, education, and the like.

9to5, Southeast Regional Office, 250 10th St, NE, #107, Atlanta, GA 30309; 404/876–1604. Cindia Cameron. National membership organization of office and clerical workers to promote better pay, policies, and working conditions.

Southeast Women's Employment Coalition, 140 East Third St., Lexington, KY 40508; 606/233–9481. Cynthia Brown. Research and coalition building around issues of gender and racial discrimination. Publishes booklets and reports on economic issues involving Southern women and the quarterly *Generations.*

Southerners for Economic Justice, P.O. Box 240, Durham, NC 27702; 919/683–1361. Leah Wise. Organizing and advocacy to link workplace and community issues.

Southern Neighborhoods Network, Inc., P.O. Box 121133, Nashville, TN 37212–1133; 615/292–1798. Verna Fausey. Networking, economic analysis, research, and education. Publishes the bimonthly *Southern Communities* and various community action guides.

Southern Regional Council, 60 Walton Street NW, Atlanta, GA 30303–2199; 404/522–8764. Steve Suitts. Research, education, and advocacy on civil rights and voting rights. Publishes the bimonthly *Southern Changes.*

United Mine Workers of America (UMWA), 900 15th Street, NW, Washington, DC 20005. 202/842–7200. Organizing mine workers in the coalfields. Publishes the monthly United Mine Workers *Journal.*

Women and Employment, 1217 Lee Street, Charleston, WV 25301; 304/345–1298. Pam Curry. Research, advocacy, education, and technical assistance for women workers, especially self-employed or in nontraditional jobs.